SHACKLETON BOYS

VOLUME 2

SHACKLETON BOYS
VOLUME 2

TRUE STORIES FROM SHACKLETON OPERATORS BASED OVERSEAS

STEVE BOND

GRUB STREET • LONDON

Published by
Grub Street
4 Rainham Close
London SW11 6SS

Copyright © Grub Street 2019
Copyright text © Steve Bond 2019

A CIP record for this title is available from the British library

ISBN-13: 978-1-911621-33-1

Design by Lucy Thorne

Printed and bound by Finidr, Czech Republic

DEDICATION

Roy Chadwick CBE FRSA FRAeS
1893 – 1947
Avro's masterly designer behind the
Manchester, Lancaster and, Lincoln, and
who was working on the Shackleton design
before his untimely death in an Avro Tudor crash

CONTENTS

FOREWORD

The phrase 'close-knit' is regularly in use these days. Though seen more often than not in reference to families or to small communities, there is no reason why it cannot apply to large organisations as well, if they can claim a sense of shared purpose and togetherness of spirit, an essential brotherhood in fact. The stories in the first volume of this book clearly showed the bond felt among the home-based Shackleton crews of the late 1950s and the 1960s; it shone through the pages as the warm nostalgia of St.Eval, St. Mawgan, Ballykelly, Kinloss and Lossiemouth stirred the spirits once again.

Those units spanned the length and breadth of the United Kingdom, but this second volume shows that even the separation by half a globe and endless tracts of ocean between its squadrons overseas did nothing to dent the essential character of the maritime force. The postings available reflected the closing days of Empire. Gibraltar was – and is – a special case, but Malta, Aden and Singapore beckoned, until the shutdown east of Suez brought us all home; but not before Majunga and Sharjah, too, had become household names for Shackleton boys, while Gan, that Indian Ocean stepping-stone paradise, and forays up the South China Sea to Hong Kong, put extra spice into crews' travel bags.

Let's take a closer look at these famous bases via a leisurely west to east drone in a Shack – at 1,000 feet of course. From the UK we would probably fly the well-trodden route down 10W – practically visible on the waves so often was this sea pathway used – arriving after a mere six hours at the iconic Rock of Gibraltar, though crews were just as likely to 'pay' for their Gibex with the dreaded 12-hour overnight LROFE (long-range operational flying exercise), staggering onto the 6,000-foot runway soon after dawn and praying they didn't meet the vicious wind shear caused by a strong south-easterly breeze. No. 224 Squadron, 'Faithful to a Friend', was in residence from July 1951 to October 1966. Perfectly placed to carry out the unit's motto to 'Guard the Gateway', you turned east into the Med or west into the Atlantic to do your business, more often than not the counting in and out of Soviet submarines to and from their northern base. In your leisure time you might turn south for beer then fish and chips in Irish Town, and much later north, where you might listen to the haunting notes of the blind guitarist in Dick's Bar across the border in La Linea. Good memories, but sadness, too, when it all ended. Harold Wilson gave little notice for the squadron to quit the Rock, and when they did, that October all those years ago, they arrived at the mess at Ballykelly with not much more than their flying kit. We made them feel at home in the bar that afternoon, treated them like returning brothers, which of course they were.

Our nostalgic drone now takes us due east another six hours. RAF Luqa's motto, 'An Airfield Never Beaten', could not be more appropriate, given Malta GC's astonishing resilience in World War 2, so 38 Squadron had a proud home from

September 1953 to October 1965, and at Hal Far for a further eighteen months. No. 38's main business was in the Med, but it was also a frequent visitor to the Gulf, supporting 37 Squadron's adventures from Aden. In addition, Luqa's Shackletons were, perhaps, the main players on the Beira patrols of the period, when the island of Madagascar was the improbable host to a maritime detachment at its north-west base of Majunga. It's a regret of mine that I never visited that Indian Ocean outpost. Sadly, the operating parameters of the Mk.3, on which I flew at the time, were found to be rather too cissy for the peculiar requirements of Majunga. Heathrow International it was not. The flavours of that detachment are wonderfully well catalogued in Volume 1 – the flying stories, that is. There is little record of the social whirl of Majunga. I wonder why…

Now, after a final social soiree in Malta's 'Straight Street', or 'Narrow Street', or 'Strada Stretta', oh – all right then, 'The Gut', a rite of passage for maritime crews, we must rumble on, now a little further east but a long way south, to the rock and desert of Aden, where for ten years from 1957, 'Wise Without Eyes' 37 Squadron held sway with the Mk.2 at RAF Khormaksar. This base boasted 'Into the Remote Places' as its motto, to which many of our aircrew might have added… 'You can say that again!' No. 37 had had its share of maritime operations during its previous tenure, at Luqa from 1953-57, but in the baking heat of the south Arabian Peninsula, there was not so much growling over endless seascapes, thanks to the charged local politics. Yemeni rebels targeted the colonial oppressor from 1958, and the RAF's largest ever unit responded via the might of its nine squadrons. 37's bomb bays were cleared of sonobuoys, torpedoes and depth charges to make room for 1,000-lb bombs and leaflets, while the Hispano-Suizas on the nose were aimed at more serious targets than the humble flame-float, ensuring lungfuls of cordite, and ears even more deafened than usual, after a sortie in the Radfan Hills. Brother squadrons came and went, but the atmosphere was increasingly taut and tense, and perhaps there were less feelings of regret here, than any other overseas outpost, when the time came for the final return to base – to the UK – in 1967.

Time to move on, and the need to tip the hat to Sharjah, 1,000 miles north-east up the Arabian Peninsula, where so many UK squadrons carried out three-monthly detachments through the 1960s. But in 1970/71 for the final year of British presence, a repositioned 210 Squadron took over the mantle. Was it hot? Just a bit! Certainly a little warmer and drier than Ballykelly, from whence it had come. But it made the sea swimming in the Dubai creek bathwater all the better, and anyway, the humidity never threatened that of the soggy blanket experienced in the Far East. On then, ever south and east, and Singapore's great base at Changi awaits. But how to get there?

An unending sea passage over the Gulf of Aden, Arabian Sea, Indian Ocean and Malacca Strait is none too attractive a proposition, and anyway we don't do 23-hour flogs anymore, so we'll settle for a rest along the way. Katunayake, in verdant Sri Lanka (then Ceylon) is a possibility (not forgetting to make the famous call 'abeam Ratmalana') but much more likely is Gan, that coral paradise 40 miles north of the equator. Nowhere beat it as a battery recharger, even for the one night which is all we can spare. For that short stay we might even be allowed to savour the rattling symphony in the rooms with a prehistoric air conditioning system usually reserved for visiting crews – usually the transport 'shinies'. An early morning start, and how comforting to know that our bosom pals from the 205 Squadron detachment, who had looked out for us on SAR standby during the transit from Aden, would now do so again on the final, 11-hour haul east. And so to Changi, and figures imprinted on my brain. All sorts of clever satellite measurements on Google pages may say slightly different, but 0122N 10359E was good enough for me, and for the API (air position indicator) I wound them on before every flight. From late 1963 to mid-1966 Changi worked hard to deliver its motto, 'We Shelter Many' while 205's 'First in Malaya' could well have been adapted to suit the newly formed Malaysia, which had so irked Indonesia's President Sukarno that his antagonistic operations occupied British and Commonwealth forces for three years.

Who among 205 aircrew and the invaluable, almost permanently featuring re-force squadrons from the UK will not recall middle of the night sweat-stained Hawkmoths in the Malacca Strait at 500 feet, endless Kuching recces, climbing away from the Tawau area for the night return – 'must make it before the bar closes' – to Labuan, dodging the giant thunderstorms always threatening over Sabah? Yes, there was ASW as well, of course, and the ever-present SAR (search and rescue), plus the eclectic detachments, shrinking that corner of the Far East: Hong Kong needless to say, and 205's second home at that time, Labuan. There was too, Sangley Point and its extraordinary neighbourhood, Cavite City; there were make-believe campaign medals suggested by aircrew; a gong for operations conducted from Gong Kedak up in Malaya, and a star for a couple of mosquito-infested nights at Alor Setar. There were flits – if you can call 21 + hours to Darwin a flit – to Australia, stopping halfway at Cocos, but not catching sight of the self-proclaimed king. Silly stuff, maybe, but all part of a rich seam of memories.

Although our droning odyssey through maritime units overseas has reached its final destination, we must pay tribute here to the long and honourable Shackleton service of our South African friends, the colleagues of 35 Squadron at Ysterplaat, in beautiful Cape Town. We have neither the time nor the endless diplomatic clearances which would no doubt be needed, to visit them, but their stalwart 27 years of service with the Mk.3 makes us more than happy to share our memories. We were all in this 10,000-rivet formation together, after all.

So time to reflect and take final stock of things. Just a few more lines must suffice as time is pressing, though an engine change – that perennial delayer of transits which could bring exclamations of joy (i.e. in Hong Kong, or Honolulu on westabout) or opposite expressions of Anglo-Saxon (Djibouti springs to mind) – would come in handy.

Some more warm thoughts come easily to the fore... Gibraltar, crossing Spanish Road. Well, at least we had preference over pedestrians and road traffic, unlike Ballykelly, where the thanks we got after a 12-hour LROFE could be holding for 20 minutes to let the train go through. The boys of 38 in Malta will have fond memories of their Marsovin nectar, and so will others. 'Marsovin wines are shipped directly to consumers worldwide', says the current blurb. Yes, and years ago it even reached us down in Masirah, thanks to the weekly Argosy, and was unmissable at two shillings and three pence a bottle in proper money.

Phil Styles, the eloquent Shackleton historian, put service on 37 Squadron in Aden in true context: certainly, the often quoted 'moments of extreme terror', as pertaining to military life, were not unknown, but there was precious little evidence there of the epithet's other half – the 'interminable boredom'. Apart from the endless sweating, the 205 boys will remember Changi for the village, where Chinese tailors could measure you for KD (khaki drill) in the morning and apologise that it wouldn't quite be ready that afternoon – it would fit perfectly and last for years. There was Bedok Corner, where you sat by the sea and ate late night Chinese food, the best in the world. No doubt they will hold disturbing memories too, as I do, of seeing Changi Jail, a brutal reminder of a time when guys weren't so fortunate as us.

But enough of bare reminiscences of the places. Let the men lucky enough to serve in them as Shackleton Boys bring them to life with their stories, which are many and varied, and told with feeling, warmth and humour. No, we weren't shiny, and we may have been a long way down the batting order of the commands. But yes, we were close-knit all right, and I don't know anyone who would have changed the years we had together.

Wing Commander Jerry Evans RAF (Retired)

INTRODUCTION and
ACKNOWLEDGEMENTS

At the end of World War 2 the Royal Air Force (RAF) possessed a substantial maritime reconnaissance (MR) force, which had been developed and refined throughout the conflict. The value of the MR force was recognised, and although the service then went through a considerable downsizing, it was still seen as essential for the protection of British interests overseas. These areas were primarily the Mediterranean, Middle East, Far East to Hong Kong and all associated trade routes linking them to Britain and each other.

Operating locations.

OPERATING LOCATIONS

The MR force based overseas in July 1945 was largely made up of squadrons equipped with Consolidated Liberators, which under the terms of the lend-lease agreement with the United States had to be returned. In addition, there were Wellingtons and Warwicks which were quickly withdrawn, and a substantial force of Sunderland flying boats which continued in service, albeit in smaller numbers until the late 1950s. Replacements for the Liberators primarily emerged as converted Lancasters, together with a small number of similarly adapted Halifaxes. A little later, a single squadron of Hastings was added in the weather reconnaissance role. With the arrival of the Shackleton in increasing numbers from 1951, re-equipment with the new type initially concentrated on the home fleet of Coastal Command. The first unit to station them overseas, albeit for a limited period, was 269 Squadron which operated out of Gibraltar from January to March 1952.

By early 1953 much of the re-equipment of the overseas MR force was complete, and units then stationed outside the UK were: 37 and 38 Squadrons in Malta (flying Lancasters as part of the Middle East Air Force [MEAF]), and 88, 205 and 209 Squadrons at Seletar, Singapore (flying Sunderlands under the control of the Far East Air Force [FEAF]). In addition Coastal Command at Northwood retained control of 224 Squadron at Gibraltar, who had only changed over from the RAF's last Halifaxes to the Shackleton two years previously. In July 1953 37 Squadron also re-equipped with Shackletons at Luqa, followed two months later by 38 Squadron at nearby Hal Far. By 1962 control of the units in Malta had switched from MEAF to the Near East Air Force (NEAF).

With the Mediterranean area well covered it was next the turn of the Middle East. 37 Squadron relocated to Khormaksar, Aden in August 1957, followed by the Far East with 205 Squadron at Changi in May 1958. The final new overseas location to acquire a permanent Shackleton presence was Sharjah, in what is now the United Arab Emirates. When all British forces were withdrawn from Aden in 1967, there was an urgent need to continue MR and search and rescue (SAR) coverage in the Middle East from another location. Therefore, just a month before 37 Squadron disbanded at Khormaksar, a maritime detachment (MARDET) started operations at Sharjah, which had been selected as the closest available suitable airfield. MARDET was operated by aircraft and crews on rotation from UK-based squadrons until the autumn of 1970. It was then decided to move 210 Squadron there permanently from its former base at Ballykelly.

Although every MR mark of Shackleton served with overseas units (the T.2 and T.4 were only ever based in the UK), only one such squadron flew the MR.3, when 203 Squadron moved from Ballykelly to Luqa in February 1969. Undoubtedly a major consideration was the fact that the MR.3 was very overweight, and thus its 'hot and high' performance was marginal to say the least. Even with the addition of two Viper jet engines, giving an improved take-off performance, the MR.3's ability to leave the ground at maximum weight had more to do with the curvature of the earth! The experience of the team testing the Viper installation prior to introduction to service serves to highlight some of the problems, as explained by Avro flight test observer **John Smith**:

"The Viper fuel system was modified to cope with the greater explosive nature of gasoline. The only down-side was that the fuel to the Viper and the outboard Griffon had a common supply line, so interruption of this common fuel supply during take-off would result in both engines stopping. As it was essential to be able to control an engine failure at the most critical point of take-off, some flight testing was necessary. The project test pilot was Bill Else. During one week in early April 1965, and in about 12 flying hours on WR973, we accomplished all the testing necessary to establish that there were no adverse flight-handling characteristics, and the stalling speeds were not affected.

"We were then ready to attempt the critical engine failure take-off tests. There was no doubt that this would be potentially dangerous and, for optimum safety, we used the very long and wide runway at RAE (Royal Aircraft Establishment) Bedford. This turned out to be a good decision. The width of the runway was available when we needed it to accommodate some larger than expected lateral deviations that occurred after the simulated engine failures on take-off. On another test, the extra length of the runway enabled Bill to abort the take-off after failing the two engines, when it became apparent that we might not get airborne. Some fine tuning of the scheduled take-off safety speeds was required before we tried again. In Bill's own words: 'If I can get it into the air for long enough to retract the undercarriage, with the reduction of drag it will climb OK. Sometimes it just needs a lump in the runway at the right point to help it into the air!'

"This emphasised just how critical the double engine failure was at the take-off weights we were trying to approve. This situation would not be acceptable for a civil aeroplane, but the military were ready to compromise. We added a further knot to the take-off speeds for a little extra comfort. We then began flight test measurements of the actual performance: rate of climb, take-off and landing distances, which were published in the flight manual.

"The installation of the Viper was a successful modification. However, the increased operating weight had a serious impact on the fatigue life of the wing spars. Despite a frequent inspection programme to look for and repair developing cracks, it was a losing battle and the aircraft had to be withdrawn from service before the Nimrods became fully available."

The next change to the overseas fleet came in October 1966, when 224 Squadron was disbanded in Gibraltar. This left the western end of the Mediterranean and eastern Atlantic to be covered from St. Mawgan and Luqa. The situation was then largely stable until 1969, when the Nimrod fleet began arriving to replace the Shackletons. This, coupled with the continued scaling down of Britain's military commitments overseas, led to a further rethink regarding the deployment of such expensive and limited-in-number assets. The last three months of 1971 saw the final withdrawal of the RAF Shackleton abroad. In October 205 Squadron closed its doors in Changi, the following month 210 Squadron packed up shop in Sharjah and last of all 203 Squadron in Luqa waved goodbye to its last 'Growler' in December when it became the sole Nimrod squadron based outside the UK. However, Nimrod detachments from UK squadrons were maintained at nearby Tengah.

During their time overseas the Shackleton squadrons had been involved in a number of operations, in addition to their daily routine. Throughout much of the 1950s and early '60s Shackletons from Malta and Aden were called on to carry out reconnaissance and leaflet drops. This was due to on-going border disputes in the Arabian Gulf which led to drawn-out incursions by Saudi Arabian forces into Muscat and Oman.

From about 1959 political upheaval and discontent became rife in Aden. This led to an Egyptian-supported rebellion in the Radfan region, and the declaration of a state of emergency by the British High Commissioner in December 1963. Once again the Shackleton was used to support operations. This included conventional bombing of rebel-held areas, primarily by 37 Squadron, which continued until the final withdrawal from Aden in 1967.

In 1965, the Unilateral Declaration of Independence (UDI) by Ian Smith's government in Rhodesia quickly led to the establishment of a Royal Navy blockade of oil supplies attempting to reach the port of Beira. The blockade was supported by detachments of Shackletons for maritime patrol, flying from Majunga in Madagascar, and although these aircraft were mostly drawn from UK-based units, 37 and 38 Squadrons also took part. The Majunga operation is covered in detail in *Shackleton Boys Volume 1*.

The Indonesian Confrontation began in 1961 when agreement was reached to create the federation of Malaysia. This encompassed Malaya, Singapore and North Borneo. Indonesia had claims on parts of Borneo, and by 1962, an independence movement in Borneo, supported by Indonesia, was in open revolt. When the Federation of Malaysia came into being in September 1963 it was the signal for increased infiltration across the border by Indonesian forces. Malaysia invoked the Mutual Assistance Treaty which called for Commonwealth support, in response to the Indonesian aggression. Shackletons from 205 Squadron at Changi were heavily involved in lengthy patrols searching for insurgent gun-boats in the seas around the Malayan mainland and Borneo, and this included mounting frequent detachments to Labuan. The Indonesian Confrontation formally ended on 11 August 1966 with the signing of the Bangkok Accord.

THE SOUTH AFRICAN AIR FORCE

Despite extensive promotion to help Avro's efforts to secure a second customer for the Shackleton, including a number of overseas tours by Coastal Command squadrons (see Volume 1) and some encouraging noises made by Canada, they were only able to find one other buyer; the South African Air Force (SAAF). A team from the

SAAF flew in an MR.2 in November 1952, but initially ruled it out. Lockheed pushed hard to persuade them to take the P2V Neptune instead. Nevertheless, the SAAF retained an interest in the Shackleton and a number of proposals were made for changes to the aircraft. In April 1953, three MR.2s from 42 Squadron at St. Mawgan demonstrated the aircraft in South Africa and six months later an order was placed for eight aircraft. The Shackleton was considered to be the most modern anti-submarine aircraft available at that time. It provided the SAAF with an offensive capability, and the necessary range and endurance to patrol its 2,000 miles of coastline performing the same roles as the RAF fleet.

Delays in delivery included a hold-up by the South African government in granting an import licence. However, in March 1955 it was announced that the SAAF would be the first to receive the MR.3, (together with the airborne lifeboat which the RAF had abandoned in 1956). Subsequently eight MR.3s, from the initial production batch, were diverted to the SAAF with delivery expected in May 1957. In February of that year a large contingent of personnel, from 35 Squadron SAAF, arrived at the Maritime Operational Training Unit (MOTU) at Kinloss for ground training. They later moved to Avro's at Woodford for flying training.

No. 1716 was the first of the eight aircraft to fly on 29 March 1957. Nos. 1716 and 1717 were officially handed over to the SAAF at Woodford on 16 May by Avro director and general manager, J A R Kay. Also present were the South African Deputy High Commissioner to London, W D Van Schalkwyk and Commandant Matthys Johannes 'Thys' Uys AFC, commanding officer, 35 Squadron SAAF. Both aircraft were then flown to St. Mawgan, on 21 May, for further training including joint exercises with Coastal Command and the Royal Navy. Before they left for their new home, the aircraft were grounded for a short period. This followed the discovery of wing-skin cracks, which were repaired by an Avro working party. The first three aircraft (Nos. 1716, 1717 and 1718) finally arrived in South Africa on 18 August 1957 (12 days before the RAF received their first MR.3s!) So began their impressive 27 years of operation, during which time just one aircraft was lost (see Appendix Three).

These aircraft were essentially the same as those delivered to the RAF, however they did have the provision to carry 25-lb or 60-lb rocket projectiles mounted on underwing rails (although it is unlikely they were ever used in anger). This arrangement had been developed for the RAF but not taken up. In 1966 the fleet was brought up to Phase II standard by a working party travelling out from Hawker-Siddeley at Bitteswell. By 1973 they had all been further modified in-house by the squadron to virtually Phase III equivalent, although the Viper engine modification was not adopted.

With increasing difficulties in obtaining spares (especially engine parts and tyres), 35 Squadron's fleet was gradually reduced until the final withdrawal on 23 November 1984. Thus, after almost 33 years the Shackleton's overseas story was essentially over although the RAF's 8 Squadron at Lossiemouth would continue to give the type an occasional presence away from home for a further seven years.

The importance of the Shackleton to the RAF, and the SAAF, throughout its 40 years of service cannot be overstated. Its crews flew countless long, often tedious, always noisy hours scouring the oceans, whether looking for Soviet ships, exercising with submarines, or on vital search-and-rescue sorties for ships and aircraft in distress. Then, in later years, the AEW.2 (airborne early warning) patrolled the skies to seek out aircraft threatening to intrude into UK airspace, and then directing fighter aircraft to investigate. Equally demanding was the task of the ground crews. To keep their often-troublesome aircraft airworthy, they toiled away in extremes of weather from the cold and snow of Bodø, to the almost constant rain of Ballykelly and the raging heat and humidity of the Middle and Far East.

Throughout those many long years the price to pay was high. In particular, flying for hour after hour, night or day, in any weather over uninviting seas at low level, and when required manoeuvring to home in on a potential target, demanded much of both the crews and the aircraft. Sadly, many failed to return. Of the 191 aircraft built, no fewer than 25, or 13%, were written off in accidents, and 156 'Shackleton Boys' lost their lives.

The stories presented within these pages give a flavour of just what life was like, for both air and ground crew, with the 'Old Grey Lady'. At times it could become very boring, and humour was their essential antidote. However, there were occasions when life became more demanding, even exciting. But there were also times when it all went wrong...terrifying...and occasionally catastrophic. Hopefully these pages go some way to recognising and remembering their sacrifice especially in this, the Shackleton's centenary year.

The response to my appeals for contact with 'Shackleton Boys' was overwhelming with well over a hundred coming forward with their memories – thank you. It became clear at an early stage in my research, that in order to ensure that as many of their great stories as possible – be they routine, humorous (lots of that in the 'Kipper Fleet'!) or tragic – reached a wider audience, two volumes were essential. Therefore, Volume 1 covered all the units based in the United Kingdom, and included those overseas exercises, flag-waving trips and detachments that were covered by home squadrons, including the major tasks on Christmas Island and Majunga. Volume 2 covers the units based overseas at, and deployed to: Changi, Gan, Gibraltar, Hal Far, Khormaksar, Labuan, Luqa and Sharjah, plus many other small detachments and visits. The SAAF operations from Ysterplaat/Malan are also covered in Volume 2.

All this has only been possible with the help of the following Shackleton personnel and their families, who have so enthusiastically allowed me into their homes, endured many lengthy telephone calls, answered interminable questions and granted access to their precious logbooks and private photograph collections.

Sqn Ldr Wally Allaway, Flt Lt Bob Allen, Sgt Lionel Ashbury SAAF, Sgt Alec Audley, Major John Balladon SAAF, Master Aircrew Bob Barrett, Flt Sgt Peter Bellchambers, Captain Hartog Blok SAAF, Sgt James Box, Sgt Ken Brereton, Flt Lt Roy Brocklebank, Air Cdre Jack Broughton OBE, Sqn Ldr Laurie Bruce, Sqn Ldr Peter Bruce, the late Sqn Ldr Colin Butler, Flt Lt John Campbell, Flt Sgt Jim Cargill, Sqn Ldr Ray Carran, Cpl Geoff Clift, Flt Lt Martin Coales, Major Knoppies Coetzer SAAF, Sqn Ldr Andy Collins, Sqn Ldr Tony Cunnane, J/T John Cooper, Master AEO Nev Cooper, Chf Tech David Curnock, Sqn Ldr Ray Curtis, Chris Cussen, Chief Tech Chris Dance, LAC Alan Davidson, SAC Trevor Dobson, Sqn Ldr Gordon Dodds, Sgt George Dorrington, Flt Lt Derrick Downs, Sqn Ldr Mike Dyson, J/T Cliff Edwards, Sgt Malcolm Elliott, Wg Cdr Jerry Evans, Sqn Ldr Mike Evans, Flt Lt Raymond Evans, Flt Lt Nev Feist, Mike Fisher, John Fraser, Sgt John Gibbings, Flt Lt Guy Gibbons, Flt Sgt Mike Griffiths, Brian Haining, Capt Japie Horn SAAF, Brian Howett, Flt Lt Bill Hustwayte, Wg Cdr Keith Jarvis, SAC Paul Jessau, Jim Johnson, Sgt Ian Jones, SAC Peter Kain, Peter Kendall, SAC Clive Kilgour, Bill Killick, Sqn Ldr Rob Knotts, Gp Capt Derek Larkin, Flt Lt Brian Latham, Sqn Ldr Dave Lawrence, John Lennard, J/T Norman Lindsay, Flt Lt Bob Lyall, J/T John May, Flt Lt Neville May, Flt Lt Dave McCandless, Keith McDonald, Sqn Ldr Mike McKenna, Sandy McMillan, Sqn Ldr Alan Mills, Peter Mills, Flt Lt Peter Morris, Sgt Simon Morrison, Gp Capt Mike Norris, Flt Lt David Phillips, Sqn Ldr Colin Pomeroy, Flt Lt Gerry Pond, Sqn Ldr Mike Rankin, SAC Brian Ray, Fg Off Alan Reed, SAC Brian Reynolds, SAC Gerry Reynolds, SAC Ken Rochester, Sqn Ldr Rod Saar, Sqn Ldr 'Red' Sankey, Chf Tech Lance Smale, J/T Ned Smale, Sqn Ldr Tony Smart, John Smith, Sgt Mick Speake, Wg Cdr Derek Straw, Phil Styles, LAC Bill Tarran, Fg Off Reg Turner, Air Cdre Bill Tyack, Nick Von Berg, Flt Lt Jim Ward, SAC Roger Ward, Vic Warren-King, W/O Alastair Watson, Gp Capt Andy White-Boycott, Sqn Ldr Nigel Whitling, Sgt Rex Wickins, W/O Adrian Wilson, Vic Wise, Sqn Ldr Brian Withers, Sgt Stanley Wood.

Gentlemen, I thank and salute you all.

In addition, I must once again say a big 'thank you' to the Shackleton Association, not least Bill Hercus, who edits the superb *Growler* magazine, plus Peter Dunn, Bryn Lewis and Phil Styles, who have willingly allowed me access to their archives and encouraged their membership to support my efforts. The many others who have helped along the way are listed below; if I have forgotten anybody please accept my humble apologies.

Thanks must also go to 41 Squadron Association, Peter Algar, Richard Andrews, Richard Ansley, Adrian Balch, Phil Bennett, Jean Butler, Nick Byatt; 8 Squadron Association, Colin Cooke, Les Davies; Changi-ite website, Ray Deacon RadfanHunters website, the late Colin Fair, Richard Forder, John Hughes, David Kirk RAF Fire Service website, the late Geoff Mann, Pat Martin, Dr Ray Neve who once again valiantly joined me in ploughing through many hours of recorded interviews to transcribe them, Chris Olaf, Russell Osborn, Jeff Peck, Graham Pitchfork, John Rodger, Robbie Shaw, Tim Stevens, Joe Tarrant, Michael Watson, Sue Wilson, Stephen Wolf, Brian Wood, and Keith Woodcock. I must also once again express my gratitude to John Davies and all his team at Grub Street, who continue to support and encourage my literary endeavours. Finally, and most especially of all, my thanks and love go to my darling wife Heather, who has been a driving force and great support throughout the many months of this project, giving me endless ideas and advice, sense-reading and proof-reading my draft manuscripts.

As always, I have endeavoured wherever possible to credit correctly the origins of all the photographs and other material I have used. It has to be said, that in the Internet age, the true origins and source of some material is not always possible to identify with certainty. Therefore, if I have inadvertently omitted anyone please accept my apologies and grateful thanks.

THIS BOOK IS NOT THE END OF THE STORY – there are so many stories yet to be told! Experience has taught me that long after a book has gone to print and been released, people continue to come forward to recount their untold memories. It is my intention to ensure that as many as possible get the airing in print they deserve in some future work.

Dr Steve Bond
February 2019

HOME FROM HOME – LIFE IN A SHACKLETON

20,000 RIVETS IN LOOSE FORMATION

Pete Bethell and his crew after an SAR flight in 205 Squadron's WL741 from Gan, 21 March 1964. (Gordon Dodds)

Gordon Dodds – pilot 204, 205 and 206 Squadrons

"Since before the Second World War our maritime air forces have been considered the 'Cinderella Service'. They were assigned leftover, old, noisy, uncomfortable aircraft with out-of-date equipment. 'Front-enders' might be forgiven for looking enviously at other roles equipped with the latest, fast, shiny, glamorous 'planes. This is not my view! In a curious way the noise, vibration, smell, long, and sometimes tedious hours on Shackletons bound crew members together. We shared long, uncomfortable flights, day and night, which helped us become teams of ten men together. I was privileged to work and fly with a huge range of characters from all walks of life. The comradeship was very special, the Shackleton squadrons' greatest strength.

"The tailwheel undercarriage and balloon tyres of the Mk.2 Shackleton were notorious for causing pilots problems. They contributed to many exciting arrivals over the years. The one golden rule when making an asymmetric landing was, even if you bounce, do not go around again. Once, we were doing night circuits, and on an asymmetric approach we bounced badly. For some reason, my colleague decided to ignore the golden rule, he thrust the THREE throttles forward and we clawed our way back into the air. At such low speed the rudder did not have enough bite to counteract the asymmetric thrust, so we started to yaw slowly to the left. Out of the gloom appeared a hangar, just to the left of the nose. I had time to wonder what new career I should choose if we survived. The speed slowly crept up, the rudder became more effective, then we lurched past the hangar with a roaring of Griffons, a shuddering airframe and a shaking crew. We staggered back into the night sky; the hangar, the aircraft and the crew survived to fight another day. Whoever said that flying the Shackleton was boring?"

CHAPTER ONE

'GUARD THE GATEWAY' – RAF GIBRALTAR

What is now the airport at Gibraltar began life as a racecourse. It was in the years between the two world wars that it started to be used as a flying field, primarily for aircraft disembarking from Royal Navy ships visiting the harbour. By 1942 it had been fully developed into an active airfield, and became RAF North Front, a title it retained until 1966. It was heavily used throughout the war as a fighter station and a staging post for traffic transiting to and from Malta. Maritime units were first stationed at North Front in late 1942 with the arrival of 500 and 608 Squadrons with Hudsons, and 179 Squadron with Wellingtons.

Post-war the maritime role from Gibraltar was primarily the remit of 224 Squadron. It was first formed in 1918 but disbanded a year later, re-appearing in 1937 in the general reconnaissance role (later renamed maritime reconnaissance). At that time it flew Ansons, then Hudsons and finally Liberators. In 1946 it re-equipped with Lancaster GR.3s (general reconnaissance) at St. Eval, disbanding on 10 November 1947. The squadron re-formed on 1 March 1948 at Aldergrove flying the Halifax GR.6 on meteorological reconnaissance duties, which were soon expanded to take on the full MR role. In October 1948 it began a detachment to North Front, and in 1949 it was renumbered as 224/269 Squadron receiving its first Shackleton in July 1951 when the whole squadron was relocated to Gibraltar.

In January 1952, 269 Squadron split to become independent, moving back to Ballykelly two months later. At the same time 224 Squadron gave up the last of its Halifaxes to become an all-Shackleton MR.1 unit, replacing them with MR.2s from May 1953 (although the last MR.1 did not leave until August the following year).

Bill Hustwayte – navigator

"At the end of March 1953, I was posted out to 224 Squadron in Gibraltar which had only recently changed over from flying the last Halifaxes in the RAF. In those days the squadrons were commanded by squadron leaders. No. 224's boss, when I arrived, was Sqn Ldr Gordon Mattey DFC,

North Front Gibraltar circa 1965. 224 Squadron pans on the right, Four Corners Mess on the left. (Derek Straw)

MR.2 WG533 224 Squadron, turning finals to land North Front Gibraltar.
(via Rex Wickins)

and when he left in October 1953 Sqn Ldr J G Roberts DFC DFM took over and was still there when I went home in April 1955."

Sqn Ldr Mattey had been awarded the DFC in 1941 while flying Coastal Command Whitleys with 51 Squadron at Dishforth. Sqn Ldr John Roberts won his DFM in 1942 whilst with 106 Squadron which flew Hampdens from Finningley, and added the DFC a year later when he was with 150 Squadron at Blida in Algeria, flying Wellingtons. **Bill Hustwayte** *continues:*

"The easiest thing about the Mk.1 Shackleton, after the Lancaster, was getting up the front – the space between the roof and the main spar was only about two feet six or something in the Lanc. The spars were polished like mirrors where all the crew had slid through! Other than that, there wasn't much difference between them. They did the same thing, flying for hour after hour at low level. It was a very short runway in Gibraltar, and there were tremendous crosswinds, so being a tailwheel aircraft it had to be put down very firmly.

"We were a constituted crew and my captain was Frank Nicholls. We had two navigators, first and second; I'd only just come out of training so I was second nav for about the first year I think; but you were still doing all the navigation. In our crew, when my first nav was posted home I became first nav. You had two main types of flight. One was combined submarine exercises with the navy which were done in Malta, where the Mediterranean Fleet was. We were also sent to Ballykelly to exercise with subs based up there. The other type of flight was LROFEs of around 15 hours duration. In fact our crew held the record for a Shackleton for some time – 22 hours and ten minutes continuous; that's a long time with one crew. Because the weather was pretty good at Gib at that time in July, they were just seeing how crews could be fed with hot food, instead of sandwiches, for all that length of time. It was also to see how men performed over a long period. We didn't just go out flying round and round, we flew out to Lisbon, picked up the SS *Vulcania* and escorted it for about 12 hours. The people on board must have thought 'I wonder

224 Squadron crew with 'Nick' Nicholls on right, Flt Sgt Johnny Johnson co-pilot next to him, then Bill Hustwayte, second nav bottom right. (Bill Hustwayte)

why that aircraft keeps going round us?' The aircraft were very reliable as far as I remember.

"We were the search and rescue squadron for that part of the eastern Atlantic, and also for the western part of the Mediterranean. In my time I only had one call-out. This was for the sinking of the *Empire Windrush* on 28 March 1954. I remember it clearly, it was a Sunday morning when we were called out. We had an airborne lifeboat fitted and flew out to Algiers, but were never used. We got over there and flew round and round the area where the ship was on fire for half an hour, but by that time there was a naval destroyer and several other ships rescuing everybody off the ship. There were only four fatalities, in the engine room where the fire had started, and the ship sank two days later."

> The Empire Windrush *was a British troopship en route from Japan to the UK carrying 1,276 passengers and 222 crew. On 28 March 1954 there was an explosion and fire in the engine room, and half an hour later the order was given to abandon ship. A number of ships rallied to pick up the survivors. A line was put aboard the ship to tow it to Gibraltar, but it sank early on 30 March when only eight miles out.* **Bill Hustwayte** *again.*

"In July '54 the Soviets exploded their first nuclear weapon. Two of our Shacks went back to the UK, going to Avro's at Woodford to have sniffing devices fitted. I think the worst of the radiation was around about 30 to 35 degrees north in a wide band. There were several Canberras flying at high level, with the Shackletons at low level. We did some very long trips. People were there from Aldermaston checking the aircraft over, and taking all the filters out to find out what sort of weapon had been exploded.

"We went to Ballykelly to compete in the Aird Whyte trophy, an anti-submarine and bombing competition between the squadrons. We also went to Ballykelly twice for the Joint Anti-submarine School (JASS). Crews were operating with Royal Navy destroyers and frigates and chasing our submarines when we found them. It was very interesting, lasting for about three or four weeks and we did a lot of flying.

"The squadron routine meant that we would fly two or three times a week. In

The Empire Windrush *on fire March 1954. (Bill Hustwayte)*

my 24 months on the squadron I flew 1,114 hours. By the time I left, we still had five Mk.1 and three Mk.2 Shackletons. The only difference was that instead of having that big bay window in the front, the Mk.2 had the guns. All my nav gear was still the same.

"I was very happy to have had a tour on Shackletons, even though you were sat between eight contra-rotating propellers – there were no bone domes in those days. After my Shackleton time I went into the night-fighter world on 141 Squadron with Venoms then later, Javelins for a number of years, before going back to multi-pistons with 48 Squadron Hastings at Changi."

The Empire Windrush *was not the only passenger liner fire that called on 224 Squadron's services. In December 1962, the Greek-operated SS Lakonia, en route from Southampton to the Canary Islands, suffered a fire which quickly spread to the point where the ship had to be abandoned. In all 646 passengers and 376 crew took to the lifeboats, although several had been destroyed by the fire.*

Flt Lt Dave Leppard and his crew took part in the SAR effort in MR.2 WL757 C, locating the lifeboats and directing the rescuing ships. Eventually, the Argentinian passenger ship Salta and the British cargo ship Montcalm, were able to rescue the survivors. Sadly, 128 of those aboard the Lakonia had lost their lives.

MR.1 S 224 Squadron Gibraltar. (Bill Hustwayte)

Derek Larkin – Air Electronics Operator (AEO)

"Derek 'Min' Larkin was coming to the end of his three years at Halton as an aircraft apprentice when he volunteered for aircrew duties. He was accepted for a five-year period, then available to former apprentices, before returning to his ground trade to complete his twelve-year engagement. He trained as a wireless operator and air gunner. In the autumn of 1953, he was awarded his signaller's brevet, his sergeant's stripes and a posting to Coastal Command.

"After three months at St. Mawgan with the School of Maritime Reconnaissance (SMR) flying in the Lancaster, he left for Kinloss and 236 OCU (Operational Conversion Unit) to convert to the Shackleton. Two months later he joined 224 Squadron at Gibraltar, which operated the Shackleton MR.2.

"The squadron flew patrols into the Mediterranean and into the Atlantic west of Portugal. NATO exercises operating with the Royal Navy's Home and Mediterranean Fleets and with the US Sixth Fleet were regular activities. An unusual task in September 1956 was to fly on a south-westerly track from Gibraltar at 18,000 feet gathering air samples following Soviet nuclear tests. He flew two similar sorties over the next two weeks.

"During the 1956 Suez crisis, the squadron found itself on the fringes of the operation but there was increased activity by Soviet surface ships and submarines and the squadron had the important task of monitoring the narrow Straights of Gibraltar, the western entrance to the Mediterranean. This was to become a regular feature of 224 Squadron's activities in the coming years as the Soviet Navy's Black Sea Fleet started to expand

Flt Lt Olaf Cussen DFC and bar. (Chris Cussen)

its operations.

"Towards the end of his tour, Larkin achieved an 'A' categorisation and was appointed the signals leader on his crew." [1]

Olaf Cussen – pilot
Flt Lt Olaf Cussen's son Chris kindly provided the following memories about his late father who died in 2009. Gib was Olaf's last flying posting, having survived the war flying 67 operations in Whitleys, Halifaxes and Lancasters, during which he was awarded the DFC and bar. In November 1942, while on 161 Squadron on special duties, he crashed Whitley Z9160 in the Algarve when on the way back from Gib due to double engine failure. He and his crew were interned. As Chris says "Well, interned is a strong word as they were asked not to run away, and stayed in a village until repatriated two months later to continue his flying."

"My father finished his Shackleton conversion at 236 OCU Kinloss in May 1955. He then flew Shacks from Gib in 224 Squadron between 1956 and 1958. He flew a Shack pretending it was a Lanc for the film *Silent Enemy*. I can remember the Shack, WL792, doing a high-speed belly landing on the runway during the Battle of Britain display on 14 September 1957. I was standing just behind the barrier as it slid past! It touched down about a quarter of the way down the runway and slid past the audience. I still remember seeing the props curl under the engine cowlings, and that the tailwheel came off and bounced alongside the aircraft. The display was intended to have Shacks fly past on four, then three, then two and finally one engine. Dad was flying 'Q Queenie' and overflew the crash on a single engine. The entry in his logbook is a rather laconic 'Formation Flying'.

"On a goodwill mission to South America [see Trevor Dobson's account below] he flew MR.2 WL753, one of four aircraft to take part. They flew along the beach at Rio de Janeiro so low that the prop wash was blowing spray off the tops of the waves!"

Trevor Dobson – armourer
"I had joined the RAF in early 1954, and after trade training at Kirkham in Lancs was posted in the autumn to Strubby, a satellite of the RAF Flying College based

---

1. 'Men Behind the Shackleton', Graham Pitchfork, *Flypast*, 2018

at nearby Manby. One of the college's various roles was to introduce senior officers, with piston-engine backgrounds, to the new jet types entering service, a novel feature of these being ejection seats. Thus, I found myself working with the explosive cartridges for the seats, together with canopy detonators, and practice bombs for the unit's Canberras. Initially I was content with this new and exciting world of RAF life in deepest Lincolnshire, but before long I began to get itchy feet. These were the days of Empire, when the possibilities for overseas postings were mouth-watering. Fired with tales of life in Singapore I volunteered for the Far East, and was posted instead to Gibraltar. But what the heck it was overseas, and January 1956 found me eagerly climbing aboard an Eagle Airways Viking at Blackbushe for the Air Ministry trooping flight to Gib. It was the first time in my life that I had set foot outside England.

"I quickly settled into the routine of the Coastal Command base, which despite its small size and single flying squadron, was a surprisingly busy host to a steady flow of visiting aircraft both scheduled and ad hoc. The armourers were kept on their toes storing, servicing and loading the Shackletons' depth charges, sonobouys, pyrotechnics and 20-mm Hispano cannons. The armament section was located on the north side of the airfield, close to the fence which marked the border with Spain. Despite a sensitive political situation the border was open, thus giving access to La Linea for recreation at the weekend. The busy working routine, in support of the generally lengthy sorties flown by the Shackletons, was an early start. Then at the end of the day, we headed for Eastern Beach if time permitted. No. 224 Squadron itself had reason to hold its head high, having won the Coastal Command Inter-Squadron Efficiency Trophy for the last two years running. To add to its good

fortune, it heard that it had been selected to showcase the RAF and the Shackleton on a tour of South America and the Caribbean – and to my great delight, I heard that I would be going too.

"Code-named Operation Southern Cross the tour would last from 16 March to 17 April 1957. The exotic itinerary would embrace Brazil, Uruguay, Argentina, Chile, Peru, Ecuador, Florida, and Bermuda, and this was to be a very

224 Squadron's WL753 2 ready for the South America tour March 1957. Left to right: Jimmy Lynch, Gordon Cowling (UK), Jim Eley, (then UK), front Flt Lt Olaf Cussen. (Chris Cussen)

prestigious project entailing meticulous preparation. Force commander for the trip would be the air officer commanding (AOC) RAF Gibraltar, Air Cdre John Miller, who had a distinguished background and who was four times mentioned in despatches. His deputy would be Wg Cdr Edward Odoire DFC and bar, AFC, the senior air staff officer (SASO) at Air Headquarters Gibraltar. The top trio would be completed by 224's CO, Wg Cdr Gordon Willis DFC AFC, who had an extensive maritime background. Four aircraft were earmarked and painted '1' to '4' on the nose: WL758 ('1' – CO plus AOC Gib); WL753 ('2' – Sqn Ldr R Flood); WL751 ('3' – Flt Lt Olaf Cussen DFC); and WL752 ('4' – Flt Lt Anthony Bluett DFC and bar). Preparations for the forthcoming odyssey began in earnest with formation flying practice heading the list. The aircraft were made spick and span, ground crew were issued with white overalls, and I was advised that I would be promoted to acting sergeant (unpaid!) for the duration of the tour, a sensible ploy aimed at ensuring me reasonable accommodation 'down route'. I found myself allocated to WL753, on which my chief task would be to manage the aircraft panniers. These contained a comprehensive range of spares plus all the baggage, and had to be winched in and out of the bomb bay as required. Lindholme rescue gear would also be taken."

*Air Cdre John Miller was OC 145 Squadron Blenheim Ifs at Croydon on the outbreak of war. Wg Cdr Edward Odoire won his first DFC with 142 Squadron when flying Battles, and the bar three years later when the same squadron had Wellingtons. Wg Cdr Gordon Willis commanded the Wellington-equipped 524 Squadron at Langham, Norfolk towards the end of World War 2. Flt Lt Bluett's DFC was won when flying Hurricanes in the Western Desert with 6 Squadron, and the bar when flying Mustangs with 112 Squadron in Italy. **Trevor Dobson** continues.*

"With so many countries on the itinerary, the currency plan and imprest arrangements involved the station accounts staff in some nifty legwork. Thus it was that on Saturday 16 March at 0700 hours the Shackletons, crammed with people and equipment, began roaring off from Gib bound for Dakar (Senegal) some ten hours 45 minutes flying time away. Dakar was the stepping stone for the Atlantic crossing. After an overnight stop in the West African capital, the detachment set off early next morning for the long, over-water leg to Recife (Brazil). It was planned this would take just under 13 hours. The main preoccupation for the ground crew in the back of the aircraft during these lengthy transit flights was to find somewhere comfortable to sit and, not surprisingly, the crew rest bunks were in great demand. My preference was for either the bomb aimer's position in the nose, or the observer's position in the tail, which 'waggled about a bit'!

"Following an uneventful crossing of 'the pond' Recife was duly reached, but this was merely a convenient landfall, and the tour proper was due to begin at Rio de Janeiro. The itinerary then took in Montevideo (Uruguay); Buenos Aires (Argentina); Santiago (Chile); Lima (Peru); Guayaquil (Ecuador); Key West (Florida); Bermuda; and the Azores. In general terms the flying programme for the tour was divided into three-day groups: day one – transit and service aircraft; day two – demonstration flight; day three – rest day. The actual displays at each location normally began with a single aircraft doing four, three, two and single-engine flypasts; then a slow flypast with bomb doors, flaps, scanner and wheels down; followed by a fast, low pass; and finishing up with a three-ship formation display. I have vivid memories of how impressed the spectators were at each venue; on every occasion 224's performance was a real head-turner. Long queues formed to inspect the Shackletons on the ground, and the hospitality was legendary wherever we went! At messes and cricket clubs (a curiously prolific British institution) along the way we were invariably feted, and barbecues followed cocktail parties in stamina-sapping succession. There was the opportunity to go up Sugar Loaf mountain, and down Copacabana beach. Banana trees, cotton plants and llamas were seen for the first time. A rest day trip took us up into the Andes to what was purportedly the highest railway in the world, at 15,800 feet.

"The tour as a whole was far from routine. I remember that flying across the Andes to Santiago had apparently caused some concern to the aircrew though of course, this was not passed on to the passengers. Similarly while at Guayaquil (7-9 April) two aircraft were detailed to visit the Ecuadorean capital Quito, some 10,000 feet up in the mountains. On take-off for the return trip the Shackletons needed the full, +25 lb boost, and water methanol injection to get off the ground due to the high altitude. From 3-5 April the programme took the detachment to Lima, capital of Peru, where I was very interested to see Peruvian air force Hunters and Canberras, only delivered the previous year.

"Leaving Guayaquil on 10 April the force flew north up the coast, and headed for the US Navy base at Key West in Florida. Here the Shackleton with its in-line Griffons, contra-rotating props and tailwheel was something of a novelty to the Americans, long used to nose-wheels and radial engines. One Shack gave engine trouble here after almost flawless serviceability thus far, which prompted a flood of volunteers in Gib to fly out a spare! However, Key West was merely a transit stop and not on the display programme, resulting in two rest days. With Miami beckoning, and Greyhound buses a-plenty, myself and my mate Ted Bunn led the field to see alligators in a swamp, and Frank Sinatra in a hotel!

"The tour was nearing its planned end, but there was one more display to perform before the team headed home, and this was at Bermuda. It was a seven-hour trip away out over the Atlantic and roughly 1,100 miles to the north-east of Florida. Transiting on Saturday 13 April, Sunday was a rest day, and the display took place on the 15th – and what a show it was! 'RAF 'Planes in Demonstration Over City' trumpeted Bermuda's newspaper *The Royal Gazette*. The following day: 'Three Royal Air Force Coastal Command 'planes roared low over Hamilton yesterday morning in a demonstration of power and manoeuvrability of the Shackleton.... Hundreds of persons, many of them on roofs and verandas, watched as the 'planes came from Kindley Air Force Base at 10.45 a.m. In their first pass over the harbour, from north-west to south-east, the 'planes were in group formation. A moment later, they came

MR.2 WL758 224 Squadron on a one-engine flypast during the South American tour, March 1957. (Trevor Dobson)

back in a line. Swooping down low over the harbour and then pulling sharply up to clear the city, the 'planes separated, the one on either end [sic] peeling off to left and right and the centre aircraft continuing in the same direction. The four-engined 'planes also made solo passes over Hamilton. First one came over with one engine feathered. Then, another came over with only two engines on one side operating. The third roared by with only one engine working, the other three propellers visibly motionless. During some of their passes, the 'planes had their wheels lowered and bomb bays opened.' The two photos accompanying the front-page report provided vivid testimony to what an impressive sight it must have been.

"That was about it. On the evening of 16 April I clambered aboard '753 for a 22.00 departure. This was the longest leg of the entire tour – 13 hours and 25 minutes to the Azores. After a most welcome night-stop at the Portuguese base, it was a mere seven hours and 40 minutes 'hop' over to Gibraltar. When we arrived back on the Rock in the late afternoon of 18 April I was very tired, but very happy to have been lucky enough to be selected for the trip of a lifetime. The month-long, 16,000-mile tour had stuck to schedule, had been a great success, and was a credit to all involved."

*Five months later, he was also a witness to the unfortunate air display accident mentioned by Chris Cussen. **Trevor Dobson** again:*

"From the airfield the towering 1,300 feet of limestone, which forms the distinctive Rock of Gibraltar, made an imposing backdrop for the station's annual, and very popular, Battle of Britain 'At Home' day. The flying display was a noisy and impressive affair, for a wide variety of UK and foreign types was on show both in the air and on the ground. Eventually, it was the turn of RAF Gibraltar's resident 224 Squadron to demonstrate its current equipment, the Shackleton MR.2. Eagerly the crowd looked out over Eastern Beach as WL792 lined up for the runway, the growl of its Griffon engines echoing off the sheer face of the Rock. But what was this? – the 'Shack' was touching down with its wheels up! There was a screeching and grinding of tortured metal as the aircraft slithered along the runway, its contra-rotating propellers instantly losing the argument with the unyielding concrete. The oft-repeated story – probably apocryphal – is that the crowd thought the incident was part of the routine and roared their approval, but a stunned air traffic control knew otherwise and immediately triggered the emergency procedures. One of the first on the scene was the duty armourer, Jeff Setterfield, who made the aircraft safe from an explosives point of view. I was another young armourer watching events that day as I was off-duty, and I caught the luckless Shackleton's unorthodox progress down the runway on my Kodak Brownie."

> *The unfortunate four-year-old Shackleton was initially categorised as Category 4 (repairable), but was re-categorised Category 5 on 11 November 1957 and broken up on site for components.* **Trevor Dobson** *continues.*

"My Gibraltar tour took me on until January 1958, after which I went home to demob and 'civvy street'. Today, surrounded by documents and photos of that overseas tour, within an overseas tour as it were, I can smile and reminisce enthusiastically about what a grand affair it all was. Exactly as it should have been for a 21-year old."[2]

MR.2 WL792 K 224 Squadron wheels-up landing Gibraltar, 14 September 1957. (Trevor Dobson)

---

2. *The Growler* issue 67.

Dave Curnock – engines

"I arrived at North Front, Gibraltar in May 1958 as a newly qualified junior technician (J/T) engine fitter, fresh from completing an apprenticeship at Halton. I was posted onto Aircraft Servicing Flight (ASF), where we were responsible for carrying out second line servicing on the Shackletons of 224 Squadron, and on the Station Flight aircraft comprising a VIP Devon, an Anson, and two Meteors. Occasionally we would also carry out rectification of defects on visiting aircraft. My first supervisor was an experienced corporal technician (Cpl/Tech) who promptly told me to forget all that 'stuff' they had taught us at Halton, and to learn how things were really done. It didn't take too long to find out what he meant.

"My initiation into the mechanical complexities of the Shackleton began rather modestly as a Man 'E' (if my recollection serves me) on a minor servicing. This lowly position was reserved for newbies like me, or for any engine man who had, in some way, incurred the wrath of the Chiefy! One of the first tasks on an inspection involved the fully de-cowling of all four engines by their respective fitters. They then placed the cowlings and panels on wheeled racks which were pushed across to the corner of the hangar where I took over the cleaning and repair (if such repair was within my scope of capability) of the items. My domain was occupied by a large paraffin bath in which the items were degreased, and an air-line which was used for initially drying them off. The final drying was achieved using large handfuls of cotton waste – not a particularly efficient material. My corporal technician introduced me to using the water/paraffin emulsion that, along with an engine cleaning brush, worked particularly well in the crevices on the insides of the panels. On completion of inspection and repair the area was closed off with canvas screens to form a spray booth. Here the panels were painted in a beautiful shade of grey! One job that was left to the engine lads who refitted the panels was to apply, using an artist's pencil brush, the fastener alignment marks in white paint.

"In due course I worked my way up through the pecking order of job cards onto the real engine work. This included the first of many changes of spark plugs, each engine had 24 of these. There were two per cylinder – one on the outside of the cylinder bank (easy) and one buried inside the vee (not so easy). Apart from the spark plug spanner, a length of low-pressure oxygen hose was useful for removing and installing the inner plugs. It fitted nicely over the end of the plug and reduced the chances of dropping a plug down the vee, a sure way to incur the wrath of the Chiefy and earn the unfortunate fitter a turn at the paraffin bath on the next aircraft in! Checking and adjustment of the valve clearances and other tasks such as examining the radiators/oil coolers and intake meshes for corrosion were relatively simple jobs; a less than pleasant job was the removal of the water-methanol pumps. This was necessary to allow removal of the snot-like residue that formed in the bottom of each tank between servicings. Removal of this slime involved using one's arm to reach into the tank through the booster pump aperture, and dragging the slime out through the same hole. Naturally some of the mess ran along your arm resulting in a change of overalls and a salt-water shower. Even the shower usually failed to remove all of the stubbornly pungent odour from the skin.

"One particularly tedious job involved the removal and replacement of all the engine control rods and cables from the roof of the bomb bay. These were often badly corroded, along with many other parts of the Shackleton. Resetting the controls, and lock-wiring the turnbuckles, was fairly time consuming. Corrosion is a major problem on any aircraft, especially on the Shackleton, with it operating for long periods at low level over the sea. Even when on the ground the airfields from which they operated were often close to the sea, particularly that in Gibraltar. We took some unofficial measures to reduce or delay the onset of corrosion on some components. Typically the engine air-intake grill meshes, and the leading fins of the coolant radiators were given a light coating of yacht varnish. This item was available under RAF provisioning from the main stores in Gibraltar, as it was used on the decks of the marine craft section rescue launches.

"On completion of the inspection there were the obligatory engine ground runs; the principal characters in this activity were the chiefs and sergeants. The remainder of the team usually ended up on hangar cleaning duties or, if lucky, a place in the sun as 'outside man' on the ground run team checking for leaks, or on fire-bottle duty. After satisfactory completion of post-hangar work the aircraft was prepared for air test. I once won the sweepstake to represent the engine trade on an air test. I spent most of the flight sitting on the floor of the aircraft with my back against the rear spar, from which position I was unable to see outside. On one notable occasion an aircraft was presented for air test on 11 separate occasions. It was rejected for a variety of reasons by the test crew, which included mag drops and radio and radar equipment problems. Rather bizarrely, one of its air tests was postponed after a bee had crawled inside the pitot head. While we were waiting for the crew to complete their internal pre-start checks, an eagle-eyed member of the ground crew actually saw the bee as it approached, watched it land on the pitot head and crawl inside. Congratulations all round (except from the instrument men who had to break into the pitot system to remove the offending insect).

"Having volunteered for Gibraltar I was (somewhat foolishly) one of the first to put my hand up when our Chiefy

MR.2 WL754 of 37 Squadron, engine change Masirah. (Chris Ashworth)

asked for volunteers to join 224 Squadron on a detachment. I was mistakenly under the impression it would be a super jolly as the squadron had, in the year before my arrival, undertaken a tour of South America [see pages 26-28] – wrong! The detachment was to Masirah, a place that neither I, nor any of the lads in the crew room, had ever heard of. A week or so working on the squadron, before our departure, served as familiarisation in the first line working life of an engine fitter on the Shackleton. In the main this consisted of refuelling, re-oiling, water-meth-anol replenishment, etc. One of the most frequent snags that cropped up on the after-flight inspection was the missing exhaust stub. This was a frequent event in the days prior to the extended tail-pipe modification to the exhaust system. The fish-tail exhaust stubs often failed around the welded joint securing them to the mounting flange, which abutted the exhaust expansion chamber. Most engine men had a sharpened GS screwdriver in their tool kit. This came in handy, as a makeshift chisel, for splitting the bronze nuts that secured the flange, thus speeding up the fitment of a new stub.

"As one of four aircraft we flew to Khormaksar, Aden in early January 1959. It was a flight time of around 26 flying hours with a transit stop en route. For the whole detachment I was allocated to fly with a crew captained by one of the senior squadron pilots. This flight lieutenant had many years' experience on the Shack-leton, and was held in some awe by many of the crew. He was a stickler for punc-tuality, and also had a rather short temper that was often coupled with some col-ourful language. He always landed freshly shaved, having brought his own shaving kit including a mug which was filled with hot water from the galley, and used the mirror of the P12 compass to great effect during this process. His colourful language was highlighted during our approach and landing at El Adem, Libya. The co-pilot, a likeable Scotsman who was relatively new on Shackletons, was flying this phase of the flight. It was not until after we had landed that the co-pilot realised that some rather explicit words of 'advice' to him from the captain had been heard by everyone over the intercom!

"The purpose of the detachment was to carry out what was known as 'colonial policing'. This involved Shackleton squadrons, on three-monthly rotations, in dropping bombs on various targets in the desolate, mountainous part of the 'emp-ty quarter' in Oman. I believe 224 Squadron was the last unit to carry out this particular duty. After a period in which the crews worked up to practise their bombing and gunnery skills at Khormaksar we set off for Masirah, a further five hours flying time away. On arrival the ground crew had to erect their tents on a fresh section of desert that formed the domestic area; the previous incumbents from a base in Cornwall had left the original tented area in a rather unsanitary condition. My billet was a six-man tent, which proved rather spacious as there were only two of us sharing. Work was a daily routine of pre- and post-flight in-spections, replenishment of systems, de-snagging, and finally, the 'armourers' ben-efit'. For this exciting production all those trades other than armament kept as far

MR.2 of 224 Squadron, piloted by Flt Lt George Etches, carrying out a low pass at Masirah in early 1959. (Dave Curnock)

from the aircraft as possible, due to them being 'bombed up' for the next day's detail. Those who were slow off the mark could find themselves providing motive power to a bomb trolley. This was not an ideal situation as there had been one instance of a 500-pounder falling from its carrier in the bomb bay, onto one of the only pieces of concrete on the dispersal.

"One day, on returning to the tented flight office following a lunch break, we came across the unusual sight of the back end of a donkey sticking out from between the tent flaps. This was one of many that roamed freely around the local village just outside the camp area. As there was no boundary fence to prevent either man or beast entering the airfield area the donkey had decided to look for some lunch. We soon found it had taken a liking to, and eaten, several pages of one of the Form 700s that were left open on the table when everybody went to lunch. These pages included some of the servicing records, and most of the major component life details. Several signals later, most of the information had been obtained from Gibraltar technical records – very embarrassing for the NCOs in charge at the time. Those of us in the junior ranks saw the funny side of it all, even though we had to carry out a fresh inspection and re-signing of the replacement F700.

"While at Masirah 224 Squadron took part in a formation flypast in honour of the visiting AOC-in-C, Johnnie Johnson, who was on his farewell tour of stations under his command. I was fortunate enough to fly on the rehearsal. My normal transit position in the front turret had been commandeered by somebody of higher rank, so I was allocated a seat in the port beam – with a large, inward-opening porthole window. Noisy, but exhilarating. However, unfortunately I leaned a little too far forward into the slipstream and lost the lens hood from the camera I had borrowed. Regrettably I only had one black-and-white film with eight shots remaining – two of these I had inadvertently 'double exposed'. My time at Masirah was broken by two trips away, one to Bahrain and the other to Khormaksar to replace an engine that had developed a coolant leak. The latter trip was at short notice as a medevac flight with a sick, locally enlisted, army chap occupying one of the crew bunks.

"All things said, although it was hard work, I enjoyed my time on the 'Shack'. There was a tremendous feeling of satisfaction when 'my' aircraft took to the air, the sound of four (usually!) Griffons roaring overhead is something I shall never forget."

Ian Jones – air signaller

"In the summer of 1962 I was at Topcliffe, training as an air signaller, when a large very noisy visitor arrived. It was a Shackleton T.4; my first close-up view of the 'Old Grey Lady' which, if I passed my training, I would most likely be serving on. My father was serving at Ballykelly, a large Shackleton airfield, so I had seen Shacks before of course. However, I had never been up close to one.

"I seemed to be transported back to World War 2. On close inspection, it might well have just returned from a bombing mission over Germany. On board, after clambering up the ladder onto the steeply sloping floor, the first thing that hit me was the smell – a mixture of oil, battery acid and vomit! What was I doing? Could I wangle a posting onto Transport Command? Unlikely, so better get used to it. So, as expected, I was duly posted to the MOTU to convert onto the Shack. My first flight was on 26 July 1962, and will be etched in my memory forever. I only had to look at one and I could be airsick. I managed to survive the training, and my mood was much improved when I was posted to 224 Squadron at North Front, Gibraltar. I flew from Lyneham to Gibraltar in a Comet Mk.2; my first jet ride. It had rear-facing seats, so the take-off and climb-out left one hanging from the seat by the belt – not nice! 224 Squadron was probably the best posting anyone could have wished for. The squadron offices were modern and on the north side of the runway, whilst the station was on the south side. We all had airfield driving permits and commuted across the runway in clapped-out old J2 mini buses. I quickly felt at home there. Here we were, young, single, living free of charge in a nice mess in a lovely climate and with money in our pockets.

"Landing and take-off from North Front could be quite exciting as the Rock created some quite serious up and down drafts. Experienced pilots on finals could see the downdrafts coming by observing the sea changing on the surface. Luckily I was allocated to crew 7 and for our crew photograph we made a break with tradition and stood in a figure seven formation. The film 'The Magnificent Seven' was all the rage. I had arranged for the station broadcaster to play the theme as we beat up the runway at low level on our return from a trip. What a life. We were captained by a super New Zealander, Flt Lt Andy Bezzant. He had flown Beaufighters in World War 2 and was a very good and safe pilot. Landing a large heavy

Flt Lt Andy Bezzant's crew 7, 224 Squadron. (Ian Jones)

'tail dragger' was really a skill and we used to form up outside the squadron to watch visiting crews land. There were hoots of derision as they bounced and sometimes had to go around again.

"Life quickly settled down, and in retrospect, it was easy. We spent a lot of time in the crew room drinking coffee, eating bacon butties and 'genning' up on the Shack's many devices (systems were as yet unknown in electronics). Flying however, was the complete opposite. It appeared that seeing how long we could stay airborne was a matter of honour. Mostly we seemed to be at a thousand feet or less, being chucked around in the turbulence, and in my case chucking up anything that I had eaten or drunk in the past 12 hours. It quickly became apparent that I could not spend more than ten minutes on the sonar positions, which were situated next to the front spar and orientated sideways to the centreline of the aircraft. So, I spent much of my Shack time avoiding these to the relief of my crew colleagues, who were rather fed up with me spending so much time with my head in a sick bag. It did not stop them sending me up a cup of what, in those days, passed for coffee, which I duly drank only to find a fag end at the bottom! Pass me a bag! In fact the only thing I could keep down, on some very rough trips, was a cup filled with tinned peaches and tinned cream – bizarre. What I do find amazing is that when I look in my logbooks, many of the trips I did more than 50 years ago, are still quite vivid in my memory.

"The RAF had a penchant for naming equipment with a colour code, so we had Blue Silk, Orange Harvest and Green Satin. We also had Autolycus, which was a large dustbin size tank in the nose, and the objective was to fly a zig-zag course ahead at low level in order that Autolycus could detect the CO_2 and exhaust fumes from a submarine, which was using its snorkel or cruising on the surface. Autolycus was in Shakespeare's 'A Winter's Tale' and was a 'Sniffer out of unconsidered trifles'. Operations when we used it were code-named 'Bisto'!

"I loved W/T and radar. The radar was ASV 21 and was housed in a dustbin-like housing which could be lowered and raised under the aircraft. It was a great piece of kit. We could, with practice and skill, detect very small objects on the surface at quite some distance. W/T was of course 98% Morse code, and most of our messages sent and received were encoded. It was the W/T signaller's job to collect the codes after the briefing. Thankfully we were not instructed to eat the books in the event of capture! We also had a top secret KL7 coding machine based on the German 'Enigma'. There was one sin that no signaller should be guilty of committing – landing with the radio trailing aerial still extended. It was just a wire with lead weights at the end and was deployed when we were at very long range and for certain frequencies.

"Stories around squadron life were many. One crew, when crossing the runway in Gib at high speed, forgot the massive storm drains along the edge and rolled the vehicle! No. 224 Squadron was the relief for 37 Squadron based at Khormaksar. This required us to send aircraft and crews down there once a year to provide relief and support. The troubles were still on in Yemen, so we were always conscious of the danger. This meant that 224 Squadron aircraft always had the two 20-mm cannons mounted in the nose, and we practised firing them regularly. On arrival we were briefed on personal defence. We all sat in a room awaiting our 'lecturer'. Around the walls were a lot of framed pictures, all turned to the wall; of course curiosity got the better of us, and someone got up and turned them around. They were all photos taken in the local morgue of the bodies of British troops. By the time our lecture started we were well wound up and prepared to kill anything that seemed a threat.

"We were billeted in the Red Sea Hotel, which was right next to the goat market. Depending on the wind direction the pong could be incredible. In fact I was there on the day President Kennedy was assassinated. After getting the important things done – buying Bata 'Bundoo Boots' (which we were allowed to wear with uniform), cameras, hi-fi and electrical goods – we flew regular missions to suppress the locals and any desire they may have had to do us harm. Of course we were very 'British'. We would fly over the selected target one day and drop leaflets telling them we would be back tomorrow to drop bombs! Gunnery practice was a bit of a failure, the target being a large hessian rectangle between two poles, set up on the range. We would fly in, set 'Guns to fire', and let rip. Certainly, in our crew, I don't think we managed to put a shot through the target, ever. The position of the two breech blocks either side of the signaller operating the guns, meant that the noise, smoke and smell were real adrenalin pumpers.

"Whilst there in 1963 two crews were called out on SAR duties. We were both scrambled to search for an aircraft carrying some Somali VIP politicians. In those days we had to collect rations from the store, and one signaller on board was duty cook. Every crew had at least one damn good cook. We duly belted over to the store in a Land Rover and scooped up as much as we could, racing back to the two aircraft and throwing it all in. We quickly got airborne and headed south for Mogadishu. A 12-hour 20-minute search was conducted, and during this time we discovered that the bulk of our rations were tinned steak and kidney pies and tinned Dundee cake; just the job for the sort of operation we were on and the temperatures we were in!

"We landed at Mogadishu where we were promptly arrested and the aircraft impounded. All very friendly I suppose, but a bit worrying nonetheless. We chocked the aircraft with the only thing available, large rocks. The Swiss consul arrived quite

MR.2 WL789A of 224 Squadron at Khormaksar 1964. (Ray Deacon)

quickly (the UK had no diplomatic ties with Somalia at that time) and sorted things out. We were taken downtown, to what was quite a smart hotel and given rooms (the only other guests were Soviet and Chinese). That evening we decided to see what night life was available in Mogadishu. A large bar on the seafront appeared to be the only night life we could find, so it was beers all round. We had only been there a few minutes when a band appeared and started playing, followed by the arrival of a stream of very beautiful women. Needless to say the evening was a huge success; we hoped we had done a lot to rekindle UK-Somali relations! On return to the hotel we discovered that we were locked out and there was no sign of any staff. One signaller took on the challenge. After clambering on his mate's shoulders, he managed to get to the first-floor balcony, in through the open door, through the bedroom of the sleeping Soviet/Chinese guest, and downstairs to open the front door.

"Next day we took off for another punishing search. I say punishing because we were flying in very high temperatures at very low level over vast areas of scrubland. Once again tinned steak and kidney pies and Dundee cake were all we had. That night we returned to the bar, and again, did all we could to ensure continuing good UK-Somali relations. Enough said. Then one bright spark had an idea – Mogadishu had Tuk-Tuk-type taxis. There was only one fairly short section of dual carriageway in the town, and it was decided that we would hire the drivers to take us on a 'chariot' race around it. Of course, we were all pretty much drunk by now but what the hell! I can't recall who won but it was a real 'Ben Hur' job, and we were lucky not to have killed anyone. The next day we set off to search again, but this time it was felt that the missing aircraft would have most likely vanished and the chance of survivors was very remote. So, after a final extensive search, we set course for Khormaksar and relatively sober evenings.

"Our return to Gib proved to be a bit of an epic as we were tasked to escort a group of Hawker Hunters back to Malta. In those days we were not permitted to overfly Egypt, so the route would take us via what was known as 'Nasser's Corner'. We all departed Khormaksar to refuel at Khartoum. When we reached Khartoum it was decided that the wind direction en route was against the Hunters, so we were stuck there until it changed. Such a shame! We were taken to the magnificent Blue Nile Hotel situated at the junction of the Blue and White Niles. Full board in a luxury hotel – really tough. Whilst there, we managed to visit the site of the battle of Omdurman, the Mahdi's, as well as a lot more local tourism. At that time the idea of tourism in the Sudan was not on the cards, so we were very privileged. Unfortunately after four days the wind duly changed, and off we went escorting the Hunters. By escorting I mean that we provided airborne SAR cover should one of them go down – even flat out I doubt a Shack could keep up.

"Other memorable flights included a liaison trip to the French base at Blida, Algeria. This was just a short hop from Gib. When we arrived we were feted by our French colleagues. After a day spent looking at their aircraft, followed by a huge lunch accompanied by a lot of wine, we set off for home. I only speak for the signallers on board but how we managed to operate I have no idea. Had we been breathalysed we might have been stuck there for some time. One of our number had even managed to swop his RAF beret for a magnificent French fireman's helmet, complete with crest, which he proudly wore en route and as he stepped off the aircraft.

"On the downside of all this was the fact that the Shack and I did not mix. I even had a doctor from the aeromedical institute come down to Gib to examine me. At the end of my tour I asked to be posted to SAR helicopters, where I found my true love of excitement fulfilled. I was involved in many rescues, and was lucky enough to be decorated by the Queen for gallantry.

"Despite everything life as a signaller was good. Life on a Shackleton squadron was enjoyable, and friends were made for life. I am still in contact with a fellow signaller, from 224 Squadron, who was best man at my wedding some 52 years ago. This is just a snapshot. Even though I only served one tour on Shackletons, I could go on and on – amazing, what a life!"

Rex Wickins – air signaller

> *A South African by birth, Rex had decided to come to England to join the RAF.*

"We completed 104 flight-training hours during our time at MOTU. One particular exercise was relevant for two reasons. It was to be the first time we would endure a flight of over ten hours. By now we were getting used to the gruelling conditions and this would prepare us for the future; we would later fly for up to 15 hours on a sortie. The other reason was that instead of always returning to our base at Kinloss we had a destination. Increasing the excitement of a different terminus, we would also spend three days there. The final 'cherry on the top' was that we were flying to Gibraltar. This would be over the weekend of 17 November 1961. As I had hardly seen any sun in the northern latitudes of Kinloss, I was ecstatic.

Tony Perkins, Jack Austin, Rex Wickins (without a tie as usual), Roy Garrett. (Rex Wickins)

"Gibraltar was the home base of 224 Squadron, and everything about the place turned me on.

It was the closest point of Europe to Africa, but that was the least of its attractions. It was a dream posting, but my chances were hopelessly small. If I had been of the Catholic persuasion I would have said a thousand Hail Marys a day to get there. I could but dream.

"Eighteen months of effort was about to come to fruition. The most nerve-wracking thought that occupied one's mind as the course neared its end was, where and to which Coastal Command squadron you would be posted? All maritime squadrons came under the control of Coastal Command. On graduating from MOTU there were nine squadrons, to any of which you could find yourself being posted. Some were highly desirable, while four were to be avoided like the plague. This had all to do with location. The two prize postings were Singapore and Gibraltar; Malta wasn't too shabby either. Three of the booby prizes were in Northern Ireland; 204, 206 and 210 Squadrons were all based at a bleak airfield, Ballykelly near Londonderry. The weather there was seriously crap, the place needed to keep pumps running to prevent the airfield submerging from all the rain. NO place for a South African! Finally, 37 Squadron was in Aden. A more dismal existence and place would be difficult to find. It was possibly the worst of all; Khormaksar was as dry as Ballykelly was wet.

"Six of us were now fully trained aircrew members, ready to take up our positions on operational squadrons. At the final briefing there was not much ado from the commanding officer, except to hand out the official letters containing our postings. For me – the 'dreaded lurgy' struck. It could not have been worse – 206 Squadron Ballykelly. Besides the beastly weather to contend with, relations between Her Majesty's Forces and the IRA (Irish Republican Army) had reached an all-time low. I dejectedly considered my fate: the next two and a half years in a place that was not my cup of tea. At least I would be flying in Mk.3s, considerably quieter and more comfortable than the Mk.2.

"From out of the blue came a sudden change. For reasons beyond my knowledge my posting had been re-allocated. I was to proceed by rail to London, and then to Lyneham which was close to my original base at Hullavington. From there I would be flown by Britannia to…Gibraltar. My posting had been altered to 224 Squadron – unbelievable! This seemed to be just another occasion where someone up there was looking after me. I arrived as the very first of the new draft of signallers

MR.2 224 Squadron, no exhaust stubs and no soundproofing. (Rex Wickins)

to have come out of the batch trained at Hullavington. My contemporaries on 224 already had a couple of tours under their belts. On average they were all at least five years older than me, so they could be described as young 'hairys'. My arrival was viewed much the same as a new boy on his first day of school. The initial scepticism was alleviated when it was learnt I was a South African, played rugby and was good at sport. I was immediately nicknamed 'The Wild Colonial Boy'.

"After the pre-fabricated bungalows at Kinloss, my new accommodation could only be described as five-star. The sergeants' mess was nothing less than a hotel. All the rooms were on the second floor, large with substantial windows and a view. I was almost in the centre of the mess building overlooking a large sand square (around which were many of the other station buildings), which was actually the football ground. The ground floor of the mess consisted of a large, comfortably furnished lounge, separate TV room and dining room. In the middle of this was the heart of the establishment, the bar, and that goes for anywhere in the world. Now this would be my home for the next two and a half years.

"The 224 Squadron buildings at North Front were situated across the runway, virtually on the border. If you threw a stone out of the crew room back window, it would have landed in Spanish no man's land. Not a good idea to do this at that time of course. After breakfast we would calmly walk from the mess crossing the runway to the buildings, obviously taking heed of any aircraft activity. Here a crew room looked out over the runway, and back at the Rock. When not flying, or carrying out other activities, it was a wonderful place to drink coffee, make small talk and play cards. Sooner or later this 'hectic' morning would end, and we would casually wander back across the runway to the mess for lunch. In the afternoon – sport.

"Flights, consisting mainly of training, happened about once a week. The training varied, consisting of radar-homing and bombing runs, sonar and navigational exercises, etc. When Soviet naval activity was taking place in the eastern Atlantic or the Mediterranean a number of reconnaissance trips were ordered. These flights were often well over 12 hours long. Exercises would take place a number of times a year, involving a 'live' submarine, or a full NATO exercise. Our relaxed lifestyle would be rudely interrupted during these big occasions. It was virtually a 12-hour flight; 12 hours off, and then back in the air for another ten to 12 hours. This would happen continuously over 14 days or more. Considering the reputation of the scary runway, landing after a long all-night flight did not seem to faze our pilots at all.

"Within days of joining my first crew on the squadron I was involved in a 12-hour reconnaissance flight. It eventually landed at El Adem in Libya, which was still a friendly country to Britain's military. The communists, not Col Gaddafi, were our main concern. Tobruk was the nearest town and we made a visit. I knew South Africans had been very involved in this part of the world during the Desert War so I made a point of touring the war cemetery. This was virgin territory for me being a few miles from the Egyptian border. The return flight to Gib only took ten hours.

Six weeks later we made a similar recce trip also landing at El Adem."

*Navigator **Reg Turner** also recalled getting a friendly reception in North Africa, this time in Algeria.*

"We were showing the flag at a special lunch at Blida in Algeria in 1963. There were 21 courses each of small portions. A smorgasbord of a variety of foods including prawns, sausages, snails, fish, assorted vegetables and cold meats. Each course came with a bottle of wine. It lasted four hours; the whole crew was drunk. Somehow the Shackleton got us home on the first attempt at landing at Gib. Had the crew been tested for alcohol consumption we would have certainly been found 'drunk in charge' of a Shackleton."

Rex Wickins *continues.*

"After a short NATO exercise in May we found ourselves at Ballykelly. This was for almost a month for live exercises with submarines based in Scotland. Now I realised how incredibly lucky I was to have missed this initial posting. During the stay there we completed my longest flight (so far) on a surveillance recce – a ball-aching 15 hours plus shadowing Soviet ships. Unless you have experienced one it is impossible to convey what a 15-hour Shack flight was like. The extraordinary noise from the four Griffon engines prevented any communication, unless over the intercom. Any conversation was thus audible to all ten crew members, and so would be mainly restricted to relevant flight talk. All casual communication would be by sign language or screamed straight into a person's ear. The vibration was of a high frequency and not particularly noticeable until you may have nodded off. When your head made contact with the airframe, it felt like a dentist's drill rattling your skull, and brought you smartly back to consciousness. We would share hourly shifts on different equipment, and then depart to the beam lookouts or maybe up in the nose gun turret. I rather fancied the tail lookout where one would lie prone, on a mattress of sorts, and stare out at the endless sea sliding beneath. At least if you sneaked a kip your head would be spared a bone shake! We made endless cups of coffee, and the notorious cups of tomato soup. By now we were far from that first familiarisation flight when all the new students would offer their souls to the Elsan.

"The year 1962 was an interesting time to arrive on 224 Squadron. Quite a number of pilots and navigators were left over from, or had trained in World War 2. These guys were coming close to their 'sell-by' date so I was extremely privileged to be on crews that included them. It would have been impossible to find a more typical RAF pilot than my first captain, Geoff Mannings. He was the quintessential example of the image that comes to mind when visualising a pilot climbing out of the cockpit of a Spitfire…only he was flying a Shackleton. A handlebar moustache spread over the top of his infectious smile – actually more of a grin. He was full of joie de vivre and mischievous to boot. He was the only pilot to insist that, given the chance, he could barrel-roll a 33-ton Shack. To illustrate his claim, he would carry out the manoeuvre up to the critical point, pulling out just before executing the roll. I was part of his crew on most of these occasions and have to admit it was bloody exciting. Geoff would dive bomb the Gib runway from 3,000 feet pulling up at 100 feet into a steep climb. At the top of the climb he slipped the Shack on to its right wing, pushing the column forward just before stalling. The aircraft would slide sideways as the nose slowly came around, leaving us all in a state of weightlessness for a few seconds. This must have been an astonishing sight from the ground.

"Geoff's life in Coastal Command started at Kinloss in 1951, then on to 220 Squadron based at St. Eval, which was equipped with brand-new Shackletons; as an NCO he captained the aircraft. In 1956 he found himself back at Kinloss where he was engaged in converting arriving pilots on to Shacks. In late 1962 Geoff arrived at Gibraltar, and as squadron QFI (qualified flying instructor) he took over a crew of which I was lucky enough to be a part. All good things including Gibraltar, come to an end, and Geoff's next posting was back to Kinloss as wing QFI.

"From one extreme to the other; the next captain I flew under was a much younger pilot drawn from the new officers who had come through RAF Cranwell. Dave Leppard was a tall, blonde and athletic man, and although he never showed any of the vivacity of Geoff Mannings, he was nevertheless one of the more amiable and memorable captains I have flown with. Years later he would command 8 Squadron operating the converted, airborne early warning Shackletons stationed at Lossiemouth, retiring as an air commodore.

"Arriving at Gib in February 1962 I found that the station rugby team had already played a few matches, and was starting to get its act together for the new year. The enthusiasm of the team that greeted my arrival was soon brought to a frustrating end. In the sixties it was a 'passaporte no possible' in any shape or form to have a South African passport. The recently declared republic of South Africa was not popular. Ironically, the fascists in Spain were siding with

MR.3 WR986 K of 203 Squadron with a 42 Squadron MR.2 in Gibraltar for a Gibex exercise. (Richard Ansley)

the rest of the world. My disagreeable passport was that it also excluded me from all the revelry, drunkenness and debauchery that I might have experienced in La Linea.

"The chairman of our rugby club was a wing commander and so it did not take long to get the wheels turning. An immediate application for British citizenship was submitted to the local Crown Affairs, and a couple of days later on 16 February 1962, the colonial secretary issued me with a British passport. It is interesting to note that rugby, especially in some far-flung outpost of the Empire, can take priority over seemingly other more important affairs; I vaguely remember a crucial match was imminent.

"One of the first pastimes you learnt on arrival in the mess was to play 'Kirky'. This was a game of cards similar to bridge, where small amounts of money, if you weren't an idiot or bloody unlucky, would change hands. Halfway through the game a winner would be evident, and the other players would need to gang up against the leader in order not to lose too much money. As you can imagine, the excitement or agitation could be hilarious.

"My mate Alistair Campbell Reid was as dour a Scot as was ever conceived. His humour was so dry that a traveller in the Sahara Desert would stand a better chance of finding water. In addition, this dryness was accompanied with aristocratic arrogance, personified with a look of disdain from eyes peering down a long, blue-blooded nose. Even though Alistair and I made a mean tennis pairing, the standard was pretty poor, even when egged on by attractive housewives (so this is not much of a claim to fame). More significant was that we partnered each other at centre in the RAF Gibraltar rugby team.

"Colin Isaac was another 'champion' of the tennis court. Having sustained an embarrassing injury to his upper lip, to hide the scar, he had developed a perfect RAF moustache. As he now found himself flying in the RAF this could not have been more apt. We were not sure but it seemed highly likely that he had been born in India of high-ranking, military parentage. We were convinced of this, as he spoke much like Prince Charles. He was extremely British and anything foreign was regarded with utter disdain, 'Bloody foreigners', he would remark. Funnily enough, he married a fine Spanish girl a few years down the line.

"Unless one was flying or on duty, afternoons were free for sport. Swimming and water polo were popular, and we would travel to the south end of the Rock to the military, Olympic-sized pool for this. Most weekdays would witness an inter-section football match which took place on the sandy square in front of the mess. I was not popular with some of my opponents as they considered shoulder charges too rough for their liking; especially as we played on a very hard field. After a few months three of us from the tennis clique ended up on the same crew with Geoff Mannings as our captain to become crew 6, a tightly knit fraternity.

"Even though the cold war was at its height as I joined the RAF, actual war and its consequences, specifically an atomic or nuclear one, had not really entered our thoughts; even as we patrolled the high seas interacting with the perceived enemy. Life was relaxed and we were enjoying ourselves. This was all about to alter as the squadron was brought to a high alert state of readiness...Code Yellow. The cold war had reached its highest point of crisis in October 1962 with the confrontation between President John F Kennedy and Nikita Khrushchev. NATO and the USA had become aware of the establishment of Soviet missile bases in Cuba.

"We were confined to base and briefed on the perilous situation, after which we were instructed to retire to the mess and relax. 'Relax!!!?' No drinking – the mess bar was shut. Smoking was always allowed, so my mate Bill and other addicts were adapting to the stress in the way they knew best – maybe a pack lasted for a couple of hours. For all, smokers or not, the apprehension was relieved with the inevitable card schools of 'Kirky'. Details again elude me but it is obvious that after long hours of waiting small fortunes had been won and lost.

"The situation worsened 48 hours later with the declaration of...Code Orange! We rushed to the squadron donning flying kit and listened to more briefings. Two crews at a time would position on standby in their aircraft at the end of the runway, waiting for the word to scramble whilst the others lolled about apprehensively in the crew room; the enthusiasm to play cards had waned. The next instruction could be Code Red! By then, the end of the world could be nigh. This may sound like a fictitious war story but it was in fact deadly serious.

"At this stage in my life I find it very interesting to analyse the thoughts that were going through my head at such an anxious time. Most of the world, including family and friends back in South Africa, may have been fast asleep or at work, not fully aware of the extent of the precarious situation. JFK was about to confront the Soviets who would have retaliated. God knows where I would have been. Flogging the ocean looking for submarines or escorting a nuclear fleet probably. Who knows if there would have been even been anything left to look for?

"The crisis abruptly ended. Kennedy and Khrushchev sorted themselves out. The Soviet ships with their missiles meant for Cuba went home, and we stood down. We returned to the mess for a shower and to change. By now the bar was open. I can only imagine that Pete and I would have given each other high fives. At the squadron, things took a couple of weeks to get back to normal. The severity of this situation may seem minor now, but at the time the world seemed quite capable of destroying itself. A short quote by Soviet general and member of the Soviet army high command, Anatoly Gribkov states, 'Nuclear catastrophe was hanging by a thread, we weren't counting days or hours...but minutes'.

"Circuits and bumps were, and still are, an important part of training on any squadron. Experienced pilots as well as new ones had to practise landings, specifically at night, and especially at Gib. It was known as one of the most dangerous airfields in the world for a very good reason. More than half of it protruded out into the sea. 'Manders' (mandatory training) meant lots of circuits and bumps. As part of the crew I would have to read out and receive answers to the take-off and

No. 224's B circling the Rock doing circuits and bumps. (Rex Wickins)

all the landing checks. The aircraft would not stop after landing but would keep on rolling for an immediate take-off and go-around after the wheels had touched. Hence the word bumps as you touched down, and circuits as you went around again. It would start at dusk, and go on for a number of hours into the night.

"It was regarded as being pretty boring, but I didn't mind. I was getting a sublime view of all of Gibraltar's, and the surrounding coastline's, lights. In the twilight it was easy to see the Atlas Mountains of North Africa and the lights of Tangiers and Ceuta in Morocco. When we turned the Costa del Sol would come into view, and the lights of Malaga and small towns like Torremolinos, Estepona and Marbella, all standing out against the dark outline of the Sierra de Rhonda range. The background to all of this was a slowly appearing starry, night sky. After the 'bump' you climbed and turned south. Algeciras would come up on your right and later Cape Tarifa, and the Gibraltar Straights. Also the shimmering Atlantic Ocean in the last rays of the sinking sun in the west was viewed, before completing the circle and going around again. As there was no chance of getting lost, the navigator's job was to keep the coffee going, so for me life was great.

"Of the many roles described in the Coastal Command manifesto, the last one was particularly interesting. This was the one that Colin Isaac was particularly fond of as it gave license to keep 'the bloody natives in check'. He relished the reference to the role of 'colonial policing'. Can you imagine that being an official term in anyone's book today? The United Nations would be in uproar. Nevertheless this was one of our official duties. My involvement to participate in one such action – in the Yemen – would come sooner than I thought.

"Britain had a huge military base at Aden including Khormaksar. When the tribesmen up in the remote mountains were misbehaving, 224 Squadron was required to detach two aircraft to Aden to provide additional air support. That meant off the record, to bomb them. How ironic, the Wild Colonial Boy was off to participate in 'colonial policing'.

"Spurred on by the Egyptian president Colonel Nasser, rebels were trying to cut the road to a largish inland town which was under the protection of Britain. Marine commandos and the SAS (Special Air Service) were defending it on the ground, while two Hunter fighter squadrons provided daylight support. Our job was to fly at night and attempt to keep these rebels tired and uncomfortable by looking for their camp fires etc. and dropping bombs on them. Ridiculous actually, we may as well be hunting rabbits from 6,000 feet.

"In order to try and accomplish this we carried 12 1,000-lb bombs. If we thought we had identified a light or fire, we would drop one of these ineffectual monsters on the perceived enemy – you had far more chance of winning the lottery than harming any rebel. The only thing accurate about the bomb was that it hit the ground. An almost direct hit was required if we stood any chance of causing major damage. Anything or anyone outside a ring of 30 feet, which was the extent of the eventual crater, would cause no more than a bloody big head ache and a ringing in the ears for about a year. Finding yourself within the bounds of the crater however was clearly fatal.

"This supposedly 'inhuman, ungodly attack on poor defenceless, innocent tribesmen', which some may well have been, somehow came to the notice of the British press. As a result, there was an eventual compromise. We were ordered to drop 'aerial grenades' instead, which sounded so much better than a 1,000-lb bomb! As opposed to the innocuous huge bomb, of which you carried 12, we were carrying instead, 60 aerial grenades. But they were anything but harmless. Mincing machines

A typical Yemeni village from a Shack. (Rex Wickins))

of some 20 kgs, these lethal monstrosities consisted of a coiled, heavy metal spring, surrounding a deadly concoction of explosive and ball bearings. On impact this would jump up a metre off the ground and spread a deadly spray of shrapnel that would level everything within a radius of 200 yards.

"The fickle conscience of the minister of defence, the journalists and all their shocked readers had to be placated. Now instead of the actually useless bomb, the tribesmen would panic when they heard the ominous drone of the Shack's four Griffons. They, their families, their mud houses and even surrounding crops and livestock would be in grave danger of being decimated – and we had not 12 weapons to drop, but 60 of the blighters.

"We were to visit again on more and longer occasions; in fact, whenever the natives were restless. For us this was without doubt the worst place in the world to spend a day, let alone a few weeks. Suffice to say one could not wait a moment to get the hell out of the place. We commenced our flight back to Gib, briefly transiting through Khartoum in the Sudan. On landing there, I could not help but reflect on the night I had landed in the very same place on my way to London, some three years earlier, flying in a BOAC Comet. Back then I had chatted to the captain about my aspirations of flying for the RAF. Never in my wildest dreams could I have imagined that I would arrive one day at this same airfield, only this time in a Shackleton. The flying time to London by Comet would have been around five hours; a Shack would probably take 20.

"Early in my tour, we completed a long-surveillance patrol that necessitated a landing in Malta. Another fascinating place that duly fired up my imagination and curiosity. Never to miss an opportunity, we set off to hit the hot spots down town as soon as possible. Valletta was actually inside the Knights of St. John fortress. To enter one crossed a narrow causeway over a deep but empty moat, and through an impressive medieval gate. High imposing ramparts from the Middle Ages towered above as we progressed through and into the protection of the inner sanctuary. We were finally walking the narrow ancient streets of the knights' fifteenth century domain; overwhelming for this 'wild colonial boy'. After 6 p.m. it seemed all and sundry would parade up and down the mile-long central street. I later learnt this enabled everyone to eye one another up. Being a very strict culture embroiled in Catholicism, fraternising with the opposite sex was strictly taboo.

"The Cuban crisis may have been over but the intrigue of international spying, as well as uncertainty in the Middle East kept us on the go. On reflection, the world was in a high state of flux in the sixties. The humdrum of the long, tedious, surveillance flights was spasmodically broken with the sighting of a Soviet submarine on the surface, or finding an 'electronic trawler' masquerading as a fishing trawler. We would shadow Soviet surface vessels for no other reason than to let them know that we knew where they were. Sounds crazy when you think of it. Respite and compensation came when you landed at a different airfield. At least you could go and survey the local bars and joints, and even catch up on a bit of history.

"We continued to Cyprus from Malta (which is not that far as the crow flies), but by the time we landed at Nicosia we had made a 12-hour trip of it. We were thankful not to have landed instead at Akrotiri, near Limassol. In those days, the

Soviet ELINT 'trawler'. The crew is taking a keen interest in the Shack.
(Peter Morris)

runway there was too short for a fully loaded Shack, and we would then have had to spend our time confined to base. Nicosia on the other hand, was far more preferable to me. It was an international airport with transport to a large town close by, and they had a less strin-
gent attitude than in Malta. On the way back to Gibraltar, we had to endure three days in Malta again. The novelty of the Springbok Bar and the hordes of Maltese traversing the main drag every evening had worn thin. "November 1963 has pertinent memories, mostly unpleasant. Just before my birthday came the news that the natives in Yemen were misbehaving again. Our detachment there would be for an indeterminate length. After an early take-off, and a refuelling stop at El Adem, we proceeded down the Red Sea to my least favourite place in the world, Aden. The temperatures were horrific never dropping below 40°C, and then only at around 5 a.m., which was the coolest part of the day. Our boredom was somewhat relieved by playing water polo in a local military base league. It was more like steam-bath polo, the water temp was close to that of a hot bath. I think now that the liquid we played in was 90% water and 10% perspiration.

"There was never a shortage of volunteers to fly operations in Aden, no matter what time of day or night. Getting airborne would require two crews. The heat inside the aircraft was phenomenal, so a 'start-up' crew was allocated. Getting a Shack off the ground was a long-winded procedure. Suffice to say it took about 20 minutes and the taxi to the end of the runway for 'line up', took another ten. By now the start-up crew were exhausted, feeling like they had been working in a steel smelter for a week. Flaked out, these dripping mortals were ecstatic to be replaced by the mission crew. All that was needed from the relieving crew was to strap in and gun the idling engines. The sweet sound of four Griffons roaring at full throttle lifting you off the runway was music to the ear. The higher you climbed the sweeter it got. At 6,000 feet you sat back and enjoyed the cooler air, down to around 20°C. Funny, how at times the simplest things in life can bring you such joy.

"Unexpectedly a search and rescue mission arose; and the Shack was always perfect for this occasion. [See also Ian Jones' account on page 36, Rex was part of the second aircraft crew that Ian mentions.] The foreign minister of Somalia had gone missing in his aircraft in the countryside, and there was a lot of it about! Miles and miles of nothing, and 12 hours to look at it. I do remember lying down in the tail and seeing the odd antelope being startled as the Shack came thundering over. This monster exploding out of the sky at a thousand feet was certainly not an everyday occurrence. We landed in Mogadishu at a time when the locals had not yet started killing each other, or Americans, for that matter.

"Although we experienced very little of it, Mogadishu came across as a very chilled-out place at that time. The main square, open to the sea, was memorable for the open-air bars and eating houses, with their attendant ladies. They were unusually striking with fine, almost European features. Communication was almost impossible, but never became an issue. We were knackered, but were still up at the crack of dawn ready to continue the search. After another 12 hours of fruitlessly scouring the barren, desolate, featureless and empty landscape, we returned to Aden, a place hardly more inspiring. The following day we continued with this hopeless pursuit, until halfway through our search, when the mission was terminated; I don't know whether the minister was dead or alive. There was absolutely nothing memorable about this country and I spent a good 30 hours finding out.

"The only compensation to all that was running low on fuel for the return to Aden, so we were diverted to RAF Eastleigh, just outside Nairobi, Kenya. What a pleasure to be staying in a thatch-roofed lodge with a cool room and enjoying an excellent breakfast. The crew was not in a hurry to get back to Aden.

"January 1964 arrived with an early flight north via Kinloss to Bodø, Norway. From the oven of Aden, we prepared ourselves to cope with the fridge of the Arctic circle. We arrived at Bodø in the dark, and left in the dark. At around 11 a.m. dawn hardly broke. The twilight lasted until 2 p.m., then it was dark again. What I remember the most was a cold breakfast of cheese, raw herring, hard-boiled eggs, bread and milk: nothing warm. Three days and two nights were spent in virtual darkness. All I saw of Norway were the street lights of Bodø, which was not very exciting. We visited Norway a few more times, this being mostly in the summer. It was a very different story; it never got dark. For the moment it was home to Gib and the wet, but warm, weather.

"Towards the end of May my worst fears were realised: two crews were ordered back to Aden – again! Our crew was one of the unlucky ones. The route was becoming all too familiar; Gib to El Adem to Khormaksar and straight into action. This time around the situation was a lot more serious. Once again there was no room to sleep in the already full sergeants' mess. We were directed to a huge building that I believe had been converted from the old airmens' mess; in this cavernous structure slept over 200 hot and sweaty bodies. I was lucky to be able to grab a bed directly under a fan and close to a window; though the window actually made bugger all difference. It was constantly over 38°C but worse, much worse was the humidity factor, which remained over 100%. The fan was a godsend, but only to that part of your body that was directly influenced. My sheet was constantly wet from perspiration, no matter which way I lay. There was not the faintest hint of a

Aden, 12 1,000-lb bombs ready. Engineer, Alistair Reid AEO, Ken Boyd, Capt
Geoff Mannings, co-pilot Dave Perry, Rex Wickens, Nav Norman Pearson, Nav
Dai Evans. (Rex Wickins)

breeze, so you existed constantly pouring with sweat.

"At least we were able to eat in our own mess, but virtually in shifts. When not required for duty one was left to one's own devices – you just sweltered. I lay looking up at my fan, which was going hell for leather, knowing if it ever came loose I would be decapitated. To take my mind off this, and a host of other miseries, I found two excellent books which got me reading. This new-found pastime saved my bacon. We were to endure this forsaken place for seven weeks. As in previous detachments, even if it meant flying all night, one would volunteer just to get away from the heat.

"Once airborne we would set about our task, either surveillance up the Wadi Hadhramaut, where we were seeking out and reporting any suspicious looking camel trains and rebels, or bombing the daylights out of any suspected baddies. Any operation carried out at night was made possible as the Shack carried a bank of 36 flare dischargers. These were fired off in succession lighting up the surrounding area for some two minutes. After being called in by a controller on the ground we would come in at about 600 feet above the mountaintops banging off the flares. Negotiating the terrain and finding the target was pretty stressful for us, but far less so than it was for the soldiers who we were providing the illumination for. The situation down there was for 'mad dogs' only. They suffered unbelievable heat and the discomfort of fighting in mountains above 5,000 feet – all the while not knowing when a bullet may come their way.

"The Radfan uprising was instigated in 1962 when a customs union in the area was created. This prevented tribesmen from collecting tolls in the mountainous area straddling the road from Aden to Mecca. This situation, which we had been involved in for a few years, reached a climax during 1964. It was by far the most intense of all the colonial policing operations conducted by Britain in recent history. It started when two soldiers of the Somerset and Cornwall Light Infantry, now part of the SAS, who were detached to Yemen, were captured and beheaded.

"The Parachute Brigade and 45 Marine Commando were called in, supported by the two Hunter squadrons based at Khormaksar. Sea Vixens and Scimitars from the Fleet Air Arm were also involved. The jets provided continual air support to the ground force which now included more SAS units. This was only during day-light hours. We continued with our night harassment and provided flare drops when requested. As opportunity presented itself we sowed death and destruction with aerial grenades instead of innocuous, 1,000-lb bombs. The volatile situation remained until we finally pulled out in 1967. The violence never ever stopped and Aden remains highly volatile today.

"After surviving seven weeks of hot-house hell, we were relieved by two exchange 224 Squadron crews. It had been intriguing and at times exciting, but mostly it was exhausting and boring. We were flown back to Gib, via the UK, in Britannias of Transport Command. It was a lot more pleasant than in our Shacks, which were left behind for the poor people relieving us.

"The return to Gib was going to be exciting for a number of reasons. My car was waiting, probably with a flat battery. It seemed as though we had been away for an eternity. I soon had it back on the road as it was needed urgently! I was due a week's leave, which I meant to spend travelling up the Costa del Sol with a WRAF clerk in the admin section who I had met previously. At this stage, the rest of my motley crewmates had completed their two-and-a-half-year posting to Gib and had departed to new squadrons. Sadly, the end of my time was also on the horizon.

"I can unequivocally describe the two and a half years I spent on the Rock (despite the detachments to Aden), as the best in my life. I had arrived young and naïve in the first of a new batch of aircrew and was initially by far the youngest on the squadron. I was thrown in with guys five years or more my senior and it was a case of growing up fast. I won't go as far as to say they led me astray, but they had certainly shown me the ropes. I had travelled and seen places I hadn't even heard off.

"By September 1964 I had been on 224 Squadron for two and a half years. Most of my good and influential friends had already departed, so my life felt empty. I was sad to leave the Rock, but to add to my despondency was my next posting. I was off to 204 Squadron at Ballykelly, in one of my least favourite places, Northern Ireland. However, life was good and Sheila's de-mob from the WRAF was also in September. We were able to arrange the return to UK under our own steam. We planned a long way home in the Triumph Spitfire via France, Italy and Switzerland. We were married in May 1966."

Derek Straw – navigator

"In May 1964 I was posted to 224 Squadron, my first operational tour. Thankfully I was not over burdened with luggage, as all my personal effects had been carried by 'Shackair'. I approached Kinloss stores to return my cold weather flying clothing issued on arrival at MOTU, but they insisted it was mine for life. So off to a hot weather posting with all my string vests, long johns and cold weather gear! The Comet trooping flight to Gib was an exciting prospect. What I did not know, until

I checked in, was that the crew were only in charge of the aircraft. There was to be a nominated officer in charge of passengers; as the junior RAF officer passenger I was selected – I tried to look confident. I fell into conversation with an elderly and distinguished-looking gentleman who was assigned to the seat alongside me. In a broad Irish brogue, he quickly put me right about what being officer i/c passengers was all about, 'Forget it! If we divert ask for the nearest British consul' was the succinct advice. This was Paddy Byrne, a master engineer, also en route to 224 Squadron and destined to be my flight engineer for virtually the whole of my tour.

"I immediately started on the 'conversion' to the Mk.2, learning the subtle differences from the T.4, and about the squadron's back-up colonial policing role. Squadron flying followed quickly with a 12-hour LROFE where I discovered the paucity, or unreliability, of electronic nav aids around 36 north, but thankfully the extra 'punishment' astro training at nav school was not wasted. My issue of KD uniform was minimal, so I bought a roll of KD cloth from stores and found a tailor in Gibraltar town who claimed he could turn it into a No.6 uniform. Unfortunately the finished article did not meet the standards of the SWO (station warrant officer); on my first station parade I was ordered off. After a couple of weeks, during which I waited to be crewed up, I was summoned to the squadron. Flt Lt Gordon Statham informed me I was to join his crew on an Exercise Coldroad leaving immediately! No time for any questions. I was told 'dig out your cold weather clothing, your blue uniform, and file a flight plan to Kinloss'. 'But I've just left there!' 'Welcome to Coastal' was the retort. Our destination was Ørland, Norway; a week of visiting Ireland, Scotland and Norway followed with lots of interesting flying as the Soviet northern fleet provided targets of interest. On return to Gibraltar it was

time to get back into KD and try for a suntan. However, within a week I was on the move again – this time to Ballykelly and thence JASS. More use for the cold and wet weather gear. Back again in time to welcome home several crews who had been detached for colonial policing operations in Aden. The party went with quite a swing.

"In early September while enjoying a film down town, I was amazed to witness a slide appear-

WL789 overflying HMS Osiris *during the 1966 Aird Whyte Trophy work-up. (Derek Straw)*

ing on the screen ordering all RAF personnel to report to their place of duty, 'with immediate effect!' I reached the squadron in the late evening to hear the usual litany, 'pack your cold weather kit and flight plan for somewhere north'. Once again we set off on the well-worn track along ten degrees west to Ballykelly, this time overnight, to participate in NATO Exercise Teamwork. The headquarters had decided to exercise our short-notice call-out procedure 'Quicktrain' to get us north all the quicker. After Ballykelly we moved to Bodø to conduct surveillance sorties. During our return to Ballykelly we suffered an engine failure necessitating a diversion to Vaernes. Our arrival with a large four-engined 'WW2 bomber' caused quite a stir locally. Waiting for an Argosy with an engine change team, we were accommodated in a temperance hotel in a village called Hell! More like purgatory. These detachments to JASS and Norway continued apace during the next two years, interspersed occasionally with 'jollies' to Malta, Lajes, Bovingdon and El Adem as well as Aden. The latter required use of the medium-level bomb sight – no more chinagraph marks on the bomb aimer's window – and lots of practice for our Hispanos with war stock ammo. What a change that was from 'Fire', bang, bang, phut. First time on the range to the surprise of our gunner every round worked, and he forgot to release the trigger until all had been fired. The range safety officer and armourers alike had words with us! After a late autumn at Khormaksar, it was time to experience a Gibraltar winter. The new year brought a rash of engine failures

Aird Whyte crew and WR951. Left to right: George Murray, Paddy Byrne, Tony Stokes, Jock Naismith, David Sheringham, Murray Frankland, Doug Cook, Derek Straw, and John Horscroft. (Derek Straw)

and south-westerly gales – together. We never diverted, but the subsequent approaches and Spanish Road touch-downs made up for the lack of fairground rides on the Rock. On one occasion the Elsan erupted up some of its contents into the aircraft beams. Landing another time the Marine Craft Unit (MCU) boat crew had to be disappointed as the aircraft stopped just short of Gibraltar Bay, so they were not needed.

"May 1966 was a month with far-reaching consequences. A new squadron adjutant was posted in: Fg Off Beth Palmer WRAF. Perhaps the first Shackleton 'Girl'? She had to 'hit the ground running' the day after her arrival. Late on the Friday afternoon she was re-called to the squadron with a message that 'eggs and milk were ready for distribution'. Needless to say this cryptic message meant nothing to her. On her return she was confronted by crates of eggs, milk, and sacks of cabbages, potatoes and sundry other vegetables. These had arrived in three Shackletons that had come that afternoon from the UK. It was the 224 adjutant's task to sell them (and in the heat they could not wait). A few of us appraised Beth of her duty to sell the food, and with a little help it was all sold by Saturday lunchtime.

"In June 1966 the Aird Whyte competition took place at North Front. As in 1965 it would be Doug Cook's crew that represented 224 – and in the same aircraft, WL789. Perhaps it was the benefit of a concentrated work-up period with the competition submarine, HMS *Osiris*, that brought our crew to a peak of training. Another win for our crew; it was Aird Whyte and bar! The target submarine's first lieutenant had been paying what I regarded as overmuch attention to our adjutant. Maybe that sharpened my bombing aim, and the win persuaded her to accept my marriage proposal? Despite all the detachment time away from the Rock there was still time to sample Spanish culture, and every year the squadron had an 'away day' to a bodega in Jerez. Afterwards we repaired to a local bistro where a squadron pianist entertained us as we enjoyed a tapas and fino lunch. I suspect it was the tapas, rather than the fino, that caused the odd arrests during the return to Gibraltar. Sadly the sunshine and the joys of Spain came to an end in October 1966 when 224 Squadron was disbanded. We had to party hard to empty the squadron fund of egg and milk profits, but we persevered."

> As part of the rationalisation of the overseas MR force, 224 Squadron was disbanded at Gibraltar on 31 October 1966 and has not been re-formed since. Its role in the area was taken over by squadrons operating from Luqa and St. Mawgan, although Shackletons and later Nimrods continued to visit the station regularly.

CHAPTER TWO

'FIRST IN MALAYA' – RAF CHANGI, SINGAPORE

What eventually became RAF Changi was originally built as an army artillery base to cover the approaches to the Straits of Johore and the naval base, opening in 1941. Singapore was overrun by the Japanese in February 1942 and was then used as a huge prisoner-of-war camp (POW) with up to 50,000 men being held there. By 1944 the Japanese had added an airfield to the site, and the POWs were moved to Changi Gaol. After the war the airfield was handed over to the RAF and was selected as a transport base. It was officially opened on 8 April 1946, and in 1950 a permanent tarmac runway was laid. It would be May 1958 before an MR presence was established when 205 Squadron re-formed at the station with Shackleton MR.1s.

With the formation of the RAF on 1 April 1918, 5 (Naval) Squadron of the Royal Naval Air Service (RNAS) was transferred to the new service and renumbered 205 Squadron, only to be disbanded with the coming of peace. In 1929 the Far East Flight became 205 Squadron with Supermarine Southampton flying boats flying from Seletar, and was the first RAF squadron to be permanently based in the Far East. Later equipment included Short Singapores followed by Consolidated Catalinas, with which it almost saw out the war. It was a 205 Squadron Catalina which spotted the Japanese invasion fleet at Kelantan in East Malaya, reporting its position and presence – the aircraft failed to return. Short Sunderlands arrived in June 1945, then in 1958 it began converting to the Shackleton MR.1 at Changi; its remaining Sunderlands still operating from Seletar as a joint 205/209 Squadron. By May 1959 the re-equipment was complete and on the 15th of that month 205 flew the RAF's last Sunderland operation. The Shackleton MR.1s were replaced by MR.2s over a three-month period from June 1962, the MR.2s staying with the squadron until it disbanded nine years later.

205 SQUADRON

Nev Cooper – AEO

"Following quite a long period on 228 Squadron, I was posted out to Singapore to help form 205 Squadron at Changi. That was a laugh a minute. I travelled out between Christmas Day 1957 and New Year's Day 1958. We didn't have any aeroplanes until May. My crew (such as it was as we'd never flown together) were bunged on a Families Trooping Flight to pick up the first Shackleton Mk.1 from Aldergrove to take back out to 205. Up until then we had what could well be called a doddle of a job. They had just built a beautifully large swimming pool, just along from Changi village, which was set aside solely for dingy drill every morning, and then for airmen's families every afternoon. There must have been more aircrew up to Channel swimming standard on 205 Squadron at the end of that five or six months, than any other squadron in the RAF."

At 0548 hours on 9 December 1958 Shackleton MR.1 VP254 B of 205 Squadron took off from Labuan on a routine anti-piracy patrol, being flown by Flt Lt Walter 'Stan' Boutell and his crew. The acting deputy police commissioner of North Borneo, Mr A R Miller, went along as a passenger. After take-off the aircraft was diverted to investigate a report of shipwrecked fishermen on an atoll, 227 miles north of Labuan. They were reported as found just after 07.00 and at 11.43 Boutell radioed that the fishermen's rescue was in progress.

At 11.57 the aircraft transmitted a brief position report – but nothing more was ever heard from them. A major ASR search was launched and continued for six days. **Nev Cooper** *takes up the story.*

"I did 60-odd hours in five days during the search for VP254 that had gone down off Sin Cowe Island, part of the Spratly Group in the South China Sea. We were immediately sent out to Labuan for the search, I think we had taken at least four Shackletons there from 205 Squadron. It always gets light out there at around 6 a.m., and so we were woken up every day at 4 a.m., given breakfast, and told our new search area. We took off in the dark, got to the search area by first light, stayed there until it got too dark to carry on a 'Mk.1 eyeball' search, got back to base,

VP254's crew in front of WB854 C. (Steve Bond collection)

landed, had a meal, went to bed and were woken up the next day at 4 a.m. again. The last time proved to be a short trip on the sixth day. We were halfway to the new search area, still in the dark, when the nav gave the skipper an alteration of heading and got no reply. He told him again and still got no reply; the nav pulled the curtain back and tapped the captain on the shoulder – both pilots were sound asleep. The nav said: 'I think your plug's come out' – 'No,' the skipper (Flt Lt James) said, 'we were both asleep!' He immediately turned around and went back to Labuan. He told the duty operations officer: 'Look you're going to have another Shackleton in the water the way we're going on.' I think it was that day that another Shack, flown by Flt Lt John Elias's crew, spotted a cross on Sin Cowe Island. He flew over at low level, and seeing that it was a Christian cross reported it.

"On 16 December a landing party arrived from the New Zealand frigate, HMN-ZS *Rotoiti* and found a shallow grave marked with a simple wooden cross, plus an aircrew watch and an RAF cap. They recovered the body of Flt Sgt David Dancy DFC, the flight engineer, and transferred it to HMS *Albion* along with the cross. Both were then transferred to Labuan. His was the only body, or wreckage, ever to be found I believe. The lost aircraft had been doing an anti-piracy patrol. Drugs were being smuggled into Borneo, possibly by Chinese fishing boats. We believe VP254 was doing tight turns around what appeared to be a Chinese fishing/pirate boat, to try and see what was on the deck, when it crashed. A Chinese fishing boat found Flt Sgt Dancy in the water, but he was already dead. His body was taken to Sin Cowe Island and buried in the sand, along with a wooden cross with 'B205' carved on it (this is what they had seen on the side of the aircraft). It was never established what had happened to that aircraft, because they never found anything else for many, many, years anyway.

"The search had involved all four Shackletons, one of the last of the Sunderland flying boats from 205/209 Squadron at Seletar, four Hastings from 48 Squadron, six Valettas of 52 Squadron, two RNZAF Bristol Freighters and two USAF Albatross amphibians. It was thought that the aircraft possibly either struck its own slipstream, or the No.1 engine 'coughed' or something during a very tight port bank. There was another theory. On the Mk.1 the master fuel cocks were in a very strange place, behind the captain's and WOp's (wireless operator) backs – in other words on the back of the captain's seat. It was reckoned that the civilian policeman they were carrying would probably have been standing between the two pilots' seats, which was a common thing to do. If the aircraft did hit its own slipstream, after doing a tight 360-degree turn, this guy's elbow which would have been resting on the back of the captain's seat, could have been jolted. They thought that if VP254 was doing a left-hand circuit, which would be cocked over at about 45 degrees, his elbow could have slipped off the top of the captain's seat – more than likely knocking No.4 master cock off (the one nearest him) thus starving the engine of fuel. Subsequently a guard was put on the fuel cocks as a modification. But it was all guess-work, no one ever proved it of course.

"When we turned back that morning, I think the cross had already been found the day before, we were still looking for wreckage or survivors. Then they called it off and we went back to Changi. I got in my car at 205 Squadron and drove home in my flying suit (by that time we were in a pretty 'whiffy' state after about six days of flying well over 12 hours a day). I turned into Bedok Avenue and thought 'What the hell?', the group captain's car, with the flag flying on the front, was right outside my house. I tooted the horn, parked the car in the drive, went in and saluted. 'Ah Cooper,' he said, 'The wife of Master Signaller Jimmy Stewart [lost on VP254] is staying with you for a few days.' She stayed with us for about a week or ten days. It was a nasty business. They gave the bereaved wives the option of two places to go – home to the UK, or anywhere else they wanted to go. They certainly didn't get a great deal of sympathy from the RAF that was for sure. The driftwood cross is now bolted to the wall in the chancel of St. Eval church in Cornwall."

Gan Chung-Huang, the Chinese captain of the fishing boat Ray Fu Chen, *had indeed witnessed the aircraft crashing into the sea and found the body of Flt Sgt Dancy floating in the water. They took him to Sin Cowe Island, made a coffin, buried him and erected a cross (mentioned by Nev Cooper). Captain Chung-Huang and his crew later received a cash reward.*

Dancy's body and the cross were taken back to Changi, where the cross was erected in the station church. In 1971 Changi was closed down, and the cross was taken back to St. Mawgan, by 205 Squadron MR.2 WR969 captained by Flt Lt Travis Spurling, where it was placed on the wall of the church at St. Eval. It remains there to this day alongside a photograph of the lost crew and many other tributes and memorials to Coastal Command, in what is very much considered to be an RAF church.

No definite cause for the accident was ever established. The most probable scenario was the difficulty of judging height, over what could be a very smooth and glassy sea, which may simply have led to the aircraft hitting the water while patrolling at low level. **Nev Cooper** *continues:*

The Sin Cowe cross outside Changi church. (Lance Smale)

"After repatriation from 205, I went to 42 Squadron at St. Mawgan for a short time. I'd done so many tours on Shackletons that I applied for a posting onto something else. They picked Transport Command for me, and I was posted up to Dishforth on the Hastings OCU. At the end of the course this guy came in and said: 'I've got your postings here.' He read them out, and he said, 'MAEO (master air electronics operator) Cooper, Changi, Singapore'. I said: 'Wait a minute, I think you've got something wrong somewhere, I've only just come back from Singapore, off the Shackleton.' 'Oh no,' he said, 'There's a note here that the others are provisional, yours is definite because you know the area.' 'Oh, OK,' I said, 'don't think I'm complaining'. Changi was a marvellous posting, and without doubt the best in the RAF. I think we had about five servants who specialised in their separate jobs. We had a cook amah, a baby amah, a dhobi amah, that's three to start with. To cap it all, my posting was onto the VIP Mk.4 Hastings of Far East Communications Squadron, belonging to the commander-in-chief Far East (four-star Admiral Sir David Luce). It was truly a marvellous posting, and indeed, on return trips when passing through, I have witnessed the island going from strength to strength. In my opinion it has never looked back since the day the British moved out."

Brian Latham – pilot

"My friend Dicky, who was in charge of postings at Coastal Command, had asked my wife Mary if I would like to go out to Changi, Singapore for my last tour. No. 205 Squadron with Sunderlands at Seletar, was being converted to Shackletons at Changi, and they wanted Shackleton pilots. Although I hadn't quite finished my tour on 120 Squadron at Kinloss my CO agreed to let me go. So we packed up in Glengormley, went on embarkation leave, then flew out to Singapore and formed 205 Squadron with Shackleton MR.1s.

"Up to the summer of 1958 there were two maritime squadrons in FEAF. They were 205 and 209 and were equipped with Sunderland flying boats. It was decided to amalgamate the serviceable 'boats into 205/209 Squadron and re-equip with Mk.1 Shackletons. As the Shacks arrived the 'boats were gradually sold to Chinese breakers...shame. Those crews who still had time to serve for their two-and-a-half-year tour were converted to Shackletons on the squadron."

> Brian was the second pilot in Flt Lt Elias's crew. They were the ones who found the markers on Sin Cowe Island indicating where the Shackleton had come down in the crash described above by Nev Cooper. **Brian Latham** continues:

"We lost Stan Boutell and crew in December '58. He and his crew had come from 120 Squadron at Aldergrove, I knew them all. John Elias and I were on SAR standby and were told, later in the afternoon, that there had been no contact from Stan since midday. If there was no news by last light at Labuan then we were to go and look, so we did.

"We followed their track around the north of Borneo as far as they would have gone, then waited around until daylight and retraced our steps to Labuan. By this time other aircraft had joined in the search. Eventually the search was closed down but we asked if we could do one last run up the islands. There on Sin Cowe Island was a grave, a wooden cross with coloured roundels and B205 on it, and in coral on the ground B205 with an arrow pointing north. We landed at Labuan after losing an engine and debriefed. We asked if we could look north in the direction of the arrow, had the engine repaired and took off the next day. We checked all the islands, including the communist ones, and found one to the north of Sin Cowe, not on the chart, which was heavily fortified. In the meantime the frigate *Rotoiti*, which was taking part in the search, had put a party ashore on Sin Cowe where they exhumed the body of the air engineer Flt Sgt Dancy. An aircraft carrier involved in the search then put a helicopter ashore on the fortified island to make enquiries – it was seen off by armed guards.

"After a long trip we landed at the new airport in Hong Kong – the first Shackleton to do so. There was no news of Stan's crew so we returned, very sadly, to Changi. Many months later we heard from Formosa, that a local fisherman had seen the crash and found the body of David Dancy, which he buried and made the cross and the arrow in the sand. He was given gold and thanks, and we heard no more. One of the navigators, Alan Moore had been to my son Jeremy's christening party the weekend before the crash. His wife, though he did not know it, was just pregnant. Of course she went back to the UK, letting the squadron know when the baby was born. Seventy-five people – wives, children, mothers and fathers – were directly affected by that crash, not forgetting their friends.

"Squadron life continued with exercises with the fleet. On an exercise up near the Philippines. where we landed at Sangley Point, we had a day in Manila courtesy of the admiral in his barge. The Duke of Edinburgh, and the Royal Yacht *Britannia*, came to Singapore and we escorted it for several days. There were also mail drops to warships and navexs in the China Sea. By now we were getting more Shackletons, and more people were coming from the Sunderlands. This was when Alan Nicol joined our crew.

"We had several trips to Hong Kong. It was a dicey approach to Kai Tak past the skyscrapers on the final approach. We could look into the windows to see what Mr and Mrs Hi Lim were having for their tea. We had to fetch a Shackleton from Butterworth, so I arranged for us to travel overnight on the train to Kuala Lumpur, then on another train up to Butterworth. The crew were not best pleased but indulged me. I had to ply them with drink on the train, and buy them breakfast. John Elias and I had a day in Penang before flying back to Changi.

"We were nearing the end of our tour which had been very interesting. The Far East is fascinating, and I think we saw it at its best. We decided to travel home by troopship, it would give us time to acclimatise and arrive home towards spring. I was 'dined out' in the mess, my crew gave me a party and a silver tankard. We all had rather a lot to drink and invaded the hairdressers in Changi village, where Mary and Barbara were having their hair done – we were not popular! So ended our Far East tour. The children and the amahs were in tears when we left Changi for the last time, to join Her Majesty's Troopship *Oxfordshire*.

"It was a great experience flying in the Far East. The Shack was hot and smelly, we were always soaked in sweat, the noise made us all high-tone deaf, the weather could be dreadful, but we stayed together as a crew and knew each other and our families. Four Rolls-Royce engines, leather seats, and a reliable aeroplane – who could wish for more?"

MR.1A WG525 E 205 Squadron at Khormaksar, May 1962. (Ray Deacon)

David Phillips – pilot

"In my second tour I was on 205 Squadron at Changi. The reason we were sent there was because they'd lost a crew (Stan Boutell), and we were replacing them. We had an interesting time during a trip to Gan when we were missing for six hours; it was all down to the signallers. We did our ground checks as usual at Changi, and the wireless operator said: 'I'm having a problem, but I'm sure I can fix it.' We took off, and I was only the first pilot on that trip, which turned out to be useful because we had a flight commander with us. He was a navigator, but he said he was captain, so that was fine by me, and he sat in the front. On the Mk.1 you had a sort of couch in the nose, which was a favourite place for people to sit, and he bagged that for the trip. He'd brought his work with him, so he sat down and opened his briefcase and that was it. He just said: 'Tell me if anything happens.'

"The first thing that happened was – we hadn't got a serviceable W/T. Had I been captain, and had things been normal, we would have scrubbed. But of course, I fortunately wasn't captain, and things weren't normal because every Sunday there was a changeover at Gan. We took off to fly there, and the crew at Gan couldn't take off until we were airborne. If we were delayed, they were delayed. If we were a day late, they had to do an extra day at Gan, and that was never very popular, so that was also an incentive to get going, and the flight commander said: 'Right, take off.'

"We took off and flew up the Straits of Malacca. After an hour we were due our first position report. The WOp said: 'I still can't get through. I think I'm getting there but could you contact Tengah?' We were more or less level with Tengah and were able to get VHF contact, so we passed our position report through them to Changi before pressing on round the northern tip of Sumatra, and out west across the Indian Ocean. When the second hour came up we were not in contact with anybody, even by VHF! The WOp said, 'I think I've got through'. He felt that he'd made a transmission and heard something garbled. He couldn't decipher it, but it seemed to him that they had accepted it.

"So once again I tell the flight commander, and he said: 'Oh well, press on.' So we pressed on and that was it, no more radio contact. We tried to do VHF contact with the Shack coming the other way, but of course once you leave base you aren't bothered about VHF. You're supposed to put it on emergency frequency, but in fact nobody bothered. We couldn't make contact with them, and we were out of contact for six hours. When we landed at Gan the wing commander came charging out and demanded to know who the captain was. The flight commander, who was first off leaving us to do the clearing up, owned up. 'Right, you've been out of contact for six hours. What have you got to say for yourself?' So the flight commander said, 'Ah, well actually, Flt Lt Phillips was the captain.' But it didn't wash, they had a Court of Enquiry as you'd expect, and I had nothing to answer. The flight commander carried the can which everybody thought was only fair.

"The worst thing as far as we were concerned, apart from the loss of the crew that we replaced in Changi, who I didn't know, was the loss of two crews on 42 Squadron at St. Eval – those chaps we did know [see Volume 1]. Though we were on 206 and they were on 42, we met in the mess and things like that; that was 20 people all in one night. We had a commemoration in St. Columb church and a march past.

"Nearly all my service was in the Mk.1 on both 206 and 205 Squadrons. When I was on a ground tour I did some flying on Mk.3s, but I never did get onto a Mk.2 which was the most prolific of the Shackleton variants. I think it's fair to say that most pilots actually preferred the Mk.2, as it incorporated solutions to many of the problems with the Mk.1. So generally it was popular, the only problem was that while in the Mk.1 the radar was right at the front, fixed in a bulge under the nose, whereas on the Mk.2 it was lowered. When you took off it was tucked up inside the aircraft, and once you got airborne it was lowered for operation. There were one or two occasions when someone forgot to raise it up again when they landed – which was rather expensive."

Ray Curtis – AEO

"In November 1960 I was posted to 205 Squadron at Changi, operating the Mk.1 Shackleton off a PSP (perforated steel plate) hard standing. In the summer of 1962 we converted to the Mk.2 Shackleton, and the Mk.1s were flown to Seletar to be broken up. I was now a flying officer and a member of the crew which flew the last Mk.1 VP267 L to the Seletar

The last 205 Squadron Mk.1 VP267 L leaving Changi for scrapping 7 December 1962. (Ray Curtis)

graveyard on 7 December 1962 (flight time 35 minutes) – beating up the 205 Squadron headquarters on our way. The captain was navigator Flt Lt Arthur Curtis, and the first pilot was Flt Lt Bob Trowern.

"We also did detachments to Katunayake in Sri Lanka (the old Negombo of Ceylon) and RAAF Butterworth (an Aussie fighter base in the old Malaya). There we participated in a SEATO (South East Asia Treaty Organisation) sponsored joint maritime exercise in the 'Jetex' series – I took part in 'Jetex' 61, 62 and 63. There were two SAR incidents of note. Firstly a 14.10-hour expanding square search over the southern Malayan jungle, for a RNZAF Canberra from Tengah. The crew had abandoned their aircraft and I think one was killed, but the other managed to cut himself free from his harness and walk to a clearing to be rescued by some Malayan lumberjacks. The second was in the South China Sea. This was for a tanker in distress, which we found broken in two with the bow and the stern still afloat about ten miles apart! All of the lifeboats had been released, but there was no sign of them. We were ordered to remain on task until PLE (prudent limit of endurance), and then diverted into Saigon. This was before the full-blown Vietnam war, but there were a lot of American 'advisers' about. We also did detachments to Jesselton to carry out coastal patrols around north-west Borneo, which had a problem with Philippine pirates high-jacking their trading dhows, chucking the crews overboard and stealing the cargoes.

"Finally 'confrontation' with General Sukarno of Indonesia blew up with the Brunei revolt in December 1962, so the ever-versatile Shack was put to trooping duties. I was called off the golf course at Changi on the Sunday morning, when it all kicked off. We dropped down to minimum crews on the squadron in order to ferry Gurkhas and members of, I think the Yorkshire Regiment, into Labuan – 22 at a time.

"As I approached the end of my tour in May 1963, having now completed two squadron tours in the maritime world, I thought I would be a 'dead ringer' for a tour as an instructor at the Shackleton OCU – but no. My posting notice came through and it was to 230 OCU at Finningley, on Vulcans! In Singapore OC 205 Squadron had put me up for a general list permanent commission, and I had had my interviews up through the station commander and group commander before leaving for the UK and disembarkation leave.

"Coastal Command had always been treated with the least regard by the Air Force Board – because the board had been predominantly comprised of fighter and bomber 'types' – who hadn't a clue what we did. Historically you could make the case that it was not the Battle of Britain that saved this country from defeat in the last war but it was the Battle of the Atlantic – with Coastal Command's relentless persecution of the German U-boat fleet. In my memory I don't think we ever got a Coastal Command man on the Air Force Board.

"Wherever we went we got the shittiest accommodation, even though we might have been airborne for in excess of 15 hours. On Gan for example there were two lines of newly constructed, air-conditioned huts reserved solely for transiting V-bomber crews – we were put into sub-standard huts with fans. In Bodø there was one hotel, the Noruna, where the Transport boys with their Hercules stayed on Rate 1 allowances, while we were billeted down town in bed and breakfast joints. Soviet nuclear submarines intrude into our seas on a daily basis but what gets the headlines? A Typhoon formating on a Soviet Bear intruding into our airspace.

"As for the different marks of Shackleton, well I must say the Mk.1 was so primitive as to be beyond belief. We carried the Mk.30 torpedo which was fairly useless. It was a passive homing torpedo and could be outrun by a Soviet submarine quite easily. As I said – it was pretty primitive. In Singapore it was so hot in the aeroplane you flew with just a pair of underpants under your flying suit.

"The Mk.2 was obviously an improvement. The Mk.3 was better, but it was a bloody dangerous aeroplane at its all-up weight (AUW). That's why they fitted Vipers to assist the take-off. You could only run them for two minutes because of the oil consumption, so if you needed them at low level to prosecute a radar contact you started them up bloody quickly. There were two accidents where pilots went through the drill of – radar contact – actions stations – turning on – and slid out of the sky and crashed into the sea. One was off the South West Approaches, the other off the Mull of Kintyre. Anyway, at AUW it had to be very carefully handled. Which did I prefer? I really don't know. As you would expect the Mk.3 had more modern equipment, eventually getting 'Jezebel' sonobuoys with AQA5 recorders – which again was very rudimentary. The Canadians must have made a fortune selling us all their obsolete AQA5 equipment, but that was our introduction to 'acoustics' big time. Of course it improved when the Nimrod was introduced.

"As we didn't carry any oxygen we were restricted in altitude, basically our ceiling was 10,000 feet. We were higher at times but no-one came to any harm. A Shack transiting from Gan to Singapore back in the late 60s (he was at 8-10,000 feet), had a translation unit failure (propeller over-speed). That was an economical and smooth level to be for transit, but I wouldn't say that caused the translation unit failure. He ended up with an engine and part of the wing on fire and had to ditch [see Appendix Three]. Those up the front were killed, but some got out and were picked up by, I think, a RNZN frigate. Our normal height for blundering around was 1-2,000 feet and we would attack visually at 100 feet by day and 200 feet by night on the radio altimeter.

"My Shackleton days were wonderful. I was a young lad and we were all roughly the same age on the squadrons – there was great squadron spirit and great inter-crew competitiveness. No, I wouldn't change any of it."

Laurie Bruce – AEO

"I moved to Kinloss in 1958 as an air instructor with the MOTU. I was commissioned during this tour, and posted to 205 Squadron in Singapore in 1960. At low level in the tropics galley work was particularly trying, and for some hot food was fairly unappealing. However for most crews the addition of curry powder to 'Atlantic stew' was their only acknowledgement of the rigours of the climate. I recall that one fortunate crew on 205 Squadron lived like lords. The admirable Flt Sgt Gus Walker enjoyed cooking, when not engaged in other duties in the aircraft (he was a top-class wireless operator), and dished up splendid meals. His wife helped by preparing dishes for him to bring to work – they were a lovely pair.

"We had two 205 Squadron aircraft at Gan on permanent SAR standby. Departing crews traditionally did a low run over the broken-down causeway between Gan and the neighbouring island – at a very low height!

"I returned to MOTU in 1963, and remained there until early 1966 when I went back to 205 Squadron as air electronics leader and gunnery leader. A squadron review was held at Changi in 1966. For me the highlight of the review was meeting Gp Capt Gerald Livock DFC AFC. He gained his pilots wings on 20 December 1914 and served around the world with the RNAS and RAF, achieving many 'firsts' in aviation throughout the Middle East and Far East, including being the first RAF man to fly in Singapore, Hong Kong and North Borneo. He went on to select sites for the future airfields at Dum Dum, Calcutta and Mingaladon among many others along the route from the UK to the Far East. On discovering that the Shackleton was a very noisy aircraft his advice to me was to do what he did in his early flying days – 'Young man, if I were you I would soak some cotton wool in engine oil and put it in your ears whenever you fly!'

"In late May 1966, along with two other RAF officers, and three RAAF officers, I was detailed to join the USS *Salisbury Sound*, a seaplane tender operating in Vietnamese waters. The intention was that we would work with the USN crew as operations officers helping to control an ongoing SEATO maritime exercise. The *Salisbury Sound* would, at the same time, continue with its operational task of searching out Vietcong gun-runners operating along the east coast of Vietnam. In order to join the ship we were flown by USN P-3, from Sangley Point in the Philippines to Cam Ranh Bay on the east coast of Vietnam. Our first surprise was the descent into Cam Ranh Bay – we arrived overhead at transit height and then made a very, very steep circling descent to avoid surface-to-air missiles – apparently the Vietcong were at large in the area all around the base. Cam Ranh Bay

A typical Gan flypast by a 205 Squadron MR.1. (Laurie Bruce)

SS Salisbury Sound *with SP-5A Marlins anchored alongside, Cam Ranh Bay Vietnam, May 1966. (Laurie Bruce)*

turned out to be a huge natural anchorage, cluttered with a wide variety of USN ships. Ashore there was one very long, very narrow runway made of alloy planking with a coarse, sandblasted surface. This was in constant use, night and day, often by strike aircraft pounding the Vietcong. Buildings of all shapes and sizes were scattered around the edges of the bay. Some of them were inflatable because apparently the sand in that area was almost spherical, thus making building foundations problematical.

"The ship itself, which was anchored well out in the bay, was of World War 2 vintage, and supported a squadron of Martin SP-5A Marlin flying boats which were anchored nearby. Apparently part of the crew remained on board the aircraft at all times as anchor watch, while the remainder lived on the ship when not flying. The unfortunate enlisted men were in tiers of bunks in the vast hangar. We quickly learned that in calm waters it was impossible for the SP-5As to get airborne, so they were fitted with 'jet bottles' placed at an angle just below each of the beam hatches. To take off, the aircraft would charge across the water on full power, and then fire both jet bottles simultaneously. This launched the aircraft into the air quite violently. As the thrust was largely upward it made little difference to the aircraft's speed, so that it staggered along towards the horizon fighting to remain airborne and gain height. I did not volunteer to fly with the SP-5A crews!

"A major flaw in the ship's teleprinters made it almost impossible to decipher the incoming signals, and thus our task as controllers was something of a non-event. I recall my 'run ashore'. A tannoy announcement was made that any crew members who wished to do so could go ashore. Surprisingly only about 30 or 40, of the crew of 700-800, took up the offer, including all six RAF/RAAF officers who jumped at the chance, partly to get a closer look at the war, and partly to get a drink (USN ships are 'dry'). As Australia was engaged in the Vietnam war the RAAF officers were free to go ashore. However, the UK had refused to take part, so we RAF types were in a different situation. Without discussion, we concluded that it was our duty to examine and assess the conduct of the war in order to widen our military knowledge!

"I saw lots of activity but heard no shots fired in anger, and ended up enjoying the magnificent hospitality of a US Army Air cavalry unit. They were based, with their helicopters, towards the edge of the US-controlled enclave and, after a quick look around I was directed to the officers' club. This was a large marquee surrounded by thick stacks of sandbags. It didn't look much from the outside, but inside it was very comfortable – a well-stocked bar, tables with tablecloths, the best of food, a row of one-arm bandits, waiters – the works. The only sign that there was a war on was the constant procession of helicopter pilots in flying kit wandering in and out, festooned with pistols and revolvers of all shapes and sizes, while choppers whirred overhead. Eventually, stuffed with steak, and awash with dry Martinis, I decided to return to the *Salisbury Sound*. To my dismay when I staggered outside it was pitch dark. Fortunately, one of the chopper chaps pointed me to the road towards the beach where I could hitch a lift to my ship.

"What seemed like hours later and much more sober, I found myself on the beach surrounded by gun-toting US marines. They seemed not at all surprised to find an RAF officer wandering about in their midst and, with typical American can-do spirit, I was soon ushered aboard a heavily armed landing-craft, of the type used for up-river 'adventures', and we put to sea to find the *Salisbury Sound*. This was something of a problem in a very large, very crowded anchorage in the dark, not least because there appeared to be the occasional muffled explosion out at sea. Eventually we found the ship, but the officer of the watch refused to lower a gangway because he feared that the rather knobbly landing craft would damage his hull. Instead, he called up one of the patrol boats which were touring around looking for Vietcong 'swimmers' and were launching the odd hand grenade into the sea (the bangs in the night I'd heard), and I transferred to her. She went alongside, and I was helped up the garbage chute, rather untidy but none the worse for wear.

"I thought that was the end of the matter until I was summoned to appear before a US Navy admiral following the exercise debriefing. Thoughts of court martial loomed, possibly even questions in Parliament about an RAF officer poking about in Vietnam. To my astonishment the admiral greeted me like an old friend, gave me a large cigar, and said I was welcome to look around Vietnam whenever I was in the area. He closed by saying something along the lines of 'we have some difficulty getting people to volunteer for service in Vietnam, it's nice to meet someone who goes there off his own bat'. Sadly, I never got the opportunity to take up his offer."

CONFRONTATION WITH INDONESIA STARTS

"I was sitting at home with my family, in our flat in the Katong suburb of Singapore, in the late evening of Thursday 14 February 1963 when an RAF driver arrived. He told me he had been ordered to drive me to Changi Operations immediately with kit for a 14-day detachment. When I arrived at Ops my crew (captained by Flt Lt Ken Haining) arrived in dribs and drabs as mystified as I was. We were even more

Crew Charlie 205 Squadron 1960-61 in front of MR.1A WG530.
(Laurie Bruce)

mystified when we were each issued with a .38 Smith and Wesson revolver and a small box of ammunition. All became clear when briefing started. Apparently, a war (subsequently titled 'Confrontation') had broken out in north Borneo, between Indonesia and Malaysia, and we were required to fly to the small airport at Labuan, an island just off the Borneo coast, to provide assistance. Details of the assistance needed were scant.

"We were allocated Shackleton Mk.2 WL786 which had no bomb load, but as usual had 600 rounds of 20-mm ball ammunition loaded in the nose turret. Unfortunately the aircraft was not ready for us as it was undergoing a propeller change, and we did not manage to take off until 04.55 the following morning. We arrived at Labuan at 08.45, feeling a little tired, to be told that a task was awaiting us after we had had some breakfast. Breakfast was a strange affair, the airport terminal was hutted, and the food was served in what I presume was the lounge. We had bacon and eggs, but there was a shortage of cutlery and we were only allowed one item each – I ate my breakfast with a spoon!

"We were called to briefing immediately after breakfast. A wing commander, who seemed to be the senior officer present, told us that a patrol of Sarawak Rangers had gone missing in the mainland Borneo jungle and that all available aircraft were to be launched to look for them. Besides our Shackleton, there were also some Twin Pioneers and Army Air Corps Austers. His search plan appeared to take little account of the abilities of the various aircraft so, after some discussion, it was amended to make best use of the Shackleton's endurance and the crew's experience in the SAR role. It was pointed out to the powers that be, however, that the chance of seeing some soldiers through the dense jungle canopy was very, very slim.

"Although feeling very jaded, we were airborne at 10.45 and started our search. This was a somewhat 'hairy' affair as the jungle below was largely uncharted, and well dotted with steep peaks, and we were operating in broken cloud. Not surprisingly, we could see nothing through the towering rainforest trees. Eventually, to our relief, we were diverted to another task. We were routed to a remote jungle airstrip at Long Semodo to look for a Twin Pioneer aircraft that had crashed after take-off. We found the Pioneer almost as soon as we arrived at the airstrip. The wreckage was burning on the side of a steep hill with no survivors evident. [209 Squadron Twin Pioneer C.1 XN318, all five on board were killed.] Having reported the circumstances we were tasked to await the arrival of a rescue helicopter, but it did not turn up (we learned later that it had suffered some problem and had to make an emergency landing).

"Our next message was a strange one – it instructed us to feather an engine and return to Labuan immediately. This we did, landing at 1655 hours. We were told that an eagle-eyed airman at Changi had spotted a propeller part lying on the pan. This was where our aircraft had undergone a prop change some 14 hours earlier and he had put two and two together. We were grateful that the airman had done his job so thoroughly.

"After landing it was back to the airport building to join the Pioneer crews. They had a makeshift bar in a nearby hut they had nicknamed 'The Pink Palace'. Things then became a little hazy (we had been out of bed for some 36 hours), but I do recall one of the Pioneer chaps firing his revolver, and another lighting his Tommy Cooker on the wooden floor!

"Rather the worse for wear, we fell asleep on the floor of the airport building. We may have had camp beds and we slept until lunchtime, by which time the lost patrol of Sarawak Rangers had appeared unharmed. Later that day we were taken to a hotel, which had been commandeered for military use, for a well-earned night's rest in proper surroundings. My room was surprisingly small, almost like a cell, containing a narrow single bed, tiny bedside table and even tinier washbasin – nothing more. Despite feeling exhausted I slept badly. The constant tramping of feet in the corridor, which I assumed were reinforcements arriving, kept me awake.

"I awoke feeling very sweaty and dirty, as I hadn't washed properly for more than two days. I wrapped a towel around my waist and wandered into the corridor – now quiet – to find a shower. Almost directly across from my room I found a large open washing area with showers and a few washbasins. After a quick shower I was just leaving when I heard footsteps behind me and heard a soft greeting. I turned to find a stunningly pretty, and totally naked, young Malay lady standing beside me. She greeted me with a radiant smile before disappearing into one of the show-ers. Very much awake and refreshed, I left. Apparently, the authorities, desperate for accommodation as reinforcements arrived, had taken rooms in a hotel which, they probably didn't know, doubled as a brothel.

"We were recalled to Changi the following day, and shortly thereafter I was repatriated to the UK. 'Confrontation' was still going on when I returned to Changi for my second tour. By this time 205 Squadron officers were billeted in a comfort-able down-town bungalow, and were honorary members of the very attractive Shell Club.

"By an amusing coincidence, on my second Changi tour something similar to the brothel incident occurred. My family and I undertook a two-and-a-half-day rail trip from Singapore to Bangkok. At the final Malaysian railway station before the Thai border a large and colourful group of Thai prostitutes were gathered on the platform waiting to be deported on our train. Apparently this was a regular occurrence. The Malaysian police routinely deported the girls – and they returned on later trains! Again our sleep was interrupted by footfalls in the night. It transpired that they had wasted no time in setting up a mobile brothel in their compartments, and many of the train staff had enjoyed their favours."

Colin Butler – pilot

"My second tour on Shackletons with 205 Squadron was fabulous. Not only did we suddenly get marriage allowance when I became 25, but that also coincided with our trip to Singapore, where we got local overseas allowance. It was relatively cheap to live there; it was the very, very best tour in the world and lasted for precisely two and a half years. We went out in July 1962 and came back in January 1965 – with an extra son. We had a maid, we had a handyman who helped with the garden, cleaned the car and swept the drive. All our free time was spent at the officers' club and in the swimming pool.

"Not long after we arrived, we had to escort a Pioneer from Kuching, Borneo to Seletar. It was a single-engine Pioneer. They were in a bit of a 'shtuck' flying over shark-infested waters – so we just had to stooge around with them, it took forever. We later did the same thing for an army Beaver, and also had to escort a Britannia coming in on three engines.

"It was very dull compared with my fighter days. However, we did have some exciting times. There was one incident when we found a Chinese (?) submarine close to some disputed islands in the South China Sea. There were an awful lot of little islands that they were disputing but they weren't entitled to, so we had to do surveillance there. We had a wonderful tracking exercise on those things. They didn't run away, they just poodled along in the same direction they were going before; they probably didn't even know we were there.

"We had a lot of trouble with the Indonesians. For weeks we used to fly all night to spot any traffic that was coming across to Malaya. It was suspected that the Communists were trying to put people behind our lines to cause problems. These patrols were known as 'Hawkmoths'. Once in the middle of the night, in the Malacca Straits, radar back in Singapore thought they had seen an Indonesian fighter coming after us. We had to go under radar control, doing turns and just trying to get away from this shadow that was following us; that was quite exciting.

The 'thank-you' card sent by school children after a visit to 205 Squadron. (Bob Barrett)

"Aircraft serviceability was

surprisingly good I suppose. Serviceability problems hit us when I was in Malta on Nimrods. We started off with the best set of ground crew that Coastal Command could provide, plus we were out on our own. But then suddenly it all changed, and they stopped sending us these chief techs, and we got more of the run-of-the-mill guys. The serviceability went haywire."

Jerry Evans – navigator

"Leaving MOTU in December 1963, the choice of overseas postings in the maritime force was exciting – Gibraltar, Malta, Aden and Singapore. Ken Lamb, a new boy like me, and I awaited ours to come through; he heard first, it was 205 Squadron, Changi. But Ken preferred to stay in the UK, whereas I would have loved Singapore. He said: 'I don't know about this Jerry, 205 in Changi.' He didn't want to go, so I said: 'Let's go and talk to the mysterious 'them', the adjutant or somebody. We're both of the same rank and experience, or lack of it. Provided I haven't got my first choice, which was Gibraltar, we'll ask if we can change.' That's what we did, they were very happy either way; my posting would have actually been to St. Mawgan, and Ken was very happy to go there.

"Not long after I got out there we were given these Australian flying suits to trial. They were a sort of light cotton, a very light greenish colour and they felt beautifully soft to the touch. The only trouble with these bloody things was that they didn't breathe. From getting on board the aeroplane to getting airborne was normally about 45 minutes, because we had so much kit to test. We had no air conditioning, and you'd only been on board for less than ten minutes when the whole flying suit just looked black with sweat. It poured down your arms in little rivulets. What a relief when you rolled down the runway, we had the portholes open at the back and you had airflow through the aeroplane as you got airborne. It wasn't nice, but we just lived with it. My skin got red and blotchy all over, and didn't recover properly for about 18 months after I got back to the UK.

"At the end of '64 I became 25 and my pay doubled. Salary, married allowance, flying pay and overseas allowance all shot up. Overnight, this changed our economic conditions from comfortable to well off, and of course we got a married quarter.

"We had two patrol areas, one north of Kuching in the north-western corner of Borneo, operating from Labuan. We were patrolling sea areas to report on boats coming up from Indonesia to cause mayhem in Malaysia. We used to do the Kuching patrol with one aircraft. The other patrol was round the north-east corner of Borneo, right on the border with Indonesia; they used to get quite a few aggressive boats coming up that way. We had crews at Labuan the whole time the confrontation was on. For the same reason we had patrols in the Malacca Straits. Every night for two or three years we had one aircraft on patrol, starting at about one o'clock in the morning, through to about five or six. We had a preventive role and I think we did pretty well. We used to find more boats in the Malacca Straits because they came across from Sumatra. It was quite a short run and they had these fantastic boats doing about 40 knots across the Straits. When we found one we gave them hell, over the top at about 100 feet – with 2,400 rpm it must have put the fear of Christ in them! Great fun, fantastic flying.

"In general our Shackletons were very reliable and serviceable aircraft. A big part of the navigation system was the Doppler equipment. This measured speed and was supposed to give your ground position via an old analogue computer. If the Doppler wasn't working properly, then you had to inject all your estimated values into the thing and it computed from those. The Doppler often let us down; that was because it measured sea state, and the ocean out there was often so flat calm that it had nothing to 'bite' on. We were quite used to it not working out there, it was much better in the UK.

Jerry Evans on dispersal at Changi with 205 Squadron wearing a trial RAAF flying suit c.1964-66. (Jerry Evans)

"We went to some terrific places. I went to Australia, and we visited Hong Kong a few times. I had a brilliant detachment up in Manila. The flying was what I mainly remember. I had a terrific amount of night hours, nearly two thirds as many as I had day hours, which was really very unusual. The flying was extremely tiring, especially at night, when it was still but incredibly humid."

205 Squadron whimsy

"The Shackleton squadrons all had mottos. Irreverent aircrew, needless to say, were wont to adapt them. My favourite remains MOTU's 'Teagaisg Sealgair na Fairge' – 'Teach the Hunter of the sea' – which in my day was always known as 'We teach seals how to fly'. On arriving at Changi I discovered that 205 Squadron was 'Pertama di Malaya', which was 'First in Malaya'. Funny that, I'd always thought of it as it was widely known – 'Where is Malaya?' This was no doubt intended as a back-hander to the many 'temporarily uncertain of position' navigators such as myself, who from time to time had difficulty in locating a land mass half the size of Asia. Be that as it may, its crest of 'kris and trident in saltir' will never subvert for me the unofficial title of 'knife, fork and spoon club'.

"Flt Lt Duggie Burke, a larger-than-life character, was the 205 Squadron nav leader. Endless squadron members, not required for flying, would be 'drawn like bees to a honeypot' to be regaled with stories from him and other old hands. His Mosquito adventures from late World War 2, and post-war, were particularly riveting. It was then, I believe, that I first appreciated that great truism of squadron life – 'you should have been here last week'. Life of course, was more exciting, and you had just missed... Hong Kong, Thailand, Australia, last tour, Sunderlands, etc., etc. Of course much of it was in the mind, but given the number of second tour Shack men there, we few wet-behind-the-ears first tourists such as myself and Gordon Dodds were obvious targets for their daily nostalgia.

"As there was an unspoken pecking order to have a chair and I was way down it, I would find a corner of Duggie's floor to sit on, and spend many an entranced hour when I should have been revising the Inter Tropical Convergence Zone for my met check. Tales of Hong Kong, which was everyone's favourite detachment, were delivered with a sorrowful shake of the head, 'You need to be experienced, lad. You can't go to Hong Kong unless you've been before!'

"Once, on the long sea leg from Gan to Sumatra, I managed to spill half a plate of sausages and onions, beautifully prepared by the boys in the galley, on an area of the chart ahead of us. I could not stop plotting – what would the nav leader say? I solved the problem with a three-drift wind, extended to about ten minutes each leg. We had endless fuel, and the wind calculated turned out to be supremely accurate, so all was well. By the time we regained track the pool of sausages and onions was well behind and drying in the steamy atmosphere, leaving just a soupçon of its haunting fragrance on the chart.

"Who has not enjoyed the holiday of a lifetime then reflected wistfully that 'I need a holiday to get over it?' Well, the 205 programmers had no trouble obliging the troops in this way. The schedule was rigidly adhered to as much as President Sukarno's efforts would allow. Fourteen weeks comprising operations, occasional detachments – more and more regularly to Borneo – training and SAR standby, would be followed by crew leave for a fortnight. After that, imagine being told you had to go and lie on the beach on Gan, that beautiful coral island, and swim in piercingly blue, bathwater warm water for two weeks. Throw in the excellent mess and even the Mickey Mouse golf course, to name but two other attractions, and it was indeed a taste of paradise. Even time for cool beer when the aircraft in our area of responsibility were safely on the ground. Yes that was our lot, but someone had to do it.

"I was on 205 for exactly two and a half years. We came back in June '66, and like so many people, it was back up to Northern Ireland to 203 Squadron. They still had Mk.2s, but only for a short time because we were just about to start converting. I joined the squadron in July, and we disappeared down to St. Mawgan in about October to the Mk.3 conversion unit. The rest of my 18 months at Ballykelly was all on Mk.3s. They were more comfortable, and were probably better equipped, but it was a bit underpowered. I always preferred the Mk.2, I loved it."

Jim Ward – AEOp

"I was at MOTU until February '65 when I got posted to 205 Squadron. My wife enjoyed it tremendously. We had two boys; they had all the fun of being out there, except that I was away quite a bit. This was at the time of the Indonesian trouble so we went to various places to give support. We used to go up and down the Straits of Malacca looking for Indonesian boats coming across. One morning they told us they had a report that we'd been shot at, but we never found any bullet holes.

"One of the nice things was when we used to go to Gan for search and rescue standby. As long as you were available and weren't drunk, you had two weeks of swimming. In all the times we went there we were only called out once. We got to the end of the runway but it was cancelled. The guy had lost all his HF but when he got near enough he was able to use his VHF, so that was that. Even at Changi the squadron aircraft were all geared up for SAR and people were used to doing it. When we got to Singapore we had to stay in the mess if we were on SAR standby, later on they said that if we'd got a phone at home we could go home and they'd phone us. That made it a bit easier.

"We also had two-week attachments to Labuan in Borneo, mainly to fly trips over the jungle; it wasn't much, but we had to put on a show there. The only trip that made me nervous was when we came back one night with the co-pilot acting as captain. As he landed he literally froze at the controls. It was a short runway there, with only jungle at the end. We bounced a lot, but the captain took over and the crash tender followed us up. That was the only nervous time."

Guy Gibbons – pilot

"205 Squadron was a great place to learn the 'trade' of flying the Shackleton in the maritime role – and boy did I have to learn quickly. We had people who had flown during the war. My first flight engineer was an honorary member of the Caterpillar Club (those who had left an aircraft by parachute), having been blown out of an exploding Stirling at low level. Others had flown Lancasters, Halifaxes, Sunderlands and Neptunes. The range of tasks was everything from SAR, to intelligence gathering, to long-range patrols, as well as 'normal' ASW (anti-submarine warfare). ASV 21 was the best radar going at the time.

"Maritime Ops were good fun. You were flying the aircraft to its limits most of

Labuan from the nose of a 205 Squadron Shack. (Lance Smale)

the time. OK, there was a lot of transit flying. We did a lot of work and exercises in the South China Sea, around the Paracel Islands (these were international waters), and all the other islands that the Chinese are now claiming as their own.

"Every month we took an aircraft out to Gan, and brought one back. We were flying across the top of Sumatra, which meant climbing to 10,000 or 12,000 feet. Whether we were allowed to do that politically, I don't know, but we just did it anyway. But an issue with the spark plugs meant that, for about a year, aircraft were only allowed to do one crossing over the hills, because there was a tendency to blow a plug out. We used to climb out, go down the other side, and then transit to Gan at 1,000 to 2,000 feet. When you landed all the plugs were checked.

"When Apollo 13 blew up in April 1970 and started coming back towards this end of the world, the Americans didn't really know where it was going to land. So they announced a worldwide search and rescue effort. 205 Squadron's area of responsibility was effectively the Indian Ocean, South China Sea out to about as far as Christmas Island (which was where the Australians took over), and then all the way down as far south as you could go. So the squadron was deployed. The Gan aircraft was sent to Mauritius, as we were the standby aircraft at Changi we were sent to Gan; other aircraft were sent to places all over the area in case they were needed.

"We flew over the hills; the aircraft fully laden with the addition of a bomb-bay fuel tank. The extra 400 gallons of fuel gave us some two and a half hours more flying time if necessary. It was obviously much heavier, plus all the SAR kit. Having crossed over Sumatra, we went to feed the wing tanks from the bomb-bay fuel tank, and nothing happened; we couldn't get the fuel out of the tank. Because we were heavier than normal we didn't have enough fuel, without the bomb-bay tanks, to make it to Gan. As we'd flown over Sumatra, and weren't allowed to go back over the top (the spark plugs), we then started flying round the top end of Indonesia to Butterworth.

"We were two hours out of Butterworth when the engineer said we didn't have enough fuel to make it there. We then started looking at how we were going to lighten the aircraft – who was going to be thrown out first! I was the co-pilot, so I think I was number one on the list. We were just about to start throwing stuff out, when the

No. 42 Squadron MR.3 WR977 (now in the Newark Air Museum) taxiing at RAAF Butterworth, January 1967. (Adrian Balch collection)

engineer came up and said: 'Sorry folks, made a mistake. We've just about got enough fuel to get there,' and we did. We landed with well below what we would normally have as diversion fuel, with 400 gallons stuck in the bomb-bay tank. We then had to wait for someone to come up from Changi with the right kit to sort out the tank or defuel it. Of course everybody had flown away, so we had to wait for three days.

"We were tasked to film Icara ASW missile launches from HMAS *Parramatta* prior to the Royal Navy buying some; we ran in to overfly the ship immediately after firing, so we could follow the missile with a camera. They counted down, and our aim was to overfly some 20 seconds after firing. The first one worked (although we were slightly disconcerted to find we were lower than the cruise height of the missile), but the second one didn't go on the first press, so they pressed the firing button again. It came off the rails just as we reached the overhead. The missile duly fired and came up just in front of our outboard engine, leaving an exhaust marking on top of the wing!

"We were going up and down to Hong Kong quite a lot, and two aircraft diverted into Vietnam. One was my crew (without me as I was sick at Changi). They landed at Phan Rang Bay (an Australian base) with an engine fire. They had to wait three days for a new engine, keeping a very low profile because there were no RAF personnel there. I flew into Hong Kong on the day the first 747 landed there, and got a nice photo taken from the nose turret, of it taxiing past with our two 20-mm cannons pointing at it. We couldn't believe the size of this thing.

"We flew LROFEs which meant you were supposed to go and fly for 12 hours. In those 12 hours, the nav would do nav plotting, the radar would do radar watching, and everybody else would go to sleep. As pilot we flew two hours on, two hours off, swapping seats every two hours. The left-hand seat was the flying seat, so whoever sat there took command of the aircraft. If we suddenly found ourselves hunting a submarine, or something like that, and you were in the left-hand seat, it was your aeroplane and you ran the hunt. But oh God it was a long 12 hours.

"I will admit that we didn't always do 12 hours flying; this was a hangover from Sunderland days. Apparently, quite frequently they'd get airborne on an LROFE, then land somewhere up the coast, near to Singapore to pick up the families. They then flew further up the coast, landed on and all had a swimming party – apart from the poor radio operator who'd have to go aboard every hour and send an 'ops normal' message. Then they'd get airborne again, drop the families off, and go back to land at Seletar. We didn't pick the families up, but we did occasionally land at Labuan, which was very nice, and it was only about four hours flying to get there. There was a good restaurant in the airport terminal, much better than the food we produced, and there was a duty-free NAAFI. The poor old radio operator still had to go back on every hour to send an 'ops normal' on HF. We'd all have a leisurely lunch, stock up with duty-free, then fly back to Changi. The navigator would have to alter his maps a bit to show that we'd done 12 hours, it was totally useless flying.

"There was intelligence to suggest the Soviets were building, or had built, a base on the Andaman Islands with air defence radar and various other things. The squadron was tasked, three days running, to fly up there to do electronic eavesdropping. The big 'spark plug' on top of the aircraft was the 'Orange Harvest' radar warning receiver, which came in two versions, X band or S band, with two different-shaped spark plugs, depending on which frequencies you were trying to ascertain. We were tasked to fly around the islands at low level, with both these ECM pods going to see if there were any signals. It was a close formation of two aircraft. We went down to about 80 to 100 feet at a given point, flying all the way round but with absolutely nothing happening. Then we flew back in loose formation. It was a longish duration trip, I think we flew for 14 hours.

"In 1970 a big military exercise, Bersatu Padu, was held in Malaysia. This was to prove we could pull out and still support them by flying in F-4s, Buccaneers, etc., from the UK. We could, but we needed a squadron of Shacks for SAR cover and a squadron of Victors for in-flight refuelling; they needed a lot of aircraft to get the coverage. No.74 (Lightning) Squadron went home at the end of it. We covered them going back to Gan. We'd go halfway in case one of them fell in the water, and the Gan aircraft then took over. They just refuelled from the Victors overflying Gan and continued on to Bahrain (Muharraq). There was a lot of SAR flying for things like that, I must have done 70 hours in one week flying a sortie every day.

"Prince Charles came out on a trip to New Zealand, and we were tasked to do VIP escort – he was in a VC10, and we were down at 2,000 feet in a Shackleton! We were tasked to get airborne and fly to Darwin; he would get airborne in his VC10 and fly over the top of us when we were halfway along. He then continued to Darwin, and we'd follow. We took off at about 4 or 5 a.m., and he landed at Changi about an hour after we'd got airborne. He took off again and duly flew over the top as we passed the halfway mark, said 'hello' to us, which was nice of him, and we landed at Darwin mid-afternoon, it was quite a long trip.

"We got in to a bit of trouble there because all our windows were open, as they always were. We were supposed to have everything closed so that we could be fumigated with DDT spray; the Australians were very keen on everything being killed – including the aircrew. We duly debunked from the aircraft and went across to the officers' mess. We were told by the air attaché, who was there to meet us, that Prince Charles had left a crate of beer for in the mess as a thank-you. Well he might have left it, but he didn't tell the Australians what it was for, so when we got there they'd drunk it all!

"Every year there was an ASW exercise flown from the USN base at Sangley Point, Philippines. Our last exercise was in 1971, and the area covered most of the South China Sea (now claimed by China), and involved USN, RAAF and RNZAF P-3s and ourselves, plus subs from the UK, US and Australia. I was lucky to be co-pilot on a very experienced crew (we were already the high scoring crew on the exercise), so when the radar operator called a DRC (disappearing radar contact) we had no qualms about throwing a sonobuoy in the water. The sonar guys clearly heard a sub travelling away on a steady track, so we dropped a line of passive (listening only) buoys in the water some way ahead. Sure enough, the sub came towards the right-hand one of the pattern, so as it was in the exercise area, we dropped two SUSs (small bomblets that went 'bang' to simulate depth charges) on top. The sub didn't really like this and immediately turned hard left and accelerated, thus showing it was a nuclear boat which we hadn't realised until then. Having turned left it now went under every buoy we had in the water, so we dropped SUSs on top every time. A CERTSUB message (found and simulated kill) was sent to exercise control and we continued on task, not realising the ramifications until we landed back at Sangley Point. We were now treated to a fairly boisterous welcome, and an awful lot of beer – we had apparently caught a Polaris boat in open water, which had not happened before, so a party was now in full swing. Unfortunately the USN was somewhat unhappy at us catching their submarine. As we were on a USN base, they decided we needed to be interrogated, and dispatched a specialist team from the USA to carry it out. Luckily our boss heard of this, and we replaced the crew on the next exercise sortie. At 06:00 the following morning we were dragged out of our pits (or the party) to get airborne ASAP and divert back to Changi! The less said about drinking and flying the better, but we made it. Cue another party.

"I didn't quite complete a full tour at Changi. When the squadron was disband-

'The Gathering Storm' – 205 Squadron disbandment flypast rehearsal with Don Wimble leading.
(Guy Gibbons)

ed we did a flypast with six aircraft; I was number four. We flew over in line abreast, two 'V's really, then line astern over the parade as the flag was lowered, then finally flew past letting off all the flares. During the practice formation our leader took us into a cumulonimbus which we could all see coming – I suspect he was busy trying to put his cigarette out or something, he was always smoking. As his co-pilot you used to sit and watch the length of cigarette ash get longer and longer; he always had a paper cup to put it in, and he'd wait until it was really long, but it never ever made it to the cup, it always dropped off all over his flying suit, or onto the floor.

"Before the pull-out we had to get rid of all the war stocks of weapons at Changi. Rather than put them all onboard a boat and sail off somewhere, we went out and dropped everything. There were 21 carriers in the bomb bay, each of which could take a 1,000-lb bomb, as many as the Vulcan. We looked at dropping all 21 in one go to see how big a bang we could make! This was until it was pointed out that under the peacetime bombing rules you had to allow 1,000 feet between each bomb. The shockwave from one could set off the next one and so on up the chain towards you. We had to go up to about 25,000 feet to drop all these bombs a few at a time. Nobody thought we could go that high – we weren't even sure if the oxygen would work. It also meant that nobody could smoke. Although we didn't carry Lulu nuclear depth charges out there, we were still 'bucket of sunshine' trained.

"Going through the bomb dump they found a room chock-full of what were probably the last long, thin CLEs (container light equipment), the things, with little parachutes on the end, they used to drop to SOE agents during the war. They had long since disappeared off the inventory, but were fitted with the right kit to go on the aeroplane. We trialled what we could drop in them, and had sort of bombing competitions on the airfield to see who could get closest to the bullseye – they weren't fit for anything afterwards. We fired off all the 20-mm cannon shells; great fun, with the smell of cordite in the aircraft. I think we had the last 20-mm cannon shells ever to be fired from a Shackleton – I don't think 204 Squadron had any after that. It was a shame a lot of things got thrown away when we pulled out of Singapore which, in retrospect, would have been historically interesting.

"I actually flew the last authorised 205 Squadron aircraft out of Changi to Gan – WL750 – on 1 October with John Trout (two flying officers). As soon as we got airborne, 205 Squadron became a detachment of 204 Squadron Strike Command, and I think we were the last FEAF aircraft to leave, so what was FEAF then became part of Strike Command. However we did get into a bit of trouble leaving Changi when we did a flypast. The squadron dispersal was on the old Japanese runway, which was at right angles to the main runway. On the old runway at one end was 205 Squadron, the RNZAF Bristol Freighters, and 48 Squadron Hercules. At the other end was the Transport Command dispersal, which had all the visitors and passengers. Between the transport dispersal and the main runway there was also a road, which crossed the old runway at right angles. We took off from the main runway and did a wide orbit. It was about 9.30 a.m., so we assumed that everybody would be at work in headquarters. We flew around Changi Creek, then came in on virtually an attack run towards the Japanese runway, moving along it quite low – low enough! In fact we were so low that air traffic closed the gates on the road, there was a double-decker bus coming along and they thought we might meet it.

"There was a crowd of 205 Squadron personnel, aircrew and ground crew. Everyone had been there to say goodbye to us, including the wives that were left (most of them had been flown out before then). They had turned round and were walking back towards the squadron from the side of the runway. I can still remember the face of one of the flight commanders when he turned around again and saw us coming towards him. I don't think he knew whether to flee, or to flatten – he chose flatten. We were quite low as we went past and set off around the Straits to climb back over the island. Unfortunately for us the AOC had been having breakfast on his balcony, which overlooked part of the jungle to the south of the hill he was on, which was their quarters area. He saw the tailplane go past, level with the tops of the trees!

"The signal when we arrived at Gan went something along the lines of, 'AOC extremely displeased at your departure Changi. You are not, repeat not, to carry out any further flypasts en route to the UK.' We had three copies of that given to us, first by the duty ops man, the second by the squadron leader ops and the third by the station commander. On the way home we stopped off at Souda Bay, in Crete instead of Luqa. This was because 203 Squadron was there on exercise, and we were advised we would get more engineering support. The Americans there had seen the Mk.3s. When they saw us coming in they accused us of being a Liberator. The aircraft coming back from Singapore were all hand-painted with various decorations. One Shackleton was painted with 'White Knuckle Airlines' along the side of the fuselage. We all had different things painted on the side of our aircraft. It was the days of GT stripes down the side of cars, so we had aircraft with those.

"We came back to St. Mawgan having flown all the way across Europe in beautiful sunshine. The aircraft had been in the Far East for three or four years and hadn't seen any cold weather, or anything like that, but halfway across France we flew into a cold front. We turned the anti-icing on, but that was not particularly successful. We turned the heating on and just got showered with spiders. We went into cloud and popped out of it at 200 feet on finals to St. Mawgan. On normal days, we would be quite happy with that. However St. Mawgan's runway is, or was, about 300 feet wide, and we'd been used to operating off runways that were 150 or 200 feet wide – the perspective is very different. We rounded out at the height we thought we should round out at, which was probably about 50 feet, which is where we dropped from. That was our arrival back into the UK, but it worked. We were then boarded by Customs, who went through the aircraft with a fine toothcomb; we were all charged import duty for something or other – they got their monies worth out of us.

"We were tasked to take the aircraft to Catterick for the fire school, which only had a 3,000-foot runway. We'd both practised landing that length of runway at Seletar. If you screwed that one up, you were in the water (it just ended where they used to run the Sunderlands into the water and pull them out again). So we were happy we could do it. We'd discussed bouncing off the A1 to see if we could slow it down enough, but at the last minute it was all changed. We then had to take it to Honington on 20 October so 204 Squadron could have it. Whether they wanted it for spares, or something else, 204 were quite upset to receive it. They were expecting it to look like a standard, pristine, maritime aircraft with just 205 painted on it. They discovered all the extra markings on the aircraft; I know we had GT stripes down the side, and I think we also had the number of horsepower painted on it somewhere (four times Griffon 58s at 2,435 hp each with water-meth injection). Our total time bringing WL750 home had been 45 hours and 55 minutes; 12:50 Changi to Gan, 12:00 Gan to Muharraq, 10:00 Muharraq to Souda Bay and 9:45 to St. Mawgan; finally, 1:20 to Honington. Sadly they were less than impressed with it and it was eventually reduced to spares to help their own aeroplanes out."

Bob Barrett – AEO
"I joined a 201 Squadron crew with a really great captain, and flew my first sortie late in the night of 9 March 1966 (I remember that because 10 March was my birthday), not long before the end of the Indonesian Confrontation. 205 Squadron

WR966 G – 'Grunt' of 205 Squadron at disbandment time. (Mike McKenna)

in Singapore had been flying support, and were kept very busy with their SAR commitments, etc; detachments went out from various squadrons in the UK to support them. I went out with 201 for two to three months, flying from Changi and Borneo. Part and parcel of the Borneo detachment was looking for infiltrating boats, but we got various kinds of jobs. We also did detachments in Sharjah, where we were chasing Arab dhows with illegal immigrants, smuggling, etc. It all went under the general heading of maritime reconnaissance, but it wasn't the same as tracking submarines, or playing games with Soviet warships.

"The ASV 21 radar that we operated was extremely good – superb in the way we used it. When you were doing a radar homing you would start by just picking up the target, and then we had a set procedure to take us to the target. As you approached you lowered the radome right the way down to the attack position. The maximum range setting was 170 miles, however it wasn't always the most efficient range to operate from. If the target is at a lot shorter distance than that, you would set it to the range which would give you a better performance.

"There wasn't that much to tune on the radar. You could tune noise in and out to a degree, there was also an electronic bearing marker unit on it. For example, if a contact came up you turned the marker to cover the contact – that would give you an instant indication of the contact's bearing. You had range circles which you could wind in and out. Then you could quickly tell the navigator and/or the captain, what range and bearing the contact was at.

"As for exciting moments, everything was exciting in the Shackleton – you only had to cough and something happened! On one exercise the chap who was listening out on the wireless (our long-range communication was in Morse code), was sitting there, fat, dumb and happy. He'd isolated himself on the intercom from all the patter that was going on amongst the crew. The trailing aerial was out (it had pieces of lead shot on the end of it to keep it taught).

Bob Barrett on his final MOTU exercise. (Bob Barrett)

"We got a radar contact, and the radar operator came up, 'Captain, radar, contact…' When that happened on an exercise all hell broke loose, and you cleared the decks for action. The intercom calls would then start – 'Roger, turning on…', 'action stations!', etc., and a bell rang to get everybody's attention, and so on. So we turned on for this contact, which wasn't that far away from us and we were homing in on it. The wireless operator was still quietly sitting there. Because he'd isolated himself off the intercom he'd not heard anything that was going on, and he'd still got all the trailing aerial stuck out the back.

"Then the bomb doors opened, which caused God knows how much turbulence underneath the aircraft, and the starboard beam look-out said that the trailing aerial was whipping to and fro. The engineer who was sitting across the gangway from the wireless operator shook him to tell him what was happening. The wireless operator started trying to wind the aerial in, but it got caught in the rudder. We were trying to do a straight line into the target, with the trailing aerial trying to pull the rudder one way, and the captain, swearing like mad, 'What the hell's happening with this ****** rudder!', as he was fighting it the other way. Eventually the beam look-out had to yell: 'Stop the homing. Wireless, let some aerial out. Let's close the bomb doors.' We had to let the contact go while we cleaned everything up. That sort of thing was just par for the course in the Shackleton.

"We had a new, young AEO posted on to our crew. We were a crew of old hands who'd been working together for quite a long while, we just got on with it, had a good time, and had a beer afterwards. But he wanted to change everything and of course it didn't go down very well. We were on the first night long-range sortie that we'd done with him as the AEO when, shortly after take-off, a good-humoured, Bristolian member of the crew called up on the intercom from the galley, to ask who wanted coffee and tea – so everyone had a hot drink before we got on task. We each answered, the last being the new AEO, who had decided to put himself on the radar, and said 'I'll have OXO'. Our man in the galley eventually found a little packet of OXO in the crew box. He also found some little jars of spices, amongst them a bottle of cayenne pepper – lethal stuff! The radar position was very dark with a curtain surrounding the operator, in order that no light could get in to spoil his concentration on the screen. A paper cup containing a hot drink was passed under the curtain and accepted. A few minutes later the radar operator called the galley to ask what had been put in the OXO. On being told it was cayenne pepper (and it was a very liberal amount), he said: 'You never put cayenne pepper in OXO!' The answer just came back 'We do in Bristol'. That was the AEO's introduction to flying night sorties.

"We had some wonderful characters in maritime. One of them, with his colleague, had a gag that they used to pull on a new co-pilot who'd just done his training, just done his conversion and come onto his first squadron. We would get aboard the aircraft prior to start-up, start getting sorted out, sit down and plug in, the intercom warming up and things like that. These two old hands would be sitting in the beam seats, and before the engines started one of them would call up on the intercom to say, 'Nose, this is tail', and there'd be no answer (as it was the beam chap who was calling!) Once again, he'd call 'Nose, this is tail…nose, this is tail!', sounding as though he was getting a bit flustered.

"By this time the young co-pilot in the starboard seat would be stretching and trying to get his head down underneath the coaming to look towards the nose, then realising there was no-one in the nose. So, he would then come up on intercom, 'Tail, this is the co-pilot'. Well of course there was no-one in the tail, and he'd call again. 'Tail, this is the co-pilot.' Then, someone in the beam would come back, 'This is the beam. Who the **** is calling the tail?' The co-pilot's voice would come back, 'Beam, this is the co-pilot. Who do you want? I'm trying to call the tail to tell him there's no-one in the nose.' The beam would then reply 'Well that's funny, because there's no ******* in the tail either!' The whole crew knew what was going on, even the captain; they'd practised and rehearsed these gags over the years.

"I did an extended tour on 201; I went right through from March '66 to December '69, and then got posted out to 205 Squadron. There we went backwards to Mk.2s, but the electrics side of it was all the same as the Mk.3. We used to carry a broom down the back. This was because sometimes, when the tailwheel was lowered, it got out of kilter. So you removed the panel over the top of the tailwheel, shoved the broom handle down and straightened it out before you landed. This was the kind of thing you took for granted.

"We still had a search and rescue commitment, and our patch covered the transport aircraft that were coming from Cyprus or the Gulf across the Indian Ocean, to Singapore. For that we had one aircraft detached to Gan – it was quite something to be paid to go to the Maldives for two weeks. Most of the single guys enjoyed it, with its nice coral beaches and so on, but it was quite a burden for the married families.

"One search and rescue incident that I was involved with was over the other side of the peninsular in the South China Sea. We were coming back from a night of practice bombing, and heard a lot of R/T chatter between Changi and a 74 Squadron Lightning that had an engine problem. He had lost one engine and thought he might be able to nurse the aircraft down, but then he started getting massive vibration from the other engine, and decided to get out. He was at a good altitude, and we were down in Shackleton territory at about 150 to 200 feet above the sea. We thought the Lightning was going to come down in our vicinity, so we turned round and beetled back off out of the way while it came down."

The Lightning was F.6 XS893, flown by Fg Off Mike Rigg. It came down in the sea 19 miles east of Changi, the pilot deciding to abandon it when the undercarriage failed to lower. **Bob Barrett** *continues:*

"It crashed into the sea, and we listened out for the SARBE (search and rescue beacon) signal from his life jacket. We picked it up, no problem at all, and started homing in on it using the normal procedure. We got to the appropriate distance and set off the flares to light up the night sky, and sure enough there's the chap sitting in his dinghy. They launched a helicopter from Changi and picked him up. From the time he banged out of the aircraft to the time he was walking into Changi hospital, was something like an hour. It was always very satisfying when search and rescue was successful like that, but sometimes it could be tragic.

"I was out there until the squadron started its close-down in 1971, and was on the official disbandment parade, although the squadron went on for a little longer. It was a good tour, in a nice climate and an area that was heaving with activity. When I came home I was posted to Kinloss, and went on to the Nimrod tactical simulator being built by Marconi. Then it was all changed. When the air force accepted the first full mission simulator, it was decided it would go to St. Mawgan, so once more I packed my bags and was off to the south-west again. The Nimrod did everything bigger, better and faster – nothing like the fun we had in the Shackleton, and of course, a lot of the characters had gone by then. Yes we had fun, but not everything was done for a giggle – our work was always completed successfully."

Mike Dyson – pilot

"In '66 I wound up on 205 Squadron. That was a plum posting; if you got that you were set up for two and a half years of sheer luxury. We did two-week spells on Gan, search and rescue standby, ten-day spells in Labuan, flying around Borneo supporting whatever was going on with Indonesia. There were a lot of night patrols at 1,000 feet up the Straits of Malacca – no air conditioning – looking for fast launches that might be shipping God knows what. We were away from the families a hell of a lot.

"On 4 November 1967 one of our Shacks was returning from Gan, which meant going east and then down the Straits of Malacca and into Singapore. About 120 miles west of Indonesia, at about 7,000 or 8,000 feet, they had an engine overspeed and fire. This burnt half the wing off, and after a spiral descent they landed in the water with the radar scanner deployed. Only three people survived; a flight sergeant passenger attending his son's wedding in Singapore, the flight engineer and a signaller. The AEO was pulled aboard the 13-man dinghy that inflated from the wing, had a heart attack and died in the dinghy. The nose had broken off when it hit the water, and although the engineer damaged his hand he was able to go forward. He stepped down into the nose section, to find the two pilots dead in their seats, got out and came up to the surface. [See Appendix Three.]

A 205 Squadron MR.2 taking off from Labuan in 1963. (Lance Smale)

"Some weeks later,

as I was at the end of my tour, I found myself accompanying all the widows and families in a VC10. We were to have been met at Brize Norton by the group captain, welfare officers and so on, but the weather was so bad that we diverted to Heathrow. I arrived with this group of sad and unhappy families around me. So I explained the situation to the Heathrow people and said, 'They need peace and quiet. I want a quiet room for them please.' They took us upstairs to the VIP suite, gave everyone a nice meal and then gave me a bill for about £300. I said, 'I'll sign that, send it to the ministry of defence please'.

"I had to ferry a time-expired Shackleton to England. The four engines were given a 75-hour life extension to fly this poor wreck back to St. Mawgan. It was going to be modified, with new engines, new spars, and made into a Phase III aircraft. I was given the lot of flying it eastbound around the world – Singapore, Borneo, the Philippines, Guam, Wake and so on. I was flying from Wake Island to Honolulu at 8,000 feet with about two or three hours to go when No.1 engine gave a minor cough and a splutter. The rpm dropped significantly, and then picked up again, so I immediately feathered the engine, and we continued.

"We landed at Honolulu and I said to the engineer: 'I shut it down. I've never seen anything do that before.' He said he'd have a look. With the mags off he turned the props – with no effort at all, there was no compression. I thought perhaps the props and gearbox had separated. He took a spark plug out, but when he turned the props again the piston was moving up and down, so it wasn't that. I was told it was a supercharger blow-back, but didn't have the faintest idea what that was. However, I think if I hadn't feathered it I would have had an overspeed."

Keith Baker – flight engineer

"I arrived at 205 Squadron in April 1967, and was glad to be away from the cold of northern Scotland. The squadron was located at Changi on the sea side of the runway. Our aircraft were parked close to the squadron building, which contained the administration offices, crew room, a cinema and changing rooms. The ground crew were located next door, so we were in a little world of our own; we even had our own cafe run by a Chinese family. The taxiway and parking area was simply ground covered by metal sheets with holes in them; leftovers from the war. The squadron had Mk.2s which were not in very good condition. They had old electrical systems, and when it rained (which it did most days for an hour

RAF Changi in 1966. (Steve Bond collection)

or so), they leaked like a sieve. As the aircraft did not have as much equipment on board, they were a lot lighter and therefore easier on the engines.

"I went to the stores to collect my new flying equipment and was directed to a good Changi village tailor who made my uniforms quickly – they were a good fit and looked good. It was the done thing, and nothing was said, even the wing commander had his uniforms made there. Our tropical flying suit was coloured jungle green. Our flying boots had green canvas uppers and rubber soles, the uppers going halfway up the shins and laced up to the top – they were designed to keep the leeches out. So I had a week or so to learn the systems, and a few flights as second engineer to learn the routine. Then of course a check ride, and questions to see if I had picked up the gen. Then I was on my own. It was a lot more informal than in the UK.

"I was put on a crew with Flt Lt George 'Taff' Phillips as captain. He was a tall, lanky Welsh navigator, and the most senior flight lieutenant in the RAF. We then started our Phase III training. The RAF realised that our aircraft were not in good condition, and were going to update the electrical and electronics systems. We did a few flights with the updated aircraft, and then we were given an old aircraft to take back to the UK and bring back an updated one. I was given another flight engineer, who was still Phase II trained, to work the flight to the UK – but we both worked the engineer's panel. I also worked in the galley making tea and cooking when necessary. My sandwiches were good too, so no one went hungry. It made a change from sitting at the panel staring at the gauges and engine instruments, trying to stay awake.

"As a war was being fought in the Middle East, Israelis against the Arabs, our route to the UK was eastbound around the world. This was to prove interesting. We took off on 12 August 1967 and flew a four-hour flight to Labuan, a night stopover, and then a ten-hour flight to Guam. Another night stopover, then an eight-hour flight to Wake Island. Then on again on to Hickam. There we had a day off managing to get down town and to the beach. We didn't stay very long as we found the place was very commercialised and expensive, so after a swim we came back to the base and ate and drank there.

"The next day we flew an 11½-hour flight to McClellan, California. There the aircraft went unserviceable, and we had a few days off. The next flight was to Offutt, Nebraska, where there was great hospitality. In the bar some American offered to buy our 'Lancaster bomber' – I was all for it but one of the crew stopped me. The next flight was to Gander, another night stop and then a nine-hour flight to St. Mawgan. We had a couple of days off to get ourselves sorted out, clothes washed and so on. We reported for duty only to find that the newly refurbished aircraft was not ready as the factory workers had all gone on holiday. Even when they returned the aircraft was still not ready, so our crew was given a job to keep us occupied.

"We were sent to Pershore airfield (we were all accommodated in an old pub), and were given another aircraft to air test, and then had the afternoon off. Then we started some secret trials on it. We would fly out in the evening, and when it was dark fly low approaching a ship, when we would use infra-red cameras on it. We did this for a week. After the trips we returned to the pub, had a few beers and then to bed. The captain 'Taff' Phillips, showed his colours and got sloshed every night in the bar! The trials were a failure as when the ship showed any light it dazzled the infra-red gear.

"Our little 'jolly' came to an end, and we returned to St. Mawgan where our Mk.2 Phase III Shackleton was waiting for us all spick and span. We gave it an air test. There were some things to be rectified, which took a few days to fix. On 14 September we began our journey back to Singapore. Again we were going to fly eastwards, but instead of flying across the Middle East we flew south and our first stop was Lajes in the Azores. There we did a night stop at the US Navy base. We always enjoyed this, even if their beer was a little weak their steaks made up for it, and they made us welcome. The next day we took off for Sal (Portuguese Cape Verde Islands), but we had a VHF radio failure so we jettisoned fuel down to maximum landing weight, and returned to Lajes. Fortunately the Yanks had a spare radio that they let us have, so we refuelled and continued our journey.

"We then flew on to the Ascension Islands (another night stop), and from there to Luanda, Angola. We were met with a war-like scene with the Portuguese fighting the locals who wanted independence. Although the Portuguese wanted to leave, they wanted to do so in their own good time. We landed and taxied in. The airport and airfield were surrounded with guns of all types, light cannon and heavy machine guns all manned and ready to fire. Our second navigator, leaning out of the beam window, took photographs of the defences. However, this was seen, and when we stopped the military police came over in their jeep and demanded the photographer went with them. Of course they were armed, the navigator had to go with them – and his camera. Our captain/navigator Taff Phillips was very concerned. The rest of us left them at the airport and went to the hotel where the British high commissioner was informed. He immediately went out to the airport.

"Because of this we had an extra day there, and the stupid man was released without his film. Next morning, when I was sitting in the hotel entrance watching the world go by, a local came in with a goat in tow. I asked the receptionist what the goat was for. His reply was 'dinner sah!' It didn't turn out that bad after all. I was having a shower when I noticed that the water was running down the wall over the live light switch, so I jumped out pretty quickly before I had a shocking time! After all the excitement we flew on to Pretoria. Taff Phillips was not happy with our naughty navigator. It would cost the nav a lot of drinks to regain popularity.

"We landed at the SAAF base and loaded our suitcases and bags onto the bus to take us to the hotel downtown. At the main gates the bus was stopped by a burly South African warrant officer. He stepped aboard and invited the NCOs to join him in the warrant officers' and sergeants' mess for drinks. We pointed out to him that we were dressed in lovely smelly flying suits and could do with a shower, and some clean clothes. He just smiled and said they were used to it and not to worry. The mess welcomed us with open arms, and the drinks just kept on coming. We couldn't buy a thing – the beer was good too. Eventually we managed to get away and the chap who was giving us a lift stopped at a railway workers' pub. Once again we were made welcome and the beers came thick and fast – we still couldn't buy a thing. When I said I was hungry, steak and chips appeared at the bar in front of me. We were made very welcome by these friendly people. Eventually we got back to the hotel and checked in. Our baggage was in our rooms so we had no problems – a hot shower and to bed.

"The aircraft was leaking a lot – fuel, hydraulic oil, and engine oil, a real mess. It seems that when the aircraft was put in the hangar, for electrical refit, nothing was done to the rest of it, so the various pipes started to crack and leak. The ground crew had some work to do. They could get spares from the South Africans as they also flew Shackletons. Goodness knows how long the aircraft had been in the hangar, but it must have been a year or so. As was the norm, on this trip the officers received allowances, and the NCOs were given full board – but no money. As we were not happy with this arrangement, we had a word with the head waiter at dinner and told him the story. He allowed us to swap the soup for a good bottle of wine each. We had a good fish dish, chateaubriand steak, plus a good dessert and a glass of brandy each. The officers had their egg and chips and saved their money.

"The co-pilot was taken ill, and we had to get a replacement flown out from Singapore. When he arrived, and the leaks were repaired, we continued our epic round-the-world journey. On all of these flights I had a lot to do. I was responsible for loading the bags and suitcases and doing a load sheet before take-off. Sometimes it was necessary to move things if the centre of gravity (CofG) was out of limits. The CofG was usually aft, so I had the heavy gear placed in the nose bomb aimer's position. By this time we had a routine, and a lot of the crew would help with the loading and packing away.

"From Pretoria we had a five-hour flight to Plaisance on the east coast of Africa. We did the usual night stop, and the next day flew another eight hours to Gan, where we were legally able to have a couple of beers before bed. As he knew Taff Phillips, I went to see the duty doctor in the medical centre. We decided to play a prank; the doctor put plaster of Paris over one of my legs. I then hobbled over to the transit bar where Taffy was having his ration of beer – by the look of it he had just about reached his fill. However, when he saw me his eyes nearly popped out. I hobbled over and explained that I had fallen down the aircraft steps, and would be out of action for a few months. He went very red in the face, and nearly exploded. He started swearing and shouting, and got into a real paddy. Once he had started to calm down, I told him that it was just a trick for a good laugh, but it took him a long time to come down to earth. The next day we flew back to Changi, having taken over six weeks to complete the round-the-world trip. It was good to be back in spite of the Singapore heat, rain and humidity.

"The Coastal Command Categorisation Board came out and I was put forward as a 'T' Category – I was an 'A' cat. Now I was to be the local examiner as well; I was pleased after all my hard work. My promotion to flight sergeant also came through, so my pay packet was increased. There was no way that, at the age of 28, I could have reached that rank as an engine fitter (which I had been).

"In December 1967 a Beverley flying low level over the jungle in Malaya crashed into a hill, and we were called out on SAR to fly over the crash site to see if there were any survivors. We saw the wreckage and the large scar on the hillside but there were no signs. Ground search parties were sent out but found no-one alive."

Beverley C.1 XL150 of 34 Squadron Seletar, flew into a hill 90 miles north of Johor Baru in bad weather. All six crew on board lost their lives. **Keith** *again:*

"Life continued on the squadron as usual; trips to Gan, flying exercises and a trip to Hong Kong. This was the time of the Vietnam war, and we were patrolling the coastline in case any US airmen had crashed into the sea and we could help them. The Americans already had a good rescue organisation of their own, so I think that our effort was just a ploy to show friendship. We did get a good trip to Hong Kong out of it, which we thoroughly enjoyed.

"A new captain joined us, Fg Off Gare; a great captain and a pleasure to have on board. The whole crew were sent on a jungle survival course in Malaysia, which began with a few days of lectures and demonstrations. We had to pay attention as we were to go north across the causeway into the jungle. We wore our flying clothes and boots and were each given a machete to cut down the undergrowth. A couple of hours after entering the jungle the novelty wore off – it was hot, sweaty and uncomfortable. We were advised that snakes could be eaten, but I made the agreement with them that if they left me alone, I would leave them alone. We decided on a camp site and prepared our own 'Basha' or bush bed, and a shelter made with bamboo and bamboo leaves. The bed had to be off the jungle floor to stop the insects getting at you during the night; the best barrier to them was athlete's foot powder! The navigator had a pistol in case of tigers or wild pigs – not that we saw any.

"Once you had made your shelter, and the bed frame, the next thing was to make the top as waterproof as possible. We covered the frame with springy bamboo branches, with big leaves overlapping so that the rain would not fall on you. The jungle is full of noise at night – you can hear the rustling of things crawling and slithering under your bed. I tried to sleep with my machete in my hand, but it kept slipping out of my grasp. Then in the middle of the night came a loud crashing, then lots of swearing. One of the beds had collapsed. Panic stations! With a tiny torch light shining, someone was frantically trying to repair his bed, no-one volunteered to step out and help him; you don't know what is walking about and going to grab you in the dark.

"In the morning it was up and out for a hike in the jungle without breakfast or coffee. The first navigator, who was not popular, was found to have a very large leech attached to the back of his neck – no-one came to help until his threats came. We all had leeches attached somewhere; having to get them off gently, with salt or a cigarette dog-end touching it. You did not feel them crawl, stick on and start sucking your blood. We all had condoms to protect our willies. But for those of us with average size, how do you keep one on when slack?! We had about four days in the jungle and were quite pleased when it finished. When we got back to Changi we had a couple of days off, then back for a month of training.

"In-flight food was a self-help affair. The hours to be flown determined how much money we could spend at the in-flight store. Changi was a main stopover for the flights from the UK to the Far East and had a big kitchen for the passenger meals. We tried their food, and it wasn't bad. Our favourite was a hot and tasty prawn curry. It came in a large vacuum flask and was handed round in paper cups, thus saving us having to cook on board. We stopped ordering this when we found half a cockroach at the bottom of the flask – after we had all eaten! We suspect that one of us had eaten the other half – it must have been crunchy and tasted of curry.

"To try and keep cool during the flight most of the flight engineers built themselves a draught tube. This was a used flare cartridge with a V-shaped cut sawn in the base end, and a hole drilled to put a long bolt through. This was then, with the hole facing the slipstream, inserted in the Very signal pistol mounting above my position. The bolt stopped it from going through. The resulting breeze, through the hole brought a lovely cooling down-draught onto your head and neck. You had to remember to take it out before landing, otherwise it would fall out on your head as the aircraft was in its landing roll and the airflow reduced – much to everyone's amusement. After a flight we would be rather thirsty, so after we left the squadron we would stop at the first bar and have a few Tiger beers – the alcohol would go straight to our heads.

"Our wing commander was friendly with the local navy commander and arranged exchange trips with the crews. My crew, crew six, was a lucky one. We joined HMS Forth a submarine depot ship for about five days and were put in the chief petty officer' mess; we found it rather cramped but that was to be expected. We sailed out to sea and headed north. An exercise was in progress and the submarines would come alongside to be replenished with oil, food, fresh water and torpedoes. As the crews had been at sea for a few weeks, without washing or a change of clothes, they really stank high. The routine was for them to come up to the main deck, strip off their clothes, which were thrown over the side for the sharks, and then into the showers for a good scrub. They were then given new clothes and went to the bar for a drinking session (there was no alcohol on board the submarine).

"On the ship they had the old custom of 'up spirits' and there was an issue of

Shackleton MR.2 Phase II WG530 G of 205 Squadron off the Malay coast in 1964. (Steve Bond collection)

navy rum to all of the crew, and us. The rum was very strong and always affected me. This tradition has since been stopped. We continued our way, and eventually got to Bangkok; our two days there passed quickly. We went to the airport to take over a Shackleton, with its engines kept running, the other crew taking our place on-board ship. We then flew back to Singapore to continue our routine.

"In August 1969 we went on an exercise in New Zealand. Firstly, we flew direct to Darwin, north Australia, a ten-hour flight. We arrived in the evening, and were given accommodation at the sergeants' mess. Unfortunately, we were not made welcome by the residents, so we had a few beers and left. The next day we were up early and flew to Amberley, Queensland, an eight-hour flight. After a night stopover without any unpleasantness, we continued on to RNZAF Whenuapai, New Zealand.

"It was quite an international exercise with Americans, Australians and New Zealanders also taking part. We were to protect a convoy of ships against a number of submarines. If they got within firing range they would fire simulated torpedoes, and if we caught them we would simulate dropping our weapons on them. The results would be sorted out back at base. The submarines were all modern; the other aircraft were also modern – we were the old technology.

"The exercise proved to be a success for us with our old-fashioned methods. The modern way of submarine hunting was to drop a series of sonobuoys, and climb higher listening to the noise underwater. Most subs made some noise un-

derwater when they were transiting and could be detected. However, the subma-
riners tried to be clever. They attacked on the surface, but we were hunting them
with radar and the old-fashioned Mk.1 eyeball. So we had the highest successful
attack and kill score. Our wing commander flew on all of our flights and fitted in
quite well with the crew.

"We duly commenced our return journey but had an engine failure on take-off,
a blow back. We landed again and fixed the problem with a new magneto; fortunately the engine was not damaged. The return journey began again, and we flew
back to Amberley for a night stop, then on to Darwin. We stopped at the same
mess again, but the CMC (chairman of the mess committee) must have heard of
our previous reception, and things were different with drinks on the house for us,
which was a nice gesture from him.

"The next day we flew a boring ten and a half hours back to Singapore. Once
more we settled back to the usual routine in the hot, humid climate. My two and
a half years in Singapore were nearly up, and I was posted back to England. I had
worked hard, and flown 1,323 hours from Changi; I had kept my 'A' category and
my examiners 'T' category. My memories of Singapore were good, it was a worth-
while experience. However, some of my friends were killed and they will never be
forgotten; but life has to go on"[3]

Martin Coales – pilot

"In '69 we went out to Singapore. Kai Tak, Hong Kong was one of the favoured
detachments but we had an awful job stopping our crews getting locked up! On a
few occasions, to get them airborne the next day, we had to bail them out. After a
year or so I was made first pilot to a navigator captain. We had one or two AEO
captains, not many, but there was always a smattering of navigator captains. In
1970, in the middle of our tour, we brought all the Shackletons back one at a time
to have the wings re-sparred. We transited through Gan, Sharjah, Jeddah, and
Souda Bay in Crete; then Souda Bay to Manston, Manston to St. Mawgan and finally to Kemble. It was very slippery when we landed at St. Mawgan, one of those
landings where you aquaplaned down the runway and got away with it. I had a
co-pilot Jim nicknamed 'the wallet'; wherever we went he bought gold. He did a
lot of shopping in the Middle East, and it was said that he was even advising people in the souk in Sharjah about financial affairs and how to invest in things!

"Anyway, we picked up another aircraft from Kemble WR969, and then did a
shakedown flight at St. Mawgan, just to make sure everything was working. Then
we went on to Luqa, Malta, where we picked up some of that awful Maltese wine
for two bob a bottle and put it in out night bags. We continued on to Jeddah in
Saudi Arabia where we were to refuel, but on the way we had lost one engine and
another one was overheating. While we were talking to the engineer about what

---

3. *The Growler*

we should do, the crew unloaded all the bags – including the little overnight bags with the wine in. There were three of us who had these bottles of wine, which the custom officers ceremoniously broke, then poured the contents down the drain – they then confiscated our passports. We were due to get some engineers to sort out the engine problem, and then just leave. Unfortunately we were there for a week while all this was sorted out. The chief customs man was away on safari, but luckily the air attaché at Jeddah was able to make the peace. He got our passports returned and told us to get going and not come back. We got airborne, but the same engine was still overheating so we had to turn round and go back! I said: 'We're not stopping. Whatever happens, we're not stopping.' When we got back on the ground an engineer just got a great big hose and cleaned the radiators out – we got airborne and got away, thank heavens. Later we got a letter from the ministry, which said whatever we did we mustn't go back to Jeddah or we'd be locked up. Apparently we'd been fined £2,000 per bottle but no-one ever paid. That was the reason we shouldn't go back.

"Having finally left Jeddah we flew to Sharjah, but on departure from there No.4 was overheating, so we had to return. It was an inter-shaft seal problem, which was quite common. Then it was Sharjah to Gan, where we had another overheating problem, then Gan to Changi, so we took almost a whole month to get there and back. In this day and age it wouldn't really be cost-effective. Great fun though and a real experience. I was one of those lucky pilots; luck is a vital ingredient in a flying career. In the RAF, we flew thousands of hours of flying, and ended up getting away with a lot really – we were working to the limits.

"We carried practice bombs and sometimes 1,000 pounders but I never dropped them in anger. We used practice bombs on the ranges, usually at sea, but sometimes on desert ranges. Once our crew, with the squadron commander on board, were dropping on a desert range. The second navigator was doing the bomb selecting, and he went to drop two 25 pounders. You just straddled the target and one of the crew in the tail would assess the drop. On this occasion we were doing just that. Our second nav thought he'd dropped the practice bombs, but the man in the tail said 'CLE away'. This great container missed the range hut by about five yards! As you can imagine, our squadron commander who was seated in the right-hand seat, went absolutely puce. On the range there were bits of the CLE everywhere. Our navigator wasn't too popular, but nor was our boss who was captain for the trip.

"About three months after I joined the squadron I had my annual medical. The doctor said I was grounded – just like that. I couldn't believe my ears; he told me my blood pressure was high and he was grounding me. I'd never been taken off flying and I couldn't believe it. I wondered how I was going to tell our squadron commander. The doctor told me to lose some weight, so I went and played a lot of squash solidly for about three weeks. I lost about two stone in no time and got my medical back, but it was a bit of a shock to the system. We had a hectic lifestyle with a lot of parties. I was 24 when we went out there so officially we were not married. This was crazy and a lot of young officers lived in ghettos. Knowing that I would be 25 a few months' after our arrival, my wife and I were able to find a nice little hiring. Once I got to 25 we got various allowances, including beer rations; so we had plenty of Tiger and Amstel stashed in cupboards because we couldn't drink it all!

"One of our better detachments was to Auckland, New Zealand. We went from Changi to Darwin, then straight across from Darwin to Amberley at 2,000 feet. That being the maximum height we were allowed to fly at, and at that altitude it was very turbulent. We saw almost nothing, apart from desert, on a nine-hour transit. Every so often you'd see a little shack, and perhaps an aeroplane, Land Rover or something. Then it was to Whenuapai, Auckland for an exercise. The RNZAF took us down to South Island in Bristol Freighters and also bussed us to Rotorua – a memorable trip.

"I was with 205 until not long before it finished. In the latter part of 1971, as the months passed, the crews gradually left to fly aircraft home to the UK until there were just a couple left. We brought one of the aircraft back via Gan, Bahrain, Souda Bay in Crete, Gibraltar, St. Mawgan, and finally to St. Athan where the aircraft was going to be put into storage.

"I went on to Nimrods in September '71. In July I was up at Kinloss helping out in operations a bit, waiting until we got onto a course. The Nimrod was an amazing change; the Shackleton was pretty noisy, oily and old by comparison. But, because of that, we had very close-knit crews. We did work constituted crews in general, whereas in civil aviation you knew the checklist, you knew what you're meant to do, you've each got your own job supervising each other doing it, so you had no leeway really as to what you did and worked with anyone. In the services, you just did what the captain said and as long as he got away with it, no-one worried. As long as you were honest about what you'd done if you made a mistake, your boss would tell you not to do it again and probably buy you a pint. That's how it worked, so we all used to do our own thing much more, as long as we were getting on with our jobs. Some would work nearer to the limits but it depended on what their own limitations were. That was very important for pilots, but what they had to have was the ability to know how far they personally could go. They gained a sixth sense – when they felt that something was wrong, they knew they needed to take action."

Rob Knotts – air signaller

"In 1969 two of 205 Squadron's Shacks spent a month's detachment in Australia as part of a joint naval and air force exercise. After landing at Darwin we taxied to the dispersal and shut down the engines. As soon as we did there was a banging on the door. On opening it an Australian health official stepped in, closed the door and sprayed us all in a dense cloud of what we later learnt was DDT. Welcome to Oz!

"Following receipt of a signal warning of suspected fuel contamination, we diverted and landed at RAAF Butterworth. We taxied to the dispersal and the en-

Rob Knotts. (Rob Knotts)

gines were shut down. The crew got out of the aircraft and heard an ominous hissing sound coming from one of the main wheels – it was punctured. Spare wheels were not available at Butterworth. A signal was sent to Changi requesting a replacement wheel. Late that afternoon one of 41 (RNZAF) Squadron's Bristol 'Frighteners' duly arrived with a wheel, aircraft jacks and some of the squadron's ground crew. Their task was to change the wheel. Sadly, it was not to be.

"The Shackleton had been resting on the flat tyre all day – aircraft jacks were not available to support it. When our ground crew started to change the wheel they found that the wheel's bushes had become distorted, this was due to the unusual gait the aircraft had displayed throughout the day. Unfortunately, new bushes did not feature in the equipment delivered courtesy of the RNZAF. So a set of bushes arrived the next morning, again courtesy of the RNZAF. The new wheel was fitted and we took off and returned to Changi. The fuel contamination? Our aircraft was not affected.

"A major event during the Christmas period was the station bar competition. Each section at Changi was invited to build and decorate a bar which was judged by a panel of senior officers. The squadron took over part of the ops room, converting it into a tropical setting with water, bamboo, vegetation, plants and flowers – overall it looked pretty good. However, some of the aircrew decided that it lacked a certain something. The swampland near to the squadron building housed frogs, and some of them were offered new homes in the ops room. All was well with the frogs remaining quiet and still overnight and during the day. As the judging time approached, the bar had filled with people which raised the temperature in the room. Consequently, the frogs became active with the result that they seemed to enter into a jumping competition. I'm not sure what the judges thought. Squadron members thought it hilarious and the frogs seemed to enjoy themselves.

"The world-famous Raffles is a colonial-style hotel, housing a tropical garden courtyard, a museum and a Victorian-style theatre. No. 205 Squadron held a party in the Raffles Hotel theatre just before Christmas 1969. Not only did we have a party, but

'An ominous hissing'. (Rob Knotts)

also a pantomime, with the squadron's CO playing the part of the Fairy Queen and the ground crew flight sergeant playing the Squire.

"We sometimes flew to Hong Kong landing at Kai Tak. Opened in 1927 Kai Tak was first used for seaplanes. The Japanese were stationed there during World War 2 and extended the runway at the base. The approach to Runway 13 was said to have been one of the most difficult approaches in commercial aviation. Approaching aircraft descended on an initial heading of north-east, which took the 'plane over the harbour and then over west Kowloon. This part of the approach was done with an instrument guidance system. Passengers who had not been to HK then got their first views of the place, but they were unprepared for the final part of the approach, which was necessarily flown visually, and was quite thrilling. The aircraft flew up to the 'chequer-board' marker on a hill, two miles from touchdown, and at 650 feet turned right 47 degrees. Every landing was an experience to remember!"

Alan Mills – AEOp

"Arriving at Changi was like stepping into a hot shower. We stayed in a really basic hotel for a couple of nights, then our 'sponsor' found us a house in 'Opera Estate'. It was not very clean, and we then moved to a bungalow in the estate, which was marginally better. I still did not have enough seniority for a married quarter but was able to get an apartment owned by a local, as a 'hiring', paying RAF rent. This was to be our home for the next three years. The apartment was on the third floor of a four-storey block of flats, at Ocean Apartments East Coast Road. It could be noisy during the day from the traffic, but was quiet enough at night. After a few nights there we could hear a scraping sound, which we traced to be coming from a living room cabinet, and was being caused by some sort of large woodworm. The cabinet was swapped for a quieter one. If we went into the kitchen at night for a drink we had to make sure the light was on for a few seconds. The cockroaches, which had come out of the rubbish chute, would then scurry away! The neighbour above us was Mr Liu Thai Ker, and his Hungarian wife Marta. They had a small boy called Christof who eventually rose to become the senior architect in Singapore, planning and changing the whole look and feel of the country.

"Singapore with 205 Squadron was very different from living in the UK. It took about three months to acclimatise completely to the heat and humidity. There was very little air conditioning, mainly fans. The aircraft were hot and sticky until we had some air circulating after take-off, and we tried to cruise at 2,000 feet if we could. The squadron had increased its strength to 15 crews to cope with the threats of the Indonesian Confrontation and possibly Vietnam, plus there were some Soviet ships and submarines passing through the Malacca Straits into the Indian Ocean. There were also the search and rescue duties at Gan and fairly frequent exercises taking us to the Philippines, Australia and New Zealand. The squadron took on its share of duty on the Beira Patrol, flying from Majunga in Madagascar on a two-month detachment. In other words, we were pretty busy, with quite a lot of time away. Most of these events were predictable, and the ops/planning staff had a scheme where you could see what you were planned to do on a daily basis up to at least three months ahead.

"Singapore in 1968 was unrecognisable from the modern city it has become today. The citizens lived a more basic existence, with fewer high-rise buildings and far less prosperity; Prime Minister Lee Kuan Yew was only just starting to promote his view of a more prosperous modern Singapore. The civil airport was at Paya Lebar in the centre of the island, and the road to it had high fences to obscure the kampongs (wooden villages) from view. Land reclamation had barely started and the ships at anchor off Clifford Pier were still small, offloading their cargoes onto barges.

"Everyone on 205 had done at least one tour on Shackletons, and were, in the main, very competent. This made the flying quite relaxing. My first crew was captained by a very confident and likeable Flt Lt Dave Hinchcliffe. He was a bit dismissive of the squadron hierarchy, but because he was so competent he managed to get away with it. One of the AEOps was Bruce Gunton who eventually became the owner of the Gunton motor/electronics company. He moonlighted in Singapore for Serco, fixing the electrics and radios on their boats. He also fitted an electron-

A very smart-looking MR.2 WR960 A 205 Squadron. (Dave Lawrence)

ic ignition system (which he made himself) to his battered old car, and although his clapped-out battery required us to push start it, it always fired up quickly. He would drive like a maniac in the frantic Singapore traffic, but it was no use asking him to slow down – he just drove faster!

"After a year I was moved to another crew, captained by navigator Flt Lt Bob Parrot. He was very experienced, and we always knew what the 'plan' was. We worked well with him, and for my remaining two years on 205 I stayed with them. The AEOps were Dave Watts 'DC', a thin, serious guy who could be a bit obdurate, Ben Godwin, a gentle sort of chap who I got on well with, Robbie Robertson, a Liverpudlian, who always seemed to have a scam going, and Leo Prevett, a black chap who was new to Shackletons. We had to train Leo to bring him up to speed. He was okay but seemed to see colour prejudice everywhere (not from us), and so was a bit grumpy.

"We went to Hong Kong twice, each time for three or four days, shopping for cheap goods, eating and drinking. As we were coming in to land at Kai Tak the pilot John Potts called for full flap. I was sitting in the port lookout seat at the rear of the aircraft, and called forward to say that the flaps had not moved. John realised that he needed to land at a faster speed (so as to avoid stalling), so we touched down a bit faster than normal, and stopped without any further problems. You would have thought that we might have had at least a pat on the back for my re-porting it and John's quick decision to land at a faster speed than normal. But I should not have been sitting in a seat that was not fully stressed for landing (I wanted to look over Hong Kong), and John should have overshot the runway and returned when the problem (a burst hydraulic pipe) had been dealt with. The rest of the crew said 'thanks'; the squadron seniors were not so grateful. The hydraulic pipe that had failed was repaired but failed again as we landed back at Changi.

"Once a year, the Royal Navy submarine repair ship HMS *Forth* based at Singa-pore would go on a 12-day cruise to Bangkok, mainly to exercise its crew and engines. The squadron decided that our crew sail with *Forth* to Bangkok. Another Shack would fly up there, we would bring the aircraft back and the other crew return to Singapore. One memorable part of the voyage was as we sailed from the Singapore dockyard. We were all on deck in our best khaki uniforms, the navy as it usually does when leaving port, were in white, when suddenly the ship swung around in mid channel! The steering system, from the bridge to the rudder, had failed (the ship was launched in 1938). For the rest of the voyage there were six sailors in the bowels of the ship pulling on a big wheel whenever the bridge said left or right on the intercom system.

"The way we had operated at Ballykelly, and then Singapore, was much the same. After about three months in Singapore we got used to the heat and being sticky. If you were doing a patrol, and not too worried about altitude, you tended to stay at about 1,500 to 2,000 feet where it was just that little bit more bearable. The back windows were nearly always open, including take-off and landing; which

didn't affect the operation of the aircraft. The engineers always had to think about take-off performance, especially when we were going to be on a long haul, you were full of fuel, and the high gear supercharger on the Griffons would be used. They had a tendency to drop

Bill Howard's 205 Squadron crew. Mike McKenna is in the front row, far left. (Mike McKenna)

out of high gear on the take-off run so the pilots had then to decide whether they had the speed to take off, or the distance to brake to a halt. 205 Squadron disbanded at the end of '71, a year after I had left."

Mike McKenna – navigator

"My instructors at MOTU St. Mawgan probably regarded my approach to sub-hunting and maritime bombing as somewhat cavalier and certainly unconventional. The screen navigator seemed nervous as we took off on our first live weapons sortie carrying a stick of live 1943-vintage depth charges. I think they were sweating, the instructor certainly was, until we dropped the DCs to the fishes. It *looked* impressive. Anyway, I graduated and was posted well out of the way to 205 Squadron. I could not believe my luck; a 23-year-old rookie arriving in Singapore to all that tropical sunshine, sparkling sea, sand, water-skiing and rowing (my sport). What an adventure!

"On arrival there in early 1970 as a flying officer, I became the newest second navigator and no doubt most naive member of a crew. I was immediately taken under the wing of very experienced SNCO aircrew who were jacks-of-all-trades and experts in everything it seemed, including detachment nightlife protocol. They were endearingly called 'knockers'. That was not an unflattering term in the maritime world, but one borne of genuine affection. In my distinctly inexperienced state I can thank them for being saved from myself on several occasions away from base. As a junior flying officer I was also, metaphorically speaking, 'selected and fused' to understudy the 205 Squadron standard bearer, the dapper Kevin Dillon, from whom I eventually assumed responsibility.

"The constituted crew concept worked extremely well for assimilating new crew members. My first navigator was Flt Lt Brian Dent, a sharp operator with a mischievous sense of humour. He regaled me with 'war' stories about atomic bomb testing at Bikini Atoll, and interdicting camel trains in Sharjah; a round from the nose guns worked wonders apparently. Brian also protected me from the worst excesses of crew pranks and brought me on professionally no end. Usually it was the co-pilot who suffered the worst jokes – tea bag sandwich anyone?

"Our area of operations was extensive, ranging east from Singapore out over the South China Sea, up the Malacca Straits and into the Indian Ocean and, on one occasion, halfway to Australia to provide cover for a globe-trotting woman pilot. We saw that Krakatoa is west of Java – not east as in the film title! We flew many surveillance sorties shadowing Soviet submarines orange with rust as they negoti-ated the shallow waters and choke points around Singapore. The usual navexes, land-aways and long-range flying exercises took us to Butterworth, Labuan, Kuch-ing, Kuantan and most frequently for me, Hong Kong. Others went to the Philip-pines or Majunga for the Beira Patrol; we all had our Majunga visas ready. All crews were involved in live SAR operations, rotating on a one-week 24-hour standby commitment for military and civilian events.

"One sombre task we had was to check periodically the location of the wrecks of the Royal Navy warships HMS *Prince of Wales* and HMS *Repulse*. Both were sunk on 10 December 1941 by torpedoes launched by Japanese aircraft near Kuantan, off the east coast of Malaya. The location was the last resting place of 835 RN per-sonnel. The idea was to warn off and report vessels seen to be diving on the 'war graves'. Apparently most plundering of the site has happened in more recent years.

"We would take part in an annual Hong Kong SAR exercise. This involved searching for a barrel simulating survivor, pre-positioned south of the colony. I took part in the exercise in successive years, and on both occasions ended up with emergency diversions into South Vietnam. On 4 December 1970, returning south to Changi (with a tail section full of lampshades for the co-pilot), we heard a rum-ble and felt the whole aircraft shake violently. Captain Bill Howard, co-pilot Tony Orton and the flight engineer quickly shut down and isolated the engine, a con-rod had gone through the crankcase. Our Mayday transmissions were met with a stony silence as our guest, ace navigator Don Kerr, turned us starboard for anyone who would take us. I believe we were intercepted (but we were in crash positions by then), and we landed at Phan Rang, Vietnam, a USAF fighter-bomber base.

"Our Shackleton was an object of great amusement and curiosity. But we held our heads high as operational aircrew alongside an array of RAAF Canberras, USAF B-57s, F-100s, A-1s, C-123s and Huey gunships. Rumour said that one of our crew got airborne on a Canberra mission; just as well he got back. Having just spent all our dollars in 'Honkers' we relied on the generosity of our hosts who bought us copious quantities of Budweiser. This was my eye-opening introduction to the US serviceman at war; gung-ho fighter pilots in the squadron bar after a mission, pot-smoking rife. We even managed to make a dash to the beach, which was pro-tected by slit trenches, somewhat disconcerting when you are standing there in your 'shreddies'! We 'escaped' from Vietnam on 6 December. Our presence there must have been tricky for the Foreign Office as Britain had refused to get involved with the war. A Hercules arrived with an engine and 205 Squadron fitters. When the cowlings were removed from our engine, a shower of metal fragments fell out – we were a lucky crew.

"On 21 November 1971, having completed our second Hong Kong SAR exercise (by which time we were flying from Tengah as 204 Squadron [Far East] detachment, 205 having been disbanded) we were downtown scattered around Kowloon restaurants and bars, when a live SAR alert was called. A China Airlines Caravelle had disappeared somewhere between Taipei and Hong Kong. A crew member searched the usual haunts and found enough of us to form a crew. Sqn Ldr Peter Stean was captain as we flew 11 hours, finding nothing and returning to Kai Tak where we continued to top up our fluid levels. Subsequently we heard that a fisherman had seen an explosion at height near Penghu Island (Taipei). This was one of the first commercial aircraft losses due (probably) to an on-board bomb explosion.

"On 22 November we were returning to Tengah, our new base as part of 204 Squadron and once again, Mayday after an engine had dumped most of its oil onto the tailplane. We turned right and landed at Cam Ranh Bay, Vietnam, where we stayed for four days. We were advised to take cover on the Sunday, anticipating a Vietcong 120-mm rocket which usually arrived on a Sunday, having been dragged through the jungle all week. I met a USAF engineering officer who spent most of

205 Squadron MR.2 overflying the Queen Elizabeth *en route to its short-lived retirement in Hong Kong.* (Mike McKenna)

7 September 1971, 205 Squadron's disbandment flypast. (Mike McKenna)

his time modifying a tank/trailer combo to enable him to drive around collecting ordnance in what was left of the dump, attacked a few months earlier and still littered with unexploded devices, scattered when very big bombs had exploded. Departing on 26 November another engine was shut down, so up the Mekong Delta we flew at 500 feet to Tan Son Nhut, Saigon. After obtaining an oil seal from a civilian company, we finally staggered back to Tengah with one engine on precautionary feather (restarted for landing). What a week!

"One day we were tasked to photograph a squadron aircraft against a backdrop of the 'Seawise University', formerly known as RMS *Queen Elizabeth*. The 33-year-old stately ship was transitting south along the Malacca Straits to Hong Kong to become a floating university. Sadly the ship later caught fire and sank in Hong Kong harbour.

"During my time in Singapore, the outdoor life and water sports, acclimatisation to the tropical environment and above all flying and working in an un-aircondi-tioned aircraft made us all quite fit. I found I could compete well at rowing and sculling, regattas at Changi Yacht Club, overseas trips to Colombo, Hong Kong and Brunei, racing on the Belait river (managing to avoid the crocodiles).

"Looking back at my time there, Singapore was rapidly changing under Lee Kuan Yew. I had been fortunate to see some of the remains of Empire and evidence of the wide-ranging footprint of the RAF in the Far East, flying boat ramps at Seletar, distant airfields, relics of the Japanese occupation and Changi Gaol. There were great opportunities to explore the Malayan Peninsula, Kuala Lumpur, Penang, the colonial rest and recreation centres at Fraser's Hill and the Cameron Highlands. When I returned to the UK, I took a load of 'Selangor' pewter pots with me – so many memories.

"On 7 September 1971 the commander FEAF, AVM Nigel Maynard, took the salute and Sqn Ldr Don Wimble led a formation of six Shackletons in line-astern above the Disbandment Parade at Changi. Following formal disbandment on 31 October the remaining aircraft and crews moved over to Tengah as 204 Squadron (Far East) Detachment.

"Following the arrival of the first Nimrod, the last three aircraft and crews assembled for take-off on 15 January 1972 for the first leg of our return to the UK. Bill Howard brought us back to St. Mawgan in WR966 on 24 January, after an epic journey via Gan, Bahrain, Jeddah, Akrotiri, Gibraltar and Plymouth Sound (from whence flying boats had originally departed way back); a total flight time of 53 hours 40 minutes.

"The squadron standard was displayed on 11 February at MoD Adastral House, when Wg Cdr Dick Pendry, the last 205 Squadron CO, accepted the Wilkinson Battle of Britain Memorial Sword awarded by the Air Force Board to the unit 'for making the best contribution towards the development of operational tactics'. A fitting postscript.

"As a young man in Singapore, I believed that I had found paradise. The flying, the people, the boating, BBQs and the general atmosphere of work hard and play hard, in a mostly benign, sometimes soaking wet and hot, but spectacularly picturesque environment, made for a memorable introduction to RAF service life."

*The end came on 31 October 1971 following formal disbandment of both 205 Squadron and FEAF. The RAF finally left Changi on 9 December 1971 following which it underwent extensive redevelopment to turn it into Singapore's international airport to replace Paya Lebar which could not be expanded. The remaining three Shackletons stayed on at Tengah until January 1972. Thereafter the only RAF MR presence on the island came in the form of occasional Nimrod detachments, which also operated from Tengah. Finally, from **Bob Barrett**:*

"A short comment made by a British primary school child at Changi, following a visit to 205 Squadron in 1970. The teacher asked them to write a short account of their visit and the best stories would be sent to the squadron. One very bright and alert toddler wrote as follows: 'The Shackleton has two pilots and two alligators and the alligators tell the pilots where to go!' There was often a lot of truth in the last part of that statement!"

CHAPTER THREE

LIFE ON THE LINE – CHANGI GROUND CREW

The following extract is from RAF Changi's 1969 New Arrivals Booklet 'Here's Royal Air Force Changi'. How our attitudes have changed!

"People who are used to living in a temperate climate do take some time to get used to the heat and high humidity of Singapore. The human body is a resilient machine and can adapt itself to widely different conditions, but it does take time to adapt itself. Having been conditioned to living in a fairly cold climate in Europe, it may take anything from six days to six months, depending on the individual, to adjust completely to the new heat and humidity.

"Sunbathing. If you came out by sea, during the journey you will have seen many people madly frying themselves on the decks so that when they get to Singapore they will be a dark mahogany colour. They imagine that they will not then be accused of being newcomers to Singapore. In fact, one of the first things that will be asked of them is 'How was it in England when you left it?' and on looking around you will find that most of the people who have been here for some time are only lightly tanned. The majority of people prefer to stay in the shade, not because of the un-doing them any harm [sic] but because it is so very hot! To most people, a suntan is an attractive thing to have and there is no harm in this but the sun in the tropics is very strong and must be treated with great respect. If you want a suntan, start off very, very gently indeed, with about ten minutes in the sun and gradually increase this until you have acquired the required colour. When you are in any doubt as to the length of time you should stay in the sun, occasionally rub the back of your shoulder with your hand. If it feels at all sore or tender, dive for the shade straight away. Nivea cream is an excellent antidote for sunburn. Fair-skinned people, particularly those with red hair, must be

HERE'S
ROYAL · AIR · FORCE
CHANGI

especially careful not to get burned. If you stay out of the sun for about a week, even if you are practically black, you may think that you can spend a whole after-noon on the beach without getting burned. However, you will find that, despite your colour you will burn almost as easily as if you were snow white. It is also true that one does burn much more quickly bathing by the sea than at a swimming pool somewhere inland.

"There is no such thing as sunstroke and there is no necessity to wear a hat if you do not want to; nor is it necessary for children to wear hats. Hats do shade your face and eyes from the sun, but at the same time they make your head hot and sweaty."

> *This they believed to be sound advice at the time. But the extreme conditions of heat and humidity could be very tough on the 'Shackleton Boys'. Certain-ly this was endured by the aircrew, but even more so by the ground crew who, of necessity, spent long hours working on the Shackletons in the open. Not only were the aircraft becoming increasingly challenging to maintain in an airworthy condition, but the work was often dirty, and the aircraft surface rapidly became too hot to touch during the day. Whether the engi-neer's trade was airframe, engines, electrics, armourer, radio or radar, the problems were similar – working on and in an ageing and labour-intensive aeroplane.*

Cliff Edwards – airframe

"We had six 205 Squadron Shackletons in formation over Changi for our final farewell. We actually managed to get all our seven aircraft serviceable and in the air for the practice before for the final parade. The formation was advertised as '7 Up' after the drink. It was quite a feat, we worked very hard to get them all up. We normally had about four or five serviceable; that was our usual maximum. We used to have at least one aircraft in Gan and an-other aircraft wandering around somewhere else. They even flew up to Vietnam, although I never went there.

"The Shackleton was actually a very nice aeroplane to work on. The Mk.2 Phase IIIs that we had were a good aeroplane but the Mk.3s had a nose-wheel and had to have Vipers. However, some of the servicing could be very

After considerable investigation, extensive fault diagnosis, detailed systems analysis and lengthy technical discussion; taking all factors into account, my considered opinion is that it's knackered.

Rob Knotts

challenging on all of them. Around the main spar box it was difficult because the central part went through the fuselage and you had to climb over it; there were things like heating and fuel transfer to attend to, so I suppose that was the grottiest place to work. They were very simplistic, robust aeroplanes; quite fun when flying because you could go down to the tail or up in the nose-gunner's seat. I once made an approach to Changi sitting in the nose-gunner's seat on an air test, watching it all happen right in front of me.

"The tyres were huge so doing a wheel change was a big, heavy job, but it was easy. We only did minor rectification on the squadron; any major maintenance was done elsewhere. The airframe was pretty robust; we didn't have too much repairing to do to it. I had been on Valiants and almost every time they landed they needed some bloody sort of repair. The Shackleton wasn't like that; it was very easy to work on, mostly tyre changes and topping stuff up. They had pneumatic brakes. When you changed a wheel, you changed the brake as well so we didn't have a brake problem per se because they would just go to the wheel bay. There was a wheeze once where an aircraft went to Hong Kong and they managed to find a nick in the brake pipe, so they had to stay there for the want of a 'Mickey Mouse' bit of hose for the brakes.

"The guys spent a lot more time working on the engines; the Griffon was a nice engine but it did need a bit more TLC than the airframe. I was still quite young and low in the pecking order, so I spent much of my time cleaning the aircraft; it was a big aircraft so there was a lot of work to keep it looking good. Oil leaks tended to lubricate the surroundings, so we were often either fixing oil leaks or clearing up after them. Most of the time we didn't have too much to do, so occasionally changing the spark plugs in Gan was an exciting and different job. So that was how we spent our time basically, with only seven aircraft and just four to look after most of the time. As they used to say of the Shackleton, they were two million rivets flying around in loose formation, lubricating as they went.

"We sometimes had occurrences like snakes getting up in the wheel bay; this happened a few times. It was nice and warm up there and they would curl up. We'd often open the bay and find a snake in there – 'Aahhh!!!' I only went on one big detachment, a big anti-submarine exercise in New Zealand, based in Hobsonville, just outside Auckland. We flew down in a Hercules, coming back in a Shack, from Hobsonville via Brisbane, Alice Springs and Darwin; but from Darwin I flew in a Hercules back to Singapore. What was interesting about the exercise flights was that we used to drop 25-lb bombs, which were meant to straddle the submarines. On the first day of the exercise, within the first hour, a Shackleton spotted a submarine on the surface, diving. One of our two aircraft flew down and dropped a straddle. However it managed to drop one of the bombs on the conning tower and bent the periscope so the sub had to go back into port. There were American and Australian submarines taking part, and we had managed to dent an Australian one, which we weren't supposed to do.

"We had an engineering officer called Pike, he was a very nice guy. We had a lot of fun with him and he looked after us very well. We had an ageing wing commander called Pendry, known as 'Plod', who I think was on his last tour. He was a nice fatherly old boy and very good at team spirit and things like that. However, we did get a bollocking from him when some of the squadron wags were having a piss-up in the Malcolm Club in Changi. We were at the club and there was a tame army guy, who was a brilliant, concert standard pianist, playing the piano. We were all singing and drinking, when someone decided it would be nice to have a little fun. He set fire to some smouldering beer mats and put them in the bottom of the piano whilst he was playing. The smoke was coming out through the top of the piano, and through the keys. We all thought it was terribly funny, especially when he started to play 'Smoke Gets in Your Eyes'. But the squadron got into trouble for it. The Malcolm Club were a bit upset about the damage to their piano. As a result, Plod told us that this type of behaviour had got to stop. He also said that he didn't mind if we drank Tiger but we must stop drinking heavily, so we never ordered any more Heavily! We were however, banished from the Malcolm Club for a month; not that it mattered.

"In my last months on 205 Squadron, as we were winding up, we were forever being buggered around. We didn't know what was happening and we didn't have any spares. Half the crew had already gone and Plod was very cross about that. Actually, I was there for the last parade but then three Shacks went to Tengah the next morning. The rest of the aircraft went over the space of two more weeks or so, one or two at a time, but I wasn't there right at the very end. They went back to the UK with a lot of stuff painted on them – 'White Knuckle Airlines' along the roof and the like! We got into trouble when we cut out an 'a' and stuck it over the 'o' on the side of one of the aircraft into an 'a' in 'Force' – the Royal Air Farce. Plod was not impressed – it really was a farce when we were winding up.

"I had arrived in Changi in '69, but the squadron disbanded in '71 and I then went over to the ANZAC (Australia and New Zealand Army Corps) force until mid '72. I was only supposed to do 18 months on 205 Squadron before it was disbanded and then be sent home. I was only on Shacks for 18 months and work was routine, a relatively boring existence because mostly it was cleaning, toileting, topping up stuff and the odd little job to do. That then, was my experience on the Shackleton; I thought it was smashing."

Ned 'Plugsy' Smale – engines

"It was amazing on 205 Squadron. On one trip I was the travelling engine fitter bringing a Shack Mk.2 back to St. Mawgan; Changi – Gan – Jeddah – Malta – Gib – St. Mawgan, 12 days in total. Four hours out of Malta, the engineer called me up, No.3 prop was peeing oil, we agreed to feather it. Three hours out, the engineer called me up again, all No.2's gauges were going haywire, we agreed to restart and observe No.3 and feather No.2. The SAR Shack at Malta was called out to follow

Dick Mustoe (left) and Lance Smale, 205 Squadron ground crew.
(Lance Smale)

us in. Two hours out came the call 'Fire Fire'. An actuator on the radar dome had caught fire. So into Malta at night on two engines plus a dodgy No.3. The downside of all this was that most of the snags related to the engine which I had to fix. So I never did get down the 'Gut' with my old Ballykelly cronies who were now in Malta on 203 Squadron. Four great years. Rock on Shack boys!"

Other memories from engine men abound – the 18-foot flame that a wet start on a Griffon could produce, which caused many a rooky starter crew to panic. Torque-loading propellers by using a 14-stone man and an eight-foot extension bar on the spanner – when the man's feet came off the ground, the prop was correctly tightened. Aircraft coming home from Singapore loaded with washing machines, fridges, toys and so on in the bomb-bay panniers, to the total disbelief of the customs man at St. Athan where the aircraft were to be stored – he signed the forms anyway!

Vic Wise – electrics

FROM LONDON TO SINGAPORE IN EIGHT DAYS

"By 1967 our aircraft were rapidly approaching their use-by dates. Many Shackletons had been returned to the Avro factory where they were completely refurbished. New uprated engines were fitted along with the latest electronic and surveillance suites. When it came to 205 Squadron's turn to receive these 'new' aircraft our strength was increased from eight aircraft to 12. The plan was to fly out the four extra aircraft first and then fly an old one back and pick up another new one. Each aircraft would carry one maintainer, from each of the five major trade groups, to carry out the routine inspections along the way. The elapsed time to fetch a new aircraft out was much less than the time to fly a swap-over mission, so I pulled rank and got myself allotted to the second delivery to minimise my time away from my wife Gwen and our newborn son.

"I flew to the UK in a VC10 and went to see my parents for a couple of days, picking up some warm clothing as our tour to Singapore ended in the following

January. I then reported to St. Mawgan where I met up with WL790, the aircraft that we were to deliver, and the crew that were to fly her. The aircraft had been delivered from the Avro factory the previous day, and looked magnificent with its new paint job and complete interior refurbishment. It had that nice new leather smell that you get with a new vehicle, and was full of all the latest state-of-the-art electronic surveillance equipment. The aircrew that were to fly it were a check and training crew flying out to train our squadron crews, so they were all experts. Over the next two days the aircraft was given three quick shakedown flights to ensure that everything worked properly, and we maintainers were given a crash course on the major differences with the new model, and then we were ready to leave.

"The normal route to Singapore for a flight such as ours would have been via El Adem, Aden and then across the Indian Ocean to Singapore stopping overnight on Gan. However this was mid-1967 and the Six Day War between Israel and Egypt had been raging, so this Middle East transit was closed to us. The RAF did not want to make our low-flying slow-moving aircraft a target for Egyptian MiGs, so we took the scenic route which was to be via Malta, Kano in northern Nigeria, Nairobi, Mauritius, Gan and Singapore.

"Day one dawned and we took off to fly across Brittany and the south of France, missing the Alps, and then down the boot of Italy across Corsica, Sardinia and Sicily to Luqa on Malta, a distance of about 1,350 miles. As we flew slowly across France we could hear the captain communicating with the French air traffic controllers; you could tell from their bored French replies, that they were not happy with the low and slow passage of this 'rosbif' bomber across their airspace. It took about six and a half hours to get to Malta, by which time our ears were ringing and our bodies were still vibrating in tune with the engines. Normal procedure then was for us to do a quick after-flight inspection, which involved checking that nothing had fallen off, topping up all system fluids and recharging the compressed air systems. Just before we had finished this task the captain came to see us. There was a problem with our diplomatic clearance across the Republic of Congo, therefore we would stay an extra day in Malta rather than pushing on and waiting in Nigeria. We had a bonus day off.

"Malta had never been high on my bucket list of places to visit, but we hired a cab next day to explore the city. It not very large so after that we hired a little tourist boat to take us on a tour of Valletta harbour. As I am an avid reader of historical novels especially ones about the Napoleonic Wars and Nelson's Navy and much of the action in those involves Valletta harbour, I really enjoyed our tour. The harbour was very busy, and one of the repair docks was occupied by a ship called the USS *Liberty*. This was an old World War 2 Liberty vessel that the Americans had refurbished and fitted out as a spy ship disguised as a freighter. As I mentioned the Six Day War had just broken out. The *Liberty* had been patrolling off the coast of Israel, eavesdropping despite a warning from Israel not to do so. As a result, the Israelis torpedoed the *Liberty* resulting in the deaths of 37 crew and injuries to 170 others. The ship was back in Valletta harbour for repair.

"Next day we were off to Nigeria, a distance of 1,700 miles. We crossed the North African coast near Tripoli, and then followed a bitumen highway running south for hundreds of miles across the Sahara Desert. Eventually the road dog-leg-ged to the left to go to the Sudan, and we turned right heading for Kano. The Shackleton had been designed to obtain maximum lift from the sea; so when it travelled overland things could get a little bumpy, especially over desert. To make matters worse, just after we left the road we ran into a huge sandstorm. Despite climbing through it to gain height it was a very unnerving experience for all of us. Sitting at a lookout position in the mid fuselage I could not see the wingtips, and the noise on our uninsulated airframe was horrendous. Eventually we cleared the storm and made our landing at Kano. When we disembarked we could see that it was now looking decidedly used. The new shiny paint had a very matt-looking finish in many places, and it seemed that every orifice was blocked with sand. We spent a couple of hours removing the sand and completing our inspection, and then went to the hotel for dinner and a rest. When we arrived the hotel seemed to be full of flamboyant wealthy Nigerians in national costume, the ladies wearing huge voluminous brightly coloured dresses, and very tall turban-like head-dresses.

"Almost at first light on day four we took off for what would be our longest day of the whole trip. It is about 2,200 miles from Kano to Nairobi in Kenya over some pretty rugged country. The first countries we crossed were Chad and the Central African Republic, neither of which seemed remarkable. About one third of the way into our trip we reached the Republic of Congo border, and guess what, the dip-lomatic clearance that we had obtained in Malta was cancelled! We flew up and down the border while the captain negotiated with the air traffic controllers, who in turn consulted their masters; the upshot was that they gave us four hours to cross the country. What would happen if we failed was not explained. The Congo has the second largest rainforest in the world, after the Amazon Basin, and for a while we flew along the Congo river. From 10,000 feet it looked wide and muddy with large trees right up to the water's edge. The captain had ordered that every lookout position on the aircraft be manned in case the Congolese authorities changed their minds. I was right down in the tail cone looking straight down. I remember thinking that even if we survived a crash-landing on the treetops the crocs would get us in the end.

"It was something of a relief to leave the Congo, well within our time limit, and fly into Ugandan airspace. However this brought us another problem. Between us and Nairobi were the Rwenzori Mountains (sometimes known as the Mountains of the Moon), which at their highest are about 16,000 feet with permanent snow on the highest peaks. Our navigator plotted a route through them which meant that we did not need to go higher than 12,000 feet. However the captain insisted that everyone go on to oxygen. This was the first and only time that I had ever needed to use oxygen in flight, normally we used it to cure hangovers. The contrast in terrain was amazing. We landed safely at Nairobi airport after a very long day, and while the aircrew went off to the hotel we had to do a very quick after-flight inspection. Our schedule called for a two-night stay in Nairobi as the crew had reached their mandatory flight hours limit without a rest, and the Shackleton was in need of a 50-hour service. We stayed at the New Stanley Hotel which at that time was Nairobi's finest, so classy in fact that the doorman was European. Really there was nothing new about it, having been built in 1900 it was the favourite meeting place for expats in Africa, and had hosted many world leaders, celebrities and movie stars.

"Next morning we needed to go back to the airport to do our maintenance, and so the hotel provided two very large white Mercedes sedans to take us. On arrival we discovered that the apron was full of aircraft stranded there because of the Congo's edict that none shall pass. The pilots all wanted to know how we had managed it. We had access to the facilities of East African Airways for our maintenance. We took off as many panels as we could, including all the engine cowlings, and removed a heap of sand using compressed air guns. As the engines were new we carried out an oil change and checked the old oil for metal contamination, and then we topped up all the fluid and air systems. By midday we were finished and the two Mercedes returned to take us back to the hotel. Back at the hotel we saw that the car park was full of black-and-white-striped Land Rovers. Going into the long bar and restaurant was like walking onto the set of a Humphrey Bogart and Katherine Hepburn movie; everyone was wearing bush hats, jodhpurs, safari jackets, and long boots with shotguns over their shoulders – and that was just the ladies! Not to be outdone we hired a Volkswagen Combi Van after lunch and the driver took us to the Nairobi National Park.

"Nairobi sits at nearly 6,000 feet above sea level so this creates a problem for large piston-engined aircraft, especially when they are carrying a heavy load. The air is less dense, and the problem becomes worse as the temperature increases. So, at the crack of dawn next day, we were sitting at the end of the runway with superchargers and water-methanol cooling engaged and the engines at full revs, holding on the brakes – it was like being in an earthquake. Using the whole runway length we just staggered into the air, heading for Mauritius nearly 2,000 miles away. Our transit was across Kenya to the coast, and then over the Mozambique channel and the island of Madagascar, and into Mauritius. On arriving at Mauritius we discovered that the air traffic control tower was only manned during peak hours. Outside of those hours you broadcast your intentions to land or take off on a designated frequency, and then went ahead and carried it out. We broadcast our intention to make a long, low, slow approach over the sea when an Air Malawi Vickers Viscount, full of passengers, decided that he couldn't wait that long so he cut in front of us. I can't remember if a complaint was made or not. We stayed the night at a Royal Navy rest and recreation centre. This was situated on a pristine white beach, which had a reef about 200 yards out where huge rollers from Antarctica were breaking. I'm sure the 'bean counters' at the Admiralty were unaware of this little gem. We slept in luxury cabins spread along the beach and although we tried to persuade the captain to stop an extra night he was keen to push on.

"Next morning we set off for Gan. This was a relatively short distance of 1,750 miles, but still an elapsed time of over eight hours. From here until Singapore we would be over the ocean, so nothing exciting to see. About two and a half hours out of the Maldives, the captain called me up to the cockpit to show me that one of his four electrical generators had gone offline. Now I was on a steep learning curve; digging out the new wiring diagrams and manuals for our refurbished machine, I was soon busy checking the system with my torch and multi meter. Sure enough, the relay that connected the generator to the aircraft system was not operating. This was not an item that we were carrying in our emergency spares pack, so as always in a case like this, I resorted to impact engineering; a swift tap with a hammer and everything worked again. The problem occurred again about an hour later, but after that it behaved itself for the rest of our journey. After a fairly boring trip we landed at Gan. 205 Squadron kept a Shackleton there on a permanent rotating detachment to cover search and rescue in the Indian Ocean, and our fellow squadron members were keen to inspect the 'new' aircraft.

"Another really early start on day eight. It was still another 2,200 miles to Changi, mostly across the ocean. One of the aircrew, in our case one of the navigators, was nominated as the imprest officer, being responsible for paying all costs incurred at our stopping points. He paid the hotel and fuel bills, and any other expenses incurred, including paying the agent acting for us. The agent arranged hotels, fuel, transport and rations for the journey. The Shackleton was fitted with a small galley, two sleeping bunks and a chemical toilet to help make the long journeys more comfortable, but with ten aircrew and five supernumerary ground crew on board, lunchtime was a bit chaotic. Long boring flights led to hunger, and we made lots of bacon sandwiches. We had a fairly rough passage across the Bay of Bengal, but that was pretty normal. At Penang we flew down the Malay Peninsula keeping well away from Indonesian Sumatra, and it was a big relief to land in Singapore. We had spent eight days in a slow-moving, noisy, vibrating machine and covered some 11,000 miles. Everyone was pleased to see us back, but were not too impressed with the used look of our delivery!"

There was always time to have fun at Changi. However on one occasion in January 1964, away from the daily toil, navigation instrument mechanic **Bill Tarran** *found himself on the receiving end of a 205 Squadron SAR sortie.*

"My mates and I were very keen divers, and we used to go off looking at shipwrecks. On one occasion we hired a boat and set off, but the weather deteriorated and we decided to head back. After some time we couldn't understand why we hadn't sighted land, so I went up to the cockpit and saw there was a ruddy great metal wrench lying next to the magnetic compass! Having corrected our course, we then hit rocks which took off the propeller, and we were shipwrecked on an island off the east coast of Malaya.

"We had booked out for our trip at Maritime Command. We knew that if we didn't book back in a 205 Shack would be sent to look for us. So we laid out a big cross on the beach and the number 205. Sure enough, along came a Shack which found us and before too long we were picked up by helicopter. Our Chinese boat crew had left us on the beach saying they were going to walk home, but when we got back to Changi they had not been seen. However, after a while they did turn up, with their feet cut to ribbons on the coral."

Brian Reynolds – photographer

"I was at Brampton when I got the great news that my first overseas posting would be to Changi; even our W/O told me I was a lucky so and so. After about five months in the photo section at Changi I was given the opportunity to join 205 Squadron as their photographer. Most of the time I was tasked with fitting cameras in our Shackletons and changing the film magazines after sorties. The usual fit was the F24 vertical camera in the tail cupola and F117B handheld camera used by the signaller in the door seat. Occasionally I would be told that the F97 was required for night photography using flares, and it was always important to check

Brian Reynolds far right sheltering from sun in the land of burning concrete, Changi 1964. (Brian Reynolds)

US Navy Sangley Point 1965 with 205 Squadron sharing the pan. (Brian Reynolds)

with armourers and electricians during this fit. On occasions I had to process the film on the return of a sortie at night – frequently during the Indonesian Confrontation. When that happened, it was 'ops immediate' and I was chauffeur driven to the guardroom to get the photo section keys where I processed the film. I then rang for my transport to whisk me up to ops and return via the guardroom to the squadron or if very late, back to my billet.

"One evening I was told to dispatch a Shack and given the marshalling wands as there was no other bod available. So it was with some trepidation that I made my way to the dispersal pan. On arrival I found that I had one other bod to assist me and he had already plugged in the Houchin power set, and the pilot gave me the thumbs up to show he was ready to start up. Now carefully watching the aircrew signals I started to wave my wands – Oh the sense of power as I managed to get all engines running and in the correct sequence. It was then I noticed the still-connected Houchin moving towards the tail, and I am afraid I panicked and started to wave franticly. Luckily, 'Spike' a passing rigger, noticed my predicament, relieved me of my wands and rescued the situation. Suffice to say I was never asked to marshal again – can't understand why?

"Another exciting episode took place whilst I was changing camera magazines during one of the frequent slip crew changes. As was normal when this took place, the engines were kept running and my first duty on boarding was to inform the signaller of my presence and ask him to inform the 'driver'. Then I crawled down to the camera cupola in the tail, unlocked the camera access hatch and replaced the magazine. After cleaning the camera lens I would normally depart ASAP, but on this particular day I heard the engines roar and we started to taxi towards the runway. I was a little concerned as I was hardly dressed for a seven to eight-hour flight (shorts and flip-flops), still struggling with a camera problem with the sweat dripping off my forehead in the sauna-like environment. Eventually I fixed the camera and scrambled back to a very surprised signaller to ask if they could now please let me off! He made a quick call to the captain and as we had reached the threshold the engines were getting louder, so was the captain's voice which I could hear above them – he was not a happy chap. An embarrassed signaller lowered the ladder and I made a thankful escape for a long trek back to the dispersal. On reaching the squadron I reported back to the ground-crew office and related my story to the flight sergeant. I didn't get much sympathy, and he then came out with his favourite saying – 'Stand slack lad'. I think I saw a smile on his face.

"During my posting with 205 Squadron I went on a few detachments most of which I enjoyed. Starting with the best, the Philippines – Sangley Point for two weeks, where I met up with PO John E Finkstein Jnr, USN photographer. He let me drive his Thunderbird automatic, but only on the base, and took me for a tour round Manila. There was RAAF Butterworth, Malaya, visiting Penang and Thailand. Labuan, two weeks under canvas and we sure needed those mosquito nets. We flew there by 'Shack Airways' with luxury on-the-floor seating, with a return journey by 42 Squadron Hastings. Finally, Australia – two weeks of dust storms and flies at Darwin and Townsville, with lousy beer.

"I returned from Changi in 1966. I am never without a reminder of my time with 205 Squadron as every morning I wake up and put my hearing aids in – thanks to 'Griffon ear'."

The aircrew knew only too well how much work their loyal ground crew put in enabling them to keep flying, and engineers frequently accompanied aircraft down route.

Guy Gibbons – pilot

"The aircraft by now were getting a bit long in the tooth, and a fair bit of work by the ground crew was required to keep them serviceable; engines were always interesting. We had a batch of bad spark plugs, and one of the things that happened with the engines was that if you climbed, or were under high power for a long time, there was a good possibility that the centre core of the plugs could blow out. It wasn't disastrous, the engine would keep running but the engine started making a very interesting ticking noise, which could be heard from the ground as well as inside. It was only one or two plugs that were affected."

David Phillips – pilot

"We lost an engine on a number of occasions, it really wasn't all that unusual. I think I lost four or five. The worst occasion was on a trip out to Christmas Island going eastabout. We took off from Habbaniya in Iraq, and someone hadn't put the cap on correctly on one of the fuel tanks. As we took off and got that sort of vacuum on the upper surface of the wing, the cap came off with petrol streaming out. Looking out of the window you could see the petrol streaming back. We decided we had to get down again, but of course we were too heavy to land. We'd got 14 ground crew packed into the Shackleton in addition to the crew; they'd all got parachutes stacked at the back. So once again, as the co-pilot you do all the dirty work, and I was trying to fit up 14 people with parachutes whilst we were going round and round Habbaniya – petrol was still streaming out. The engineer fed all the engines off the one tank to hasten getting it down to a landing weight, but it still took quite a while. Needless to say we're still here to tell the tale. Eventually the fuel stopped flowing, and a bit later on we managed to land at maximum all-up weight, carrying on our way a day or two later. In the context of what we were doing, it didn't amount to much."

An old Mk.1 had stood at Changi for some years, being used as a 'Christmas Tree' for spare parts in order to keep the newer (just) Mk.2s going. As the squadron was coming towards its end, it was decided to try and bring the Mk.1 home, and much work was done by the engineers to make it ready for flight.

When it was wheeled out for ground runs, all the engines steadfastly refused to turn, let alone start. Subsequent investigation revealed that during its long sojourn unwanted and out of use, the local rodents had been quietly nibbling their way through all the wiring looms that ran along the leading edge of the wing. The aircraft was deemed to be irreparable and put to the torch.

Despite all the trials and tribulations, there still remains a very strong sense of pride in a job well done amongst those who were there. Some of this pride and esprit de corps undoubtedly stems from the fact that with only one Shackleton squadron based at each overseas location, the centralised servicing principle applied to UK stations could not be used. Each squadron was able to retain 'ownership' of their ground crew who were thus highly valued and respected. To quote a wartime wireless operator/air gunner Jack Bromfield who nicely summed up how the aircrew should – and usually did – appreciate their ground crew: "I'll tell you who don't get the praise they really deserve – the ground crews. It was the ground crew's aeroplane, not the guys that were flying it – they had just borrowed it and were expected to hand it back!"

CHAPTER FOUR

'EN ROUTE' – RAF GAN, MALDIVES

Gan is one of the string of islands which form Addu Atoll in the Maldives. Its location in the Indian Ocean made it an ideal place for a staging post for aircraft transiting from Europe and the Middle East, to the Far East. A Royal Navy fleet anchorage known as Port T was built there in 1941. This was soon followed by an airstrip, first used by 160 Squadron Liberators on maritime patrol duties searching out Japanese naval units. At the end of the war the airfield was quickly closed, only to be reopened in 1957 when it was decided that a staging post was once again needed to protect the vital route for RAF aircraft heading for the Far East.

Following extensive expansion and refurbishment, which included lay-ing a new 9,000-foot runway (virtually the entire length of the island), Gan was ready for use in August 1957. The new additions included moorings and refuelling facilities for Sunderland flying boats. From that point on the airfield saw constant use, becoming especially busy in times of crisis (not least during the Indonesian Confrontation), peaking at around 350 aircraft movements per month in the late 1960s and into the early '70s. As a result of this level of activity Shackletons, from 205 Squadron at Changi, were tasked to maintain a permanent single-aircraft detachment at Gan to pro-vide SAR cover over the whole of the central Indian Ocean area.

Gan from an MR.2 astrodome. (Bill Tyack)

Brian Latham – pilot

"During the summer of 1959 there had been a revolt on Addu Atoll by rebels wishing to form a breakaway Suvadive republic. RAF Regiment forces were sent there to protect our interests. I believe that the British authorities were worried that the Soviets were interested in Gan and there may have been a Soviet cruiser in Male. My CO and I went to have a look. Flying very low, we pulled up over the palm trees expecting to be faced with hostility – there was nothing there. However, it was decided to carry out Shackleton patrols from RAF Katunayake, Negombo in Ceylon on a daily basis and check all the islands for signs of military activity and shipping. This was called Operation Gay (gay then meaning something different from today). Katunayake was also still being used by the RAF as a staging post. Gan's supplies came by sea and the food was awful. We decided to bring in fresh fruit and vegetables from Ceylon, for the various messes, and also took eggs and soft drinks. This we continued to do from Singapore when we finally moved in to Gan officially on 29 November 1959. I still have a shopping list for bicycles, cloth, reels of cotton, even an electric pump for my batman's family.

"We returned home by RAF Comet to bring back a Shackleton from Kinloss. We took off westwards from Changi at sunrise for Negombo in Ceylon, breakfast on the way and breakfast again on arrival! After a quick engine start and take-off at Negombo, we had lunch en route to Aden, another lunch on arrival, tea en route to El Adem and again tea at El Adem. Sunset at Lyneham, but no dinner there; 19 hours flying time, 25 hours elapsed. We were put up at nearby Clyffe Pypard, and the next day we went on a week's leave, to assemble again in seven days' time at Kinloss. Back from Kinloss to Malta, night trip Malta, a long trip Aden, to Negombo and finally Negombo to Changi. Five days! With a full load it had been necessary to take off from Aden before it got too hot.

"We were now about up to strength with aircraft. However, we had a new commitment – Gan. In the summer of 1959 the RAF was about to hand over Katunayake, some 20 miles north of Colombo to the Ceylon authorities. Gan had been a secret naval base during the war (although I'm pretty sure that the Japanese knew all about it). Over the years the *Queen Mary* and *Queen Elizabeth* (at the same time) and most of the British Pacific Fleet had all been in the lagoon, but it had been allowed to go back to nature. Then during the cold war the Ceylon government decided they wanted us to leave. I suppose Gan was an obvious choice as a replacement staging post to the Far East. We still had bases in Aden and Singapore, and Gan was about halfway. The airfield was built on a coral island, part of Addu Atoll one degree south of the equator. It was the most southerly atoll of the Maldives and was rather beautiful. Many of the local people were fishermen but a lot travelled to work by boat to the island of Gan, some 'commuting' three hours each way, morning and night. Their chieftain, Afif Didi, lived on the next island to Gan.

"The runway (Costain's had the contract for the runway and buildings) was 3,000 yards long and stretched the full length of the island. When there was a storm, which there frequently was, the whole island would shake and sound like a drum. From then on we kept two Shackletons at Gan for search and rescue. Changeover day was Wednesday, and the relief aircraft had to be airborne from Changi before the relieved aircraft could leave Gan. It was a big commitment for any squadron to maintain two aeroplanes out of eight, 1,500 miles from base. That, and other commitments, including search and rescue at Singapore, meant that we never had a full squadron at Changi.

"A Soviet supply ship, and three submarines, had been reported in the South Indian Ocean and we were briefed to intercept it east of Ceylon – very strange. We found the ship, which looked like a US Type T2 tanker, and reported it as such, but were told to stick with it. We shadowed it for hours, handed over to another Shack and landed at Katunayake. We still maintained that it was not a Soviet ship, but were overruled. We took over shadowing it again the following night in spite of our doubts. In the end a warship was sent up the Malacca Straits to intercept – it was indeed an American T2 tanker! We returned to Changi and were sent off to patrol the Sunda Straits from the west, and after 17 hours of horrible weather and seeing nothing we landed on the Cocos-Keeling Islands. You could see the wreck of the first war German raider *Emden* still there on North Keeling after all those years. We had 12 hours break, whilst another Shack from Changi continued the task, and then we were off again. Still appalling weather and still nothing seen except for a Royal Navy tanker which we had not been told about. Very frustrating.

"There was always a frigate based at Gan. One night some sailors came ashore, and wrote on the runway, 'Under the protection of the Royal Navy'. Another time Gan ran out of 'our' petrol so HMS *Centaur*, a light fleet carrier, came into the lagoon and topped up the tanks for us. By this time nearly all the visiting aircraft were jets. The routine Maldives patrols from Gan continued into early 1960 when they stopped, thereafter there was simply SAR standby with a single aircraft.

MR.1 A of 205 Squadron landing at Katunayake, August 1959. (John Cooper)

"My last trip to Gan was over Christmas 1960. On Christmas Eve the local headman, Afif Didi, presented the officers' mess with a turtle. Nobody had the heart to kill it, so at midnight we took it back to the lagoon. Our return trip to Changi was my last flight in a Shackleton. The trip usually took about ten to 11 hours, but could take up to 14 hours if the met man wanted a reporting trip – not a pleasant one along the Inter Tropical Convergence Zone!

"We got to know all the islands which were very beautiful with the lagoons and light and dark seas. Gan eventually become a desirable posting, but in the early days it was very primitive with snorkelling on the reef as the only activity – nobody used sunblock either. There were no boats for sailing and we were not allowed on to the neighbouring islands of the atoll.

"I know that we helped the economy of the atoll, but when the RAF finally left Gan I feel we left them in the lurch. At last Gan is becoming a tourist hot spot – it certainly has the weather."

Keith Baker – flight engineer

"I was on my way to Gan, on my second flight on my own as the single flight engineer, on search and rescue standby. On arrival we would, as is usual on SAR, prepare the aircraft for a call-out with the flying clothes and life jackets in position, the aircraft pre-flight checked and the engines run up and checked. We would then go back to our accommodation and rest. Because we were on standby we were not allowed to drink alcohol – and we did not. In fact, the stopover was like a working holiday. Once we arrived and settled in, all we did was go out to the aircraft in the morning and check it over. Every so often we would run the engines to check them out. Then for the rest of the day, as long as we were contactable, we could do as we wished. As we were in the tropics the dress was very casual, just shorts or swimming trunks, and if you were posh flip-flops. I took up scuba diving again, and used to dive in the crystal-clear water of the lagoon. If there was a call-out for search and rescue a bell would be rung under the water. It worked well, as we did get called out a few times, usually for the local fishermen who were sometimes late returning. We played volleyball at five o'clock in the afternoon, and all the crew would join in. It was great fun, with lots of laughing and giggles. A shower and then to the mess for the evening meal. After dinner we could go to the cinema if there was a film on, or back to the crew room and chat or read a book.

"The crew had a long hut with a row of two-man rooms, cooled by an overhead fan. One of the rooms had been converted into a crew room. We had a large fridge, a small cooker, a kettle, and a table for making tea and coffee etc., plus the usual coffee table and chairs. The crew would donate food from the in-flight rations (the leftovers that is). There was tinned corned beef, butter, eggs and so on, so that you could eat when you wished and did not have to depend on the messes for your meals. This was ideal if you wanted to have a lie in followed by a late breakfast; this also meant you did not have to put on a shirt or shave.

"During the day there were large fruit bats that hung under the trees sleeping; in the evening they would wake up and cruise round looking for something to eat. One of our crew was hit in the face by one whilst he was riding his bicycle at night. Some of the keen chaps actually made a nine-hole golf course alongside the runway. The game would take a break whenever an aircraft came in to land.

"As the climate was tropical it could get quite hot at lunchtime, 40°C, so around that time anyone off duty would take a rest. We just had fans to cool us down. When the sun went down life was easier. During the monsoon season the rain would pour down and make our lives tedious. In the warm, damp climate everything tended to go mouldy. About every two months we had a trip to Gan, usually lasting about ten days. The flight back was about ten and a half hours and at about 8,000 feet, 130 knots, the route taking us over Indonesia then to Changi. The crews came back all bronzed and well rested.

"On one of our visits to Gan we were once again called out on search and rescue for a local fishing boat. Although we continued the search as long as possible, we did not find it. Fuel was running short, so we diverted into Majunga. As there was not enough room for us at the mess we had to stay at the local hotel. It was the monsoon season and the rain was heavy and non-stop. The hotel was terrible; the walls were mouldy and the beds were smelly. We were there for a few days – and I had a rotten dose of the runs. I remember sitting on the communal toilet; the plumbing was in the old French style. The toilet had a very narrow soil-pipe, we were not to put used toilet paper down the pan. Instead it was put into a cardboard box next to the seat, all lovely and smelly; the flies were doing their circuits and bumps around it. Once they had had their fill they would go next door into the kitchen. Thank heavens, eventually we left. I remember doing my pre-flight checks in the pouring rain. To keep my flying suit dry I walked around in my underpants – no-one complained. My runs eventually ceased, but it was very unpleasant. I did get checked over in Gan in case it was dysentery, however it was just a bad case of diarrhoea."[4]

Martin Coales – pilot

"On 205 Squadron, we went on detachments to Butterworth, and of course Gan. Gan was different because we did two weeks there on search and rescue. It got us away from the busy squadron and gave us a bit of a break from the family. When we weren't flying at Changi we'd go in at 7.30 a.m. and at 1.00 p.m. we'd all go down the officers' club, where the wives and children would be. Then we were just swimming and enjoying ourselves – and a Tiger beer – for the rest of the day. If there wasn't much happening on the squadron, we did exactly the same thing the next day. It was a fairly idyllic and relaxed lifestyle.

"We were on search and rescue standby 24 hours a day, seven days a week for

---

4. *The Growler*

the two weeks at a time that we were on the island. We used to go out and get the aircraft ready every morning – putting our flying suits on the seats, our headsets already plugged in, check the aircraft out and then leave it to go swimming or whatever we wanted to do. If there was a call-out, they just blew the sirens, we'd walk to the road and they'd pick us up and take us out to the aircraft. One morning one of our engineers went to the aeroplane, got in and accidentally dropped absolutely everything that was in the bomb bay on to the pan – the aircraft was immediately put unserviceable. We carried CLEs which contained survival gear such as dinghies, water, and some rations. If there were any survivors, you could drop the CLEs on land or in the sea so that they could be collected. We always carried one of these in case we had to get away quickly."

Ray Curtis – AEO

"Singapore was just routine stuff; we maintained a two-aircraft, two-crew detachment on Gan for SAR duties 365 days of the year, and rotated it every two weeks. One day you were on SAR standby, and the next day you were off. On your day off you might do some circuits, some local area flying or you might do a navex down to Diego Garcia in the Chagos archipelago (when it was completely unsullied by the Americans) and the Chagos people lived there. In the Diego Garcia lagoon, you could clearly see a sunken Supermarine Walrus amphibian.

"In the summer of 1961 there was an outbreak of something (it could have been typhoid), on the island of Rodrigues, east of Mauritius. An aircraft from the Gan detachment was sent there to drop medical supplies. Subsequently I was lucky enough to be on the Gan detachment when it was decided that the RAF would go to Plaisance, in Mauritius to receive the thanks of the mayor for saving the people on Rodrigues, from whatever it was they had been ill with. So our crew was tasked with taking the station commander from Gan – a wing commander – for a three-day detachment to Mauritius, with all the associated piss-ups and whatever. It was certainly better than being on Gan.

"One very amusing experience that happened on Gan when I was there, was when the chief of Defence Staff (CDS) Lord Louis Mountbatten night-stopped on his way to a tour of the Far East. Normally, the Gan Shackleton detachment was commanded by the senior flight lieutenant, but on this occasion, because Lord Louis was coming through, one of our flight commanders, a squadron leader, came on detachment with us. The station commander decreed that a dining-in night would be held for Lord Louis, and asked our flight commander, Tony Freeborn, to have the Shack boys lined up in the ante room after the dinner to be introduced to the CDS. I was a newly commissioned pilot officer, so was at the end of the line-up. The time duly came when the station commander and CDS approached – Tony Freeborn jumped smartly forward and said, 'good evening sir' and then went down the line introducing our crew for CDS to shake hands – this is so and so … this is so and so … and finally came to me on the end. Either he didn't know my surname, or he had a complete mental block … but he said 'this is Plt Off Ray' – to which I said 'good evening sir' to the CDS and he said 'good evening Ray' to me as he shook my hand. There were a few sniggers up the line from the rest of the blokes, and CDS was whisked away to meet other people. So, my right hand is the hand that met Lord Louis on first name terms!"

One of 205's MR.1s came to grief at Gan on 15 May 1962, when VP294 N force-landed and was damaged beyond repair; fortunately without injury to anyone on board. It became a familiar sight for some time thereafter, sitting forlornly on the edge of the airfield for the fire section to play with.

Gordon Dodds – pilot

Ocean Rescue

"On 19 March 1964 our 205 Squadron crew was positioned on the island of Gan providing SAR cover for flights across the Indian Ocean. On the 21st we were scrambled to assist a Formosan fishing boat, *Chit Glonglym*, reported to be on fire and sinking in the vast Southern Indian Ocean; our captain was Pete Bethell, and the first nav was Max Dobson. As the normal standby fuel load would be insufficient for this flight the ground crew had fuelled the aircraft to maximum load, including the overload tank. We arrived at the reported location 650 miles south-east of Gan and, after a short search, located the stricken vessel which was belching a lot of smoke and clearly in great trouble. The fishermen did not appear to have enough lifeboats or rafts and were in the process of lashing together anything that would float. The captain decided to drop a set of Lindholme gear to them. Lindholme consisted of a large self-inflating dinghy attached by floating rope to a chain of floating canisters, each filled with survival equipment. We then made a low run past the ship and over the rafts, with our bomb doors open to try to indicate to the fishermen that we were about to drop survival equipment. Pete did a perfect drop; the Formosans could almost have stepped into the dinghy without getting their feet wet. Smoke and

The Chit Glonglym *trawler on fire 21 March 1964, taken from Gordon Dodds's Shackleton. (Gordon Dodds)*

flame markers were then dropped nearby to assist in a subsequent relocation by rescuers.

"We then set off westwards towards the shipping lanes off the African coast, where we quickly found a merchant ship, the British India Line *Nuddea* which was heading north. Following standard international nautical procedures we flew across his bow several times exercising our engines, then flew off in the direction of the distressed boat. In the best traditions of the sea they turned and followed us. We returned to the burning boat, which by now was well alight, and the survivors who were now sitting comfortably in our rubber dinghy. We then flashed them 'Ship coming' on the Aldis lamp and after flying around them for a while to reassure them we set our heading for Gan where we landed after 12 hours and 50 minutes flying.

"All the ground crew at Gan were waiting on the pan ready to turn the aircraft round; in fact, two or three were already in the aircraft before we managed to get out! While the aircraft was being turned round and refuelled we had a very welcome meal, then reported to operations for briefing. The met man told us he had an up-to-date weather forecast provided by an aircraft in the rescue area. He was surprised when we all laughed, until we pointed out that he was giving us our own met reports. I doubt if there was another 'plane in the Indian Ocean that day. One hour and 50 minutes after landing we took off again for the emergency scene, where we quickly located the survivors and circled the dinghies until daylight. The burning boat had by now disappeared. A search to the west located our merchant vessel still steaming in our indicated direction. We loitered in the area to be sure the ship found the dinghy then, with the fishermen finally clambering aboard the merchant vessel, we set off for Gan once again where we landed after another nine hours and 20 minutes. We were stood-down from SAR duties for a day so that we could have a beer; after 22 hours flying, I think we had two!"[5]

Cliff Edwards – airframe

"I did one trip to Gan, the most interesting thing was that we had to fly over Indonesia, over a range of mountains at up to 10,000 feet. For a Shackleton that's very high. We had two grades of spark plug in the aircraft and although I was airframes, not engines, we used to help the engine guys when we went to Gan. Spark plugs for 10,000 feet were very expensive, or so we were told, so we used them only for the trip from Singapore to Gan and back. They used to circle over the Malacca Straits to get the altitude to go over the hill to Gan but the low-altitude spark plugs were prone to splitting their cores so I presume it's a matter of the pressure on the engines. I was just a grease monkey at the time so what did I know about theory? We used the bad plugs normally and then we put the posh ones in only when we had to go over the hill. We regarded them as high-altitude plugs.

5. Pete Bethell via Gordon Dodds (*Air Clues*, March 1964).

"When we arrived at Gan, or back at Singapore, we had to change 96 spark plugs. At Gan, we had to be ready fairly quickly to act as search and rescue aircraft, so we used to change them with hot engines. As we'd be on the ground for about an hour or so standing out in the sun, they didn't cool down very much. We had to change the plugs sitting on top of the engines, which was very warm. Because the plugs were down in the engine's V-block, we put a piece of hose over the spark plug so that once we'd loosened it and the hose gripped it, you could pull it out. If you dropped it down the V-block you were definitely in the pooh because they were very difficult to get out again. But it was not such a chore when we got back to Singapore, because we could leave them overnight and change them in the morning when they were nice and cool.

"When we arrived in Gan the aircraft we were relieving buggered off back to Changi fairly quickly; we were there for two weeks. Sometimes the aircraft would stay there for a month and the ground crew would fly back and forth in a transport aircraft; but the aircrews would only stay there for two weeks. On the trip I went on we went there and back in the same aircraft. Most of our ground-support equipment was permanently situated in Gan so that you only had to carry some spares, spanners, etc., and the four extra ground crew."

Jerry Evans – navigator

"In the sixties, and no doubt for many years before, the services followed an ultra-conservative social code which would seem laughable and probably hard to believe if seen in the light of our present-day world. Examples of this are legion, but my story derives from the ruling whereby officers were encouraged not to marry before the age of 25. It was not, and could not be, forbidden, so the 'encouragement' lay in a raft of financial disincentives to wedded bliss, and there were others, too.

"Thus, in December 1963, an eager beaver en route to my first operational posting, to 205 Squadron Changi, I departed Stansted for the Far East on a British Eagle troop carrier with my great friend Gordon 'Yog' Dodds, but minus my wife Jean, and our two-month-old son David. I was just short of my 24th birthday and therefore had no entitlement for my spouse to join me on the flight; she must wait patiently at the home of her parents in Sussex until a last-minute indulgence seat (one not required for a duty passenger) became available. So while I was excited to be going, I was also apprehensive for we wanted to tackle our new life together. When would we be re-united? The overarching problem was that duty seats on transport aircraft were at a premium. This was thanks to Indonesian President Sukarno's policy of confrontation against the infant state of Malaysia, and the consequent build-up of British and Commonwealth forces in the area. Nevertheless surely it would be only a week or so before Jean was able to join me – wouldn't it?

"In late February our 205 Squadron crew was taking its turn on a fortnight's SAR standby at Gan. On the 27th, halfway through our enforced tropical island

Nirvana, there was a knock on my door soon after dawn. It was the corporal steward from the mess. 'Excuse me sir, but I thought you'd like to know that your wife is on the Comet arriving in half an hour.' Dumbfounded, thunderstruck, uncomprehending – yes, all of those. And yes, I did want to know. 'Thanks Corp,' I mumbled, as if this sort of thing happened every day. I waited on the Gan-Fedu causeway until I saw the glint of sun on wings away to the west, then, roused from my reverie, I was whisked to VASF (visiting aircraft servicing flight) in the squadron Land Rover to await arrival. CCXVI 'dona ferens' was the crest on the nose of the Comet – translating as '216 Squadron bearing gifts'. No other words are necessary.

"The 'phone call from Lyneham, announcing a sudden spare seat, had given my wife just enough time to get there from Sussex with little more than a suitcase and the baby. There was no such thing as email in those days. And to try to telephone Gan from Sussex was unthinkable. So the sequence was – Jean told the air stewardess that her husband was stationed at Gan, the stewardess relayed the news to the captain, the captain notified Gan Approach and ATC, who told the mess. After 40 minutes over coffee in the mess, she then departed east while I continued on SAR standby for my wife and some 100 others. She had launched into a different world, seeing the delights of Idris and Khormaksar before we met up. Once landing at Changi had been confirmed, and I knew that my little family was being well looked after in my absence, I could celebrate suitably. The bliss of our reunion a week later was helped by the generosity of Bob and Di Edmunds. They accommodated us until we could find a small flat; we were still not entitled to service quarters because of my age."

Rob Knotts – air signaller

"At Gan the SAR crew was on permanent standby. Basically we were on call, but had a lot of time on our hands. However, we kept busy with activities such as studying, sport, reading. We made full active contributions to the sporting scene on Gan. On one occasion the crew I was on made it to the finals of the five-a-side soccer tournament! The final match was played in the evening under floodlights. Entertainment was mostly self-made on the island with sporting events attracting large audiences. That evening there was a capacity crowd – we lost but with honour. However, the game, the cheering and the atmosphere were second to none. The SAR crew was housed in a single building, the officers had rooms at one end of the building, whilst the SNCOs were at the other.

"Gan was bathed in sunshine for quite a lot of the time with the result that air temperatures could get high. One way of cooling off was to go for a bicycle ride, with the breeze generated offering a cooling effect. One W/O was constantly in a bad mood – the heat made him so. It was discovered that he could not ride a bicycle. So station workshops welded a couple of hospital bed wheels to an RAF bicycle; these acted as stabilisers. The result – one far more even-tempered W/O.

"Gan is a relatively small island, and it can be walked around in less than an hour. The runway basically cut the island in half. For most of the time the weather is beautifully sunny, however it does get rain. It can be raining on one part of the island, but not on another. On one occasion when we were carrying out 'mandatory' pilot training circuits and bumps, one half of the runway was bathed in sunshine, while the other half it was raining heavily. After one circuit, after touching down on the very wet runway the aircraft experienced aquaplaning. Aquaplaning occurs when a layer of water builds up between the aircraft's tyres and the runway surface, leading to a loss of traction. This prevents the aircraft from responding to control inputs. If it occurs to all wheels simultaneously the aircraft can become uncontrollable. On this occasion the co-pilot was flying the aircraft. He had recently flown Mk.3 aircraft – the nose-wheel version where the rudder was required to be locked on landing; he applied the rudder lock on our Mk.2 with the result that directional control could not be exercised! The best description of the aircraft's movement was one akin to an 'elephant on ice skates'. The aircraft slid along the runway from side to side, whilst the pilot unsuccessfully tried to exercise some degree of control. Looming up ahead were two Vulcans; the concern was that the Shackleton would veer off the runway and head for the dispersal where they were parked. Fortunately the Shackleton's wheels made contact with the dry surface on the other half of the runway, and the pilot was able to regain full control of its direction.

"In December 1967 we were scheduled to fly a 12-hour training exercise from Changi. We reported for briefing at about 6 a.m., and were due for take-off at 8 a.m. The aircraft went unserviceable and it wasn't until about 5 p.m. that we actually started up and taxied out, still facing a 12-hour sortie. As we lined up on the runway we received a message telling us to return to the squadron's dispersal. There we were met by one of the flight commanders, and we were told that we had to fly the aircraft to Gan as the SAR aircraft there was unserviceable. Take-off was to be at 8 p.m. This gave us just enough time to go home, get a meal and some overnight kit. Just before 8 p.m. as we lined up on the runway, number two generator went offline. We taxied back into the dispersal. A generator drive shaft had sheared, so the ground crew worked through the night to fix it. We eventually took off at 6 a.m. next morning. I was operating the W/T on that trip. Three hours out from Gan we received a message advising us that we would be flown back to Singapore by a Hercules; take-off was scheduled for about four hours after landing at Gan. It was pointless going to bed before taking the flight back, so after handing the aircraft over to the SAR crew we made our way to the bar in the Blue Lagoon, the transit hotel at Gan.

"This was just before Christmas. At Christmas and New Year, the British Forces Broadcasting Service always ran a fund-raising event for 'Wireless for the Blind'. It involved bids to play a particular record, followed by bids to stop it being played. That year's record was 'Thank You Very Much' by The Scaffold. It started to play;

2

3

2. No. 37 Squadron MR.2 WL797 37 C at Gan in 1966. *(Steve Bond collection)*

3. No. 38 Squadron MR.2s WL758 V and WR956 W, mid-1960s. *(Jeff Peck)*

4. No. 203 Squadron MR.3 WR987 D at Luqa, 14 November 1971. (Adrian Balch collection)

5. No. 205 Squadron MR.2 at Richmond, Australia, 1962. Lance Smale is facing the camera and 'Doughy' Baker is wearing the raincoat. (Lance Smale)

5

6. No. 205 Squadron's disbandment flypast at Changi on 7 September 1971. (Steve Bond collection)
7. No. 210 Squadron in Majunga, winter 1967. Pilot Bob Lyall taking it easy. (Bill Hercus)

ROYAL AIR FORCE FAR EAST

13

bids were made to stop it being played followed by more bids to keep it playing. So it went on and on – but at the same time raising money for a well-deserving charity. Eventually it was time to leave, and we made our way to the Hercules. Ten Shack crew members clambered aboard and collapsed in a heap, sleeping all the way back to Changi. We arrived home in time for Christmas.

"In March 1968 I headed back to the UK, leaving my wife Lesley alone in the Far East. I was part of a crew returning to pick up an aircraft. We flew back in a VC10 via Gan and Akrotiri, landing at Brize Norton. Flight time was about 19 hours. On our return trip to Changi from St. Mawgan we were to ferry a Shackleton. The route was via Gibraltar, Malta, Djibouti in French Somaliland and Gan and the journey took 40 hours flying. We were one of two crews ferrying Shackletons at the time. The other crew had departed for Singapore ahead of us. In Malta their aircraft had a HF radio fault. By the time it was cleared, the crew missed its diplomatic clearance time for the flight over Egypt and had to wait another ten days for new clearance. The next problem they encountered was at Gan.

"While the Shackleton was airborne between Djibouti and Gan, an aircraft-towing tractor in Gan collided with the SAR Shackleton. The vehicle had a double-declutching system. Standing orders required tractor drivers to wear a safety belt as the double-declutch had a nasty habit of kicking the clutch pedal which could throw the driver from his seat. On this occasion the corporal driver wasn't – it did. Unfortunately, the tractor continued without the driver, colliding with the tail of the SAR Shackleton and ripping off large bits of it.

"The inbound Shackleton, modified to Phase III standard was significantly heavier than the Phase II aircraft that suffered the tailplane damage. As the SAR crew at Gan was not certified to fly the Phase III aircraft, the inbound ferry crew had to stay at Gan on SAR duty until a replacement Phase II aircraft could be flown from Changi!"

In Volume One John Cooper mentioned being a passenger aboard a Hastings of 48 Squadron. This came down in the sea on 1 March 1960 during its second approach into Gan at night, in bad weather; fortunately with no loss of life. He continues the story by describing the 205 Squadron Shackleton's SAR response.

John Cooper – engines

SPLASHDOWN ON THE EQUATOR

"The accident report on this final low-level approach to the runway reads, 'On the second approach there was a brilliant flash of lightning at about two miles, causing pilot to look into cockpit to recover his vision. Second pilot then called 'approaching 50 feet' and almost immediately aircraft hit the sea. It seems incredible that a transport aircraft other than a flying boat would be flying at this low altitude from such a distance from the runway (1.5 nautical miles), the cloud base was, we know, 420 feet.'

"In ATC the duty ATCO asked the pilot to confirm 'three greens – undercarriage down and locked' – and the last transmission was his answer, 'roger, downwind, three greens, runway in sight'. Suddenly there was what appeared to be a feedback screech, perhaps two microphones being opened at the same time. The ATC officer initiated a call without reply; he called again, no reply, and exclaimed, 'Christ, I think he's gone in' or words to that effect. At that point, controlled panic took over as the SAR drills were put into effect. All emergency teams on standby were 'called out', by great fortune an SAR Shackleton WB834 of 205 Squadron with Flt Lt John Elias as the duty captain and first pilot, was airborne within 20 minutes of the accident occurring.

"At the crash site there was organised chaos; with the sudden surge of water into the fuselage area, everyone's immediate reaction was to vacate the sinking Hastings as quickly as possible. I certainly recall taking my lap belt off, reaching immediately above my head taking the Mae West (life jacket) from its plyboard stowage, being at least ankle deep in water, buttoning up the jacket but not tightening the straps, and exiting the aircraft by the main door. At this point there was no thought of salvaging any of our personal possessions; saving lives became the priority. Once we were all in the dinghies a head count showed that a member of the crew was missing, and we could certainly hear cries of help from what appeared to be the starboard side of the aircraft – it was the flight engineer. Geoff Atherton dived into the water from a dinghy and swam after the flight engineer, who was adrift. He stayed with him until they were rescued and for his bravery that night, he was awarded a commendation.

"Only minutes had passed for all of this to happen, when we heard the engines of the Shackleton fire into life. To a trained mechanic this sound of four Rolls-Royce Griffon engines was almost heaven sent. We as survivors didn't know there was a Shackleton based at Gan, but as the Hastings slid beneath the waves, we were mighty pleased that there was. The Shack was despatched to the end of the runway to shine its lights looking for the aircraft. However, John Elias thought that rather than do this, he might as well get airborne so within ten minutes they had taken off. The aircraft started firing flares from three miles to two miles out from the crash scene on the first run, then on the second run and then running they spotted wreckage and dinghies from two miles out. Two air sea rescue launches were despatched to the scene. The flares were clear points of light, not fuzzy as they would have been if falling through cloud. The Shackleton ran in on the runway line firing off single flares one after another, then as he passed over the ditched Hastings he would fire off a cluster, pull away then repeat the procedure.

"Don Ellis was the first navigator on the Shack and recalls the atrocious tropical storm and prior to the crash, asking the operations officer what the crew of the approaching Hastings, now on its second approach, should do. The next morning Don's aircraft took off again looking for wreckage and saw a main wheel afloat. The launches later collected any wreckage they could. He also took Geoff Atherton back to Katunayake as Geoff refused point blank to fly back in a Hastings!

"With what few rupees we had left between us, we clubbed together and bought the Shackleton rescue crew a bottle of whiskey to share among them as a thank you. Without their assistance who knows what the outcome would have been. Credit must go to all those that took part in the rescue, they were all heroes. On the night they did their duty as they were trained to do in appalling weather conditions and not knowing whether they were looking for survivors, or bodies or even nothing if the aircraft had sunk without trace. It is to these people that I say a mighty big 'thank you!'"

Mike McKenna – navigator
"Squadron life was challenging and exciting, punctuated by numerous detachments to faraway places. The frequent two-week SAR detachment to Gan, was a fantastic rest-cure from the hedonistic delights of Singapore's night-life, and excessive quantities of Tiger beer and Charlie (Carlsberg). We would deploy either by VC10, or fly in to swap airframes for the outgoing crew to return to Changi. We snorkelled off the officers' beach and watched films on a Sunday night under the stars, accompanied by roosting flying foxes. However, we were required to abstain from

Final approach at Gan 1970. (Mike McKenna)

alcohol as we were in-place as SAR cover for strategic transport aircraft staging through on the UK/Far East run and exercise aircraft of various types. If we got airborne, as there was a distinct shortage of runways for diversion from the middle of the Indian Ocean, the old joke about holding off for a VC10 on 100 miles finals wasn't funny! There was a slight tendency to friction, or was it mutual respect, between the resident Shack crew in our smelly flying suits and the KD-dressed VC10 operators, swanning in from their air-conditioned aircraft; the crews did not routinely mix.

"Occasionally we would receive a surveillance tasking. Once we spent four days relocating a Soviet 'Alligator' landing craft, carrying we knew not what, as it head-ed north-west of the Maldives towards an unknown destination in the Middle East (the Yemeni island of Socotra we later heard). Using dead reckoning (DR) and astro navigation, we flew progressively further out across the Indian Ocean from our paradise atoll. On day four we finally, with a very low camera clicking approach, caught the landing-craft crew napping – their crew scurried to close the hatch covers; job done! We were slightly vulnerable as the craft's gun-crew locked-on and tracked us around the photographic run.

"In April 1971 we flew south from Gan to the Chagos Archipelago to photograph the island of Diego Garcia, still in its relatively virgin jungle. Subsequently it was developed on loan to the US as a strategic bomber base and used later in various Arabian Gulf bombing campaigns. When we returned from Gan to base, our illustrious nav leader Frank Easto would peruse our transit charts as he had a theory that Gan wasn't exactly where the navigation charts said it was. I believe he subsequently proved his point."

The withdrawal of British forces from Singapore saw a dramatic decline in traffic, and RAF Gan was finally closed down on 29 March 1976. Since then the airport has been run by the government of the Maldives, and upgraded for tourist passenger traffic. In the summer of 2018 it had five inter-island scheduled flights a day, plus a single international flight to and from Colombo, Sri Lanka.

CHAPTER FIVE

'AN AIRFIELD NEVER BEATEN'[6]
– RAF LUQA, MALTA

RAF Luqa, situated just outside Malta's capital, Valletta, was opened in May 1940 and quickly became a vital link in the chain of Mediterranean stations during World War 2. It suffered heavily at the hands of the Luftwaffe and the Italian air force during the siege of Malta. Luqa continued as an RAF station after the war and was home to a variety of units. These included the Malta Communications Flight, a Lancaster MR squadron, Meteor night-fighter and Canberra photo-reconnaissance squadrons. From 1953, the first of three Shackleton squadrons arrived and the type was based there until its final withdrawal from service. In 1956 the airfield was the major location for Canberra and Valiant bombers during the Suez campaign.

37 SQUADRON

The first Shackleton unit to arrive was 37 Squadron. It was originally formed in 1916 as a home defence unit, only to be disbanded in 1919. In 1937 it was re-formed as a bomber unit and was transferred to Malta in November 1940, by which time it was flying Wellingtons. It later moved into the Western Desert and then Italy, re-equipped with Liberator VIs. The squadron was eventually disbanded again in March 1946, only to reappear the following month with Lancasters. A further brief disbandment followed, and then in September 1947 it began flying Lancasters in the MR role from Ein Shemer in Palestine. The squadron began moving to Luqa on 31 March 1948, and by 19 May it was fully re-located. Shackleton MR.2s arrived in July 1953.

Stanley Wood – engines

"In October 1953 I flew out to Luqa with 37 Squadron in Shackleton Mk.2s. While I was there I participated in the search for a downed BOAC Comet off Sicily. In 1954 I was on board the Shackleton that was the escort for the Queen's aircraft on her Commonwealth tour, as she returned from Lake Victoria back home via Entebbe. It was a 14-day trip one way.

"In July 1954 we flew to Durban. No .4 engine had a translation unit (TU) failure and we had to stay there for three days awaiting delivery of a replacement unit. We also carried out alternate one-month deployments with 38 Squadron to

---

6. 'Mitjar Qatt Murbuh'

Stanley Wood. (Brian Wood)

Aden. We carried out bombing and leaflet dropping sorties for the Sultan of Muscat and Oman against Imam Ghalib in the Buraimi Oasis.

"My tour in Luqa finished in 1956, and I returned to the UK. That was the end of my time in Coastal Command as I now found myself on Bomber Command, and the Thor intermediate-range ballistic missiles. I trained at USAF Vandenberg, pressing the launch button on an RAF test missile when Lord Mountbatten was present."

On 21 August 1957, 37 Squadron relocated to Khormaksar, Aden.

38 SQUADRON

Just two months after 37 Squadron's arrival in Malta, 38 Squadron (already in residence), joined it in re-equipping with Shackleton MR.2s at Luqa. No.38 Squadron was another wartime Wellington operator arriving at Ismailia, Egypt in November 1940, and thereafter had followed a similar pattern of operations across the Western Desert and up into Italy. In July 1945 it returned to Luqa and re-equipped with the Vickers Warwick ASR.1. They only lasted for a year before being replaced by the Lancaster GR.3. Moving to Ein Shemer in December 1946, 38 Squadron came back to Luqa on 31 March 1948.

Hal Far, which lies close to the coast south of Valletta, was the first airfield to be built on Malta opening on 31 March 1929, and became the second largest of the three military airfields. During the war it housed a variety of both RAF and Fleet Air Arm units, then becoming primarily a temporary home for carrier-borne units transiting through the Mediterranean, and as an armament practice station. On 14 April 1946 the airfield was handed over to the Royal Navy and became HMS Falcon. It housed a fleet requirements unit with a variety of aircraft types, and in 1959 750 Squadron moved in from Culdrose for observer training using Sea Princes and Sea Venoms. This continued until the station was handed back to the RAF on 1 September 1965. It then became home to 38 Squadron, which moved over from Luqa in October 1965 and remained there until 31 March 1967 when it disbanded – it has not re-formed since then. The airfield continued for a time as a satellite of Luqa, and then for civilian aviation, until it was finally closed in 1978.

Hal Far from a Shack. (Tony Cunnane)

Gerry Pond – navigator

"I graduated as a navigator in November 1950. My first operational posting was to 38 Squadron with Lancasters and after close to two years I did a Shackleton conversion course in mid-1953 before returning to Malta. The Lancasters were struck off charge, and in June 1953 we converted to Mk.2 Shackletons.

"Compared with the Lancaster it was a lot more noisy, but we had a bit more space. As we were converting to type on the squadron we had seconded to us an Avro engineer who had officer status. He was there to help the ground crew more than the aircrew. He said to me that the aeroplane Avros were most proud of at that time was the Lancaster. During the war when the Lancaster was being produced it only had a life expectancy of six weeks. We had two squadrons at Luqa, 37 and 38. The 37 Squadron commander had actually flown one of the Lancasters, on his squadron, over Berlin during the war; before they sprayed it white and turned it into a maritime Mk.3.

"The squadron routine was just normal long-range operational flying sorties, but we had to do quite a lot of detachments to other places. We used to go to Castel Benito and Idris in Libya, Gibraltar, Nicosia/Cyprus, and we also had a submarine fleet at Malta. HMS *Forth* was the depot ship and exercised with them a lot. From a practice point of view it was an ideal place for us to operate from. It gave the navy practice in how to deal with aeroplanes whilst we had real submarines to play with. At one time, when Mountbatten was C-in-C Med, his wife wanted to go over to Tripoli for some reason; why we never knew. She ended up travelling in one of our aircraft, sitting on an officers' mess lounge seat which was strapped at the back of the aeroplane over the Elsan – we wanted to give her a comfortable seat and there was nowhere else to put it! Whether she realised it was over the Elsan or not I don't know. It was only an hour-and-a-half trip – the crew would have to cross their legs.

"In January 1954 I was the navigator on the second aircraft that found the wreckage of the BOAC Comet 1. It had been flying from Italy to London when it crashed in the Mediterranean, just off Naples. A number of us took photographs of wreckage floating on the surface, including bodies. When Mountbatten had seen these photographs he decided that the navy would salvage sections of the fuselage up to the surface, so that the cause of the accident could be established (the investigation concluded that it was a design fault). We had been the second aircraft and were probably sent as a follow-up – the first aircraft had located it. The photos taken by our signallers probably aided the investigation. A lot of BOAC crews came through Luqa, because it was a civil airport as well as a military one. There was a lot of uneasiness amongst them for a while that the Comet might have been sabotaged.

"When I came back from Malta I was sent on an air traffic tour at Shawbury!? At the time they said it was an experiment so I had to go. I left the maritime world in September '68."

Alan Davidson – air radar

"In 1956 I was an air radar mechanic, training at Yatesbury in Wiltshire. We were asked to say where we would like to go after training and my posting came up as

Sometimes life could be boring for a 38 Squadron wireless operator. (Sue Wilson)

Malta. Of the 22 of us on the course, two went to Malta, one went to Gibraltar, one or two went to the Far East, one went to Ceylon and the rest remained in England. I was apprehensive, it was two and a half years, and it suddenly came to me that it was a long way away.

"Anyway, I got there and I was in 38 Squadron almost immediately. Landing in Malta I stayed in the overnight accommodation at Luqa. One day was spent in the hangar and suddenly a flight sergeant came to me and told me I was going to 38. I was given a place in 38 Squadron's billet. They were very good billets by RAF standards at that time; four big multi-storey blocks built round a parade square. We were on the ground floor of two of them, and the other Shackleton squadron, 37, was on the first floor. One of the other blocks was for all the admin staff.

"For my day-to-day duties, the truck came at about 7.30 a.m. to 8.00 a.m. to collect those who were on duty, and we piled in. We were taken down to the dispersal and we all went to our separate Nissen huts; radar and wireless went to one, airframe and engines went to another, etc. Then the sergeant would return to the dispersal office and to check the technical logs of the aircraft that had landed the night before for any crew comments such as 'Lot of snowflakes on the (radar) screen' or 'Scanner intermittent', etc. Then we were sent out to the aeroplane to test it and rectify any faults. They used to get a sort of stardust effect on the radar screen. Our sergeant realised that the effect was caused by the salt-water spray attacking the cables in the bomb bay and setting up electrical interference when they were flying low to drop sonobuoys. He got an AOC's commendation for that work and he finished up as a flight lieutenant.

"We didn't do anything especially technical, it was mainly a case of removing a faulty unit and fitting a new one. We'd go down to the ground equipment compound, get a PE (petrol electric) set, pull it up to the aircraft, get it running, plug it in and switch it on (there was a corporal in charge of that). Then it was into the aircraft and test the radar. Occasionally we had a scanner that jammed – that was a job for the fitters, as I was a mechanic that wasn't my job. But it was very rare that we had troubles with the scanner, the main problems were with the screen.

"Sometimes quite honestly, we had nothing to do; we were referred to as the 'gash' trades. Occasionally the W/O would come and shout for three or four men for a starter crew. The airframe or engine man would be the marshaller, and we'd have two men one on each chock. The start procedure was number two engine first of all, so we plugged in a trolley-acc to get enough power into the aircraft to start it – the internal batteries weren't powerful enough. Then after a signal, whoever was on the starboard side of the aircraft unplugged the trolley-acc, fastened up the connection panel and pulled the trolley-acc clear. They then waited for the signal to remove the chocks. Sometimes it got jammed under the wheel and you had to kick the chock to get it out. The marshaller then raised his batons, at night the pilot would flash the landing lights if he was ready, and then the aircraft was marshalled away. If an aircraft was going on a special trip we sometimes gave a hand loading up equipment. When we were on duty crew and everybody else had gone home, there were only about seven or eight of us (one from each trade), under a corporal. It was our job to get the aircraft away and sometimes to see one back in.

"There was one incident when I remember being very scared. It was a bit of a long, boring night, so the corporal said, 'Does anybody want to go to the pictures? Who'll stay by the 'phone?' I wasn't really bothered about the pictures, so I said,

'I'll stay by the 'phone'. 'Thanks bomber,' (that was my nickname) and they all piled into the truck and went off. We weren't supposed to do it of course; somebody on the station had asked why they always saw 38 Squadron's truck parked outside the cinema. I was sitting reading when the 'phone rang; it was the tower saying, 'Your aircraft 'whiskey' is returning at once with hydraulic failure'. I panicked – I was on my own – I dared not tell them that – so I said, 'OK thanks'. I rang the cinema instantly and asked them to put on the screen '38 Squadron personnel to return at once to dispersal'. They all came back grumbling at me for interrupting the film. I was really sweating that the aircraft would arrive before they got back. I think the CO was in it, he wouldn't have been chuffed if he came back and found there was only me there. Actually, that happened more than once.

"I remember the Valiant bombers taking off from Luqa in the late afternoon during the Suez crisis. I had an RAF bike, so I cycled to the end of the runway to watch them go. We were given the job of painting the black and yellow stripes on their wings. It was quite a struggle, standing on ladders and somebody shouting: 'That stripe's too wide, put some more black on!' An aircrew sergeant told me I wasn't doing it quickly enough, but I did enjoy splashing on the yellow paint. Our mail was censored for a short time, and they cut out parts of our letters with scissors; our families wondered why there were bits missing. It was silly really, because all we had to do was go into town and send a postcard!

"When I first arrived in Luqa the Shacks still had a top gun turret; they were removed eventually (these were Mk.2s with the radar scanner in the middle). When the guns in the top turret were fired, they used to blast away the radio aerials that went out to the top of the fins. So, when one landed from firing practice, we always

MR.2 WL787 newly arrived with 38 Squadron Luqa. (Sue Wilson)

had to go up and put the aerials back on or replace them.

"We used to do exercises to El Adem, just outside Tobruk, Libya. They took a full crew, one from each trade, and we spent about two or three weeks there. Nobody liked Libya, it was a horrible place. Tobruk was still smashed about from the war, and the local population looked penniless – poor things. There were some really sad sights. The food was just terrible – corned beef fritters in 105 degrees in the shade, and that was breakfast! The mess tent was a big marquee, and they used to roll up the sides because it was so hot. Big black flies used to get into the butter, probably margarine, and drown themselves in it; so you'd flick them out onto the floor. One day the orderly officer came round (I think he was a dentist), a young National Service officer. He stared at the food in horror and asked, 'Is it always like this?' We said: 'Oh no sir, this is a good day.' There were two of us in each little bivouac tent, it was just big enough. One went in one end, one in the other and we just hoped the dreaded camel spiders didn't pay us a visit; they gave you one hell of a bite.

"Down the road, from El Adem, there was a huge American camp called Wheelus Field. They had plenty of money, were highly organised and had a system whereby we lads from El Adem could go there for a day. Of course the food was sumptuous there. We would tune in to AFN (American Forces Network) Europe, and they would say what the menu was in the airmens' mess that day, and it would go on and on and on! We'd sit transfixed, and then go off to our corned beef fritters. It got so bad that the CO banned any trips to Wheelus Field, because he said it damaged morale. Our lavatories were a sort of dustbin situated in a hut; the stink was unbelievable. On and off we went to El Adem for several months, a few weeks at a time.

"We had some Maltese personnel on the squadron. They had been sent to England for basic training, returning to serve in Malta. Some Maltese LACs came in gradually as I was leaving the squadron. I remember Sgt Joe Vella, I liked him, he spoke fluent Italian. During a NATO exercise an Italian aircraft had landed, and out jumped two Italian air force officers. They announced that we'd been bombed and could all go home – Joe had translated for them. We said we'd not seen any aircraft, 'Well you've been bombed', so the CO said, 'We might as well go home'. It was ruddy farce at times, it really was.

"The other detachment was to Nicosia, Cyprus. We usually had one aircraft there, but sometimes there were two, all the time when the EOKA (Greek Cypriot terrorist organisation) troubles were on. An aircraft from the squadron would circle the island, intercept and fly over any boat coming in that it had picked up on the radar. If they thought it was a suspicious vessel, they sent a message to Cyprus customs as they were trying to stop the supply of arms to EOKA. We did guard duties on the airfield and if the control tower flashed four reds, it meant an all-units bomb search had to be carried out. Nobody particularly wanted to find one of course. The first time we were ready for guard duty we were dressed any old how.

The station security officer, a red-faced flight lieutenant said: 'Right, the trucks are ready, off you go to where you've been assigned.' (I was going to guard a Shackleton.) 'Any airman failing to appear at his assigned post will be in front of the CO tomorrow morning and given a number of days 'jankers' (restrictions). Nicosia airport was a big, sprawling airfield, so I thought I'd better jump on the truck, because I didn't really know where I was. The truck stopped and men jumped out. They were probably based in Nicosia, and seemed to know where they were going. Finally I was more or less the last one on the truck, and when he stopped I thought I'd better jump out now. I suddenly realised I was miles from the squadron wondering where the hell I was. I could see a Shackleton across the other side of the airfield. The runway landing lights were off, I knew we weren't supposed to run across the runway, but I ran like hell. I finally arrived at the Shackleton, nobody had seen me. As I got there I could hear the corporal in the guard tent, saying 'His name is Leading Aircraftman (LAC) Davidson, he's failing to appear'. I said: 'No, I'm here!' 'Where have you been?' 'I got lost corporal.' 'Oh, bloody hell.'

"There was a detention camp for EOKA detainees not far from us. I was on guard duty one night wandering around with my rifle, when a truck appeared and a brand-new-looking pilot officer leaned out and said: 'Tell your corporal that someone's escaped from the camp!' and drove off. So I went back to the tent and told the corporal, and he said: 'If he comes round here mate, I'm buggering off!' and carried on reading his *Daily Mirror*. The station security officer had a habit of driving round in his Land Rover, turning the engine and lights off then gliding quietly towards you. One night, he suddenly came up right behind me; I turned round and there was this man. He bellowed at me, 'Why haven't you challenged me airman?' I said, 'Oh sorry' and he said, 'Don't point that bloody gun at me!' It was pure Monty Python. We had nine rounds of .303 ammunition in the magazine, but nothing in the breech. I used to get lumbered with quite a few guard duties, and on one occasion we saw a live round on the ground outside the guard tent. 'Corporal, there's a live round on the ground here', so he said: 'Oh some bloody twit's dropped it. Come on, everybody back, count how many you've got.' It turned out it was mine! To this day, I don't know how it got there. Happy days.

"The tents we lived in were mounted over a little old brick wall. The tent pole went into an extension, so the brick wall meant that the tent was high enough to walk round inside. The trouble was there was an opening, so animals could come straight in – we had a stray cat. I was woken up one night by a bloke shrieking his head off because this cat had come in and gone to sleep on his head. Fancy waking up at night and finding this furry thing on you; it was half on his face and half on his chest. Another night we had a stray horse!

"We had an aircraft delivered to Nicosia in a huge packing case, which we used as a store. During one of these bomb searches, the CO said to the W/O, 'Has anybody checked all the stores?' 'No sir', 'Get some men onto that then.' Instantly, 22 airmen vanished into thin air and hid – nobody wanted the job. The W/O was a bad-tempered devil. We were all in the squadron on a hot day. We were ready to start work, so I said: 'Right, all together. Come on – hi-ho, hi-ho, it's off to work we go…' and the W/O flew into a rage. 'Get that grin off your face Davidson. Any more of that and you're in the guardhouse!' He never forgot anything that came up. On the camp at Luqa we had a permanent guard of honour for visiting VIPs – I did one for the Queen Mother on her way home from Singapore, when her aircraft landed to refuel. We had to have one man from every unit on the station, and all the names were drawn out of a hat – out came my name, so I was on guard of honour for quite a long time.

"The air marshal was coming to inspect us. We were all gathered in a circle and the CO told us to get the aircraft cleaned for the AM's visit. We were given big drums of cleaning fluid, and a huge pile of rags. The engine exhausts blew backwards under the wing and covered the whole of the aircraft with a sticky black mess. It was a dreadful job, so he asked for volunteers and bribed us with an extra weekend off.

"Morale went down and down on the squadron, but to be fair to the RAF there wasn't too much discipline. There was not a lot to do, and we didn't feel as though anybody was particularly interested in our welfare. The squadron commander was Wg Cdr H M S Green, and he personally interviewed everyone to discover why there was low morale. We marched in, saluted and he asked us all individual questions. 'Do you like the officers?' 'What do you think of the officers?' Well they were OK, we didn't see much of them really. They came in their Land Rover, jumped in the aeroplane, took off and then when they landed, they jumped back in the Land Rover and disappeared; we never really had any contact with them. When we were in Cyprus, they had huge latrines there, dug as pits, which had to be emptied. We were living in tents, and the one I was in was only about six or seven feet away. When the local Cypriots, who emptied them, went on strike the stench was unbelievable. So I told the CO. He said: 'Yes I know, but I can't do anything about that.' He asked what the food was like, and I told him that sometimes it was terrible. 'Yes I know it is, ours isn't very good. But I can't do anything about that either.'

"I left the squadron on 6 September 1958; the CO called me in and said: 'I want to thank you for all you've done for the squadron.' I came back to England and as my father was quite ill, I had a few weeks' leave (I had only been back home for a day in two and a half years). Then I was posted to Upwood as an air radar mechanic on 52 Squadron Canberras, but there wasn't the camaraderie that we had on 38 Squadron. The aircraft were very different, the Canberra had two men up front and a radar operator/bomb aimer in the back. The bomb release worked from the radar. I was testing it once, and suddenly realised the release switch was down. I heard all the clicks running down the bomb bay – good job there weren't any bombs in there!

"National Service was coming to an end, people like me were coming out as well, and it was all going to be for long-term regulars. The air force was going through a great change. All the ceremony had gone, they had stopped pay parades, we were in big draughty billets and everybody went home at weekends. It was a five-day week air force really. I stayed at Upwood until June 1959, still an LAC, and that was it for me. Two or three days before I was demobbed, a member of the Royal Family came and presented new colours to the squadron. We were all given new uniforms and I was one of those formed up around the square. After that I remember walking down to the gates, turning round, two policemen on the gates staring at me silently for a minute and that was my last look at RAF Upwood."

George Dorrington – air signaller

"I was posted to 38 Squadron at Luqa, and amongst our tasks we were looking for gun-runners in Cyprus. This was the era of Georgios Grivas (leader of EOKA) and Archbishop Makarios. Amongst other things, the NAAFI had been blown up and if anybody went out of camp, they had to have an armed escort; it was like a Northern Ireland in Cyprus. We might fly up to 14-hour MARSOs (maritime reconnaissance and special operations) if we flew them from Luqa. Flying all the way from Malta to Cyprus and back meant that you only had about two hours on task. Therefore, most of them were flown from Akrotiri. This meant taking off late at night, and looking for gun-running fishing boats, anything! We investigated every contact we found as we flew right around the island, flying in to illuminate the target and photograph it. In all we did 55 MARSOs during my two years on the squadron.

"I did have one unfortunate incident at Luqa. In the roof of the aircraft was a little discharger of photoflashes (there were six in a chamber). When you were doing a bombing run and the cameras were turning (the camera was left on all the time), the photoflashes would be discharged and went off one at a time. Each time

RAF Luqa. (Rod Saar)

ten million candlepower exploded over the sea and a photograph was taken; everybody wanted photographic evidence. One day the nav asked me if I would watch and see in what sequence these discharges went, why he asked that I don't know. As I was trying to watch what was going on, one of the photoflashes went off in the discharger blowing a big hole in the roof. The discharger blew down past me, I was sent base over apex down to the back of the aircraft landing on the parachute bags – it was quite a bang. Then one of the photoflashes, lying on the floor, went out through the hole in the roof. If it had gone off in the aircraft, that would have been us! I had to go to sick quarters when we landed to get checked out. Fortunately I wasn't hurt, but I was quite disturbed. It was quite an experience.

"The duties of the signaller were focused primarily on the radio, which was W/T Morse code (and after all these years it still comes to me automatically). We had the old ASV radar – I loved it. On the MARSOs I used to, using the radar, take us right in under the cliffs. The pilots had confidence in my ability, as we were well below the cliff tops. We also did the sonics, gunnery, use of smoke floats and markers. We had to cook, make tea and coffee; considering the facilities we had, we concocted some quite decent meals. However, perhaps most of our time was spent looking with the old Mk.1 eyeball for submarines, but especially when you were on search and rescue for survivors.

"My last trip on the squadron was on 7 December '59, I was then demobbed as a sergeant. They had encouraged us to go for an AEO commissioned rank. I went up for the aptitude tests, but I didn't do very well. I was quite happy doing what I was doing, and had no real intentions of staying on any longer than my eight years, although one of my captains, Tony Talbot-Williams, wanted me, because I did spend an awful lot of time up the front, to re-muster as a pilot. I wouldn't have missed my RAF experience for the world; we were young kids learning as went. It was a growing-up time, character building amongst a lot of very nice people."

Adrian 'Tug' Wilson – flight engineer
"I did my flight engineer training at Kinloss on the Shackletons in May 1952 and then got posted to Luqa with 38 Squadron from November '52 until May '55. I regularly flew in Luqa with my captain Bob Fox.

"I was married to Daisy and whilst at Luqa she used to cook things like braised steak and apple crumble/custard, and crews used to give me a shilling and their tins of rations in return. I then heated it up in the galley – they were some of the best meals! Ours was the only crew that did this and we ate like kings on our trips. Daisy would fill the containers from the galley on the Shack (and the earlier Lancaster as I flew on both), and then I took them out to the aircraft.

"After Malta I was posted back to Kinloss as an instructor for flight engineers and pilots on the Shackleton until June '57."

Adrian 'Tug' Wilson, air engineer 38 Squadron Luqa. (Sue Wilson)

Derrick Downs – air signaller

"I left Ballykelly in August 1958, starting on 38 Squadron in Malta in early September; I was there until 1961. Our role there was similar to what we had done at Ballykelly; coastal exercises with the navy and things like that, but our primary role was to be on detachment to Akrotiri where we were to patrol around the island for gun-smugglers (this was during the Makarios troubles). When you took off from Akrotiri, watched by the 'little man' sitting on top of the nearby hill, you turned either left or right. We never actually caught anybody as the 'little man' had told his mates which way we were going round. We spent about a fortnight there every seven or eight weeks.

"Generally speaking the aircraft was very reliable. Occasionally we used to get engine problems, but quite often, even before we took off, we would get a mag drop problem. It was such a superb aeroplane that even when we lost two engines, for example on Christmas Island, it didn't really cause us any problems. Once in Malta, with the Mk.2 we had a fuel problem. Sitting in the radar seat, you looked down to see your feet covered in fuel, due to a leak from the bomb bay. The radar and W/T kit on the aeroplane was pretty good, although not by today's standards. When we went out to Christmas Island the second time, on one of our sorties, we kept on having minor fires in the radio which caused us a bit of a problem. Of course it was nearly all Morse and W/T; there wasn't much voice communication in those days. For anything over about 150 miles you relied on Morse code.

"We did a lot of search and rescue, including a trip from Malta down to Khartoum, and around what was then French Equatorial Africa. We also did search and rescue into Turkey, we were looking for an aeroplane that had crashed very near Mount Ararat; so it was all very varied. We also did a Lindholme drop once, I guess we would have dropped it from under 1,000 feet. As I haven't put any comment in my logbook, it must have been pretty uneventful.

"I left Malta in December 1961 when I got yanked off for my nav training – it was my choice to go for nav (you know what these things are like, I had to fly for about fifty years before!). It's difficult to compare the Shackleton with other types, especially with the Canberra I subsequently went on to, but the Shack was enjoyable. At times it was nice being part of a big crew and you certainly got around. It was a whole new world when I went onto Canberras. I did a tour in Brüggen, Germany, with 80 Squadron where I was the squadron commander's navigator. When I came back I did the staff navigation course at the Staff College at Manby. I then had a tour instructing at Bassingbourn, before getting posted on to Buccaneers. I finished with the air force in January '73 as a flight lieutenant."

Tony Cunnane – air signaller

"Shackletons routinely flew very long sorties. In my time with 38 Squadron (1958-59) the longest I flew without landing or refuelling was almost 20 hours. There was, therefore, a need for some kind of toilet. For this purpose, an Elsan chemical toilet was mounted, sometimes not very securely, near the aircraft's rear entrance door – for obvious reasons as far away from the galley as possible. There was a plastic curtain that could be drawn around the Elsan to provide a degree of modesty, but in my experience most users didn't bother with it – the plastic curtain, that is!

"I should mention, en passant, that in those far-off days the officers on the crew only spoke to 'other ranks' when they had to – and then only either by aircraft position (e.g. 'Captain to Port Beam'), or rank and surname (e.g. 'Co-pilot to Sgt Cunnane, where's my coffee?') – never by first name. I also can't recall ever having had a proper pre-flight briefing with the entire crew. The senior signaller was briefed by the captain, and the rest of us did as we were told.

"In the very centre of Valletta was the famous and ancient Strait Street. In 2010 an article in the highly respected *Times of Malta* included this: 'Strait Street in Valletta, popularly known as Strada Stretta, is a street which sticks like a fossilized icon in the collective memory of most members of the British forces and other navies who spent time at 'The Gut' as they called it. Alas the street is now deserted.' On one of my rare visits in the 1950s I remember seeing the 'ladies of the night' on their doorsteps beckoning passers-by with invitations such as, 'Ten shillings an hour', and 'One pound for all night including breakfast'.

"Our squadron, equipped with Shackleton MR.2s, was the only resident RAF squadron for most of my tour. No.37 Squadron, also equipped with Shackletons, had moved out to Aden a few weeks before I arrived; while 39 Squadron equipped with Canberras moved out in June 1958. Virtually all of our operational flying was done over the Mediterranean Sea or the Libyan Sahara Desert.

"We mostly flew at 300 feet or less by day, and at 1,000 feet by night. Our mar-

MR.2 R of 38 Squadron, with the 20-mm cannons fitted.
(*Tony Cunnane*)

itime reconnaissance role was supposedly anti-sub-marine warfare in conjunction with the Royal Navy. We carried out frequent exercises by day and night aiming to detect submarine periscopes, either visually, or by using our ASV 13 radar. We dropped practice sonobuoys and real flares, and then bombed the flares. We also launched simulated homing torpedoes and, on one occasion, we dropped a time-expired real homing torpedo – presumably to get rid of it. It was probably all very exciting for the pilots, with the aircraft wingtips at times seeming to be skimming the tops of the waves as the aircraft carried out steep turns at very low level. But I must confess I found it all rather boring. It was often very turbulent flying at low level and I was regularly airsick. Fortunately, the airsickness usually didn't last long and it never affected my work in the air.

"The most senior of the five signallers on the crew was designated senior signaller. His role was to allocate airborne duties to the other four (and himself), rotating them roughly every hour so that all signallers gained experience in all roles. One 'siggie' was always required to operate the HF radio, one to operate the ASV radar, and one to be cook and bottle washer in the galley. Depending on the activity, at any given time two or more siggies might be employed on visual lookout duties, one on the starboard beam adjacent to the entrance door, and one on the port beam opposite the door. Sometimes a siggie would be deployed into the bomb-aimer's position in the nose; that position was also a favourite sleeping zone because the position was fitted with a long, very comfortable 'mattress'. The signallers were also trained to take air-to-air, and air-to-ground (or sea!) photographs from several positions in the aircraft. The best positions, photographically speaking, were the port and starboard beam. This was because we could open the windows and take photographs using the large format cameras we carried without the scratchy windows intervening.

"Occasionally we signallers were allowed to fire the twin-20 mm cannon mounted in the nose of the aircraft. The target was usually a floating buoy being towed by one of the RAF air-sea rescue launches. The senior signaller only gave me about five minutes instruction on how to use the guns before I was let loose for the very first time with live ammunition on a towed target. After my initial burst the captain of the launch asked sarcastically on the radio, 'Does your gunner know which is the target and which is the launch?' Of course I did. It was just a bit more difficult than I had expected to make the guns do what I wanted them to do.

"I don't think many, if any, of the crews thought that we would ever be engaged in a war where it would be necessary to search and kill enemy submarines. That was World War 2 stuff, and the war had been over for more than a decade. A much more important role for 38 Squadron was search and rescue. Our squadron permanently maintained one Shackleton aircraft and crew on 60 minutes readiness to get airborne for SAR. The duty lasted 24 hours for each crew, and all ten crew members had to stay together to ensure that they could get airborne within 60 minutes from any scramble order. Shackletons on real SAR missions always used the radio call sign 'Playmate' followed by a number, starting at ten for the first aircraft. Aircraft using 'Playmate' call signs were given precedence by air traffic control centres over all other aircraft.

"Occasionally we were programmed to make the short flight across the Mediterranean to Idris in Libya. I had passed through Idris before, in transit to and from Ceylon (Sri Lanka). The RAF used Idris mainly as a staging post for flights between the UK and the Middle and Far East. It was also used by military aircraft operating on the nearby bombing ranges; and for duty-free shopping trips from Malta! The RAF withdrew in the 1960s after Libya became a republic, and the site was later extensively redeveloped and eventually became Tripoli International Airport.

"As there was little scheduled flying activity at Idris, 38 Squadron pilots were able to fly over there to get on with their necessary circuit and landing practices and instrument rating renewals without the inevitable air traffic delays at Luqa. An advantage for using Idris was because crew members, who were not needed for circuit flying, could get off the aircraft and do some local duty-free shopping for the whole crew and friends back at base, while the two pilots and flight engineer slaved away in the circuit. On my second sortie with my new squadron on 20 April 1958, we did just that, a shopping trip to Idris; the sortie lasted two and a half hours – including the shopping. On that occasion there was no time to go into Tripoli, on the coast about 15 miles north. However there was quite a lot we could buy, free of duty on the base at Idris, that was not available at the same price – if at all – in Malta.

"I saw far more of the Libyan desert 48 hours after our first trip to Idris when our crew was, for our first time, the duty SAR crew. On 22 April 1958 we were summoned from our beds about midnight, were airborne well within the hour and remained airborne for 12½ hours. Our task was to search for a missing Canberra B.6, WJ772 of 139 Squadron, that had left Luqa about three hours earlier with two crew members on board, en route for the bombing range south of El Adem at the far eastern end of Libya. Nothing had been heard from the Canberra after it had taken off. The alarm was raised when the Canberra's crew did not check in with ATC at El Adem when expected.

"The standard procedure for the first search aircraft on task, when searching for an aircraft missing on a routine flight from A to B, was to search across the assumed course the aircraft should have taken. We carried out the night part of the search between Malta and El Adem at about 2,000 feet, initially listening for the aircrew emergency distress beacons, and watching for emergency flares. Once dawn broke we descended to low level for a visual search over the same area. After 12 hours, having seen and heard nothing of the Canberra, we were relieved by another Shackleton. No.38 Squadron continued the search for a whole week, night and day, but no trace of the Canberra or its crew was found and the search was eventually called off.

"On 8 February 1959, ten months after WJ772 had gone missing, a group of Bedouin Arabs came across the Canberra in the desert 160 miles south south-east of Gabes in Tunisia. Some of our squadron navigators reckoned that in order to get to that position the Canberra must have flown on a heading of 200 degrees from Malta, when 100 degrees was the required heading to reach El Adem. No-one could think of any reason why both pilot and navigator of the downed Canberra could have flown all that way without realising they were well off their intended course. The Canberra was, reportedly, relatively undamaged when it was found, but the two crew members were not inside. The ejection seats had not been used, and the aircraft fuel tanks were virtually empty. Talk around our squadron when that report became known was that the crew must have deliberately force-landed in the dark, just before their fuel ran out. They had then, for whatever reason, decided to walk away across the desert.

"Aircrew were always taught that if they were forced to eject over or force-land in the Sahara they should stay with, or close to, the aircraft because it would provide shelter from the heat of the sun and the cold of the desert nights. Furthermore, search aircraft were much more likely to find a crashed aircraft than one or more men walking alone in the desert. Crucially, no-one could imagine why an experienced crew should opt to make a hazardous forced landing in darkness rather than eject from the aircraft."

> The Canberra had disappeared after taking off from Luqa and climbing to 37,500 feet. It was eventually found as described above, its location being some 360 miles off its intended track. The bodies of the pilot Fg Off George Coulson, and his navigator Master Nav James Speed, were recovered in 1959 and later buried in El Alia Cemetery, Algiers. **Tony Cunnane** continues:

"In May 1958 our crew flew off to Nicosia in the north of Cyprus for MARSO operations. During my time on 38 Squadron there was always at least one Shackleton and crew on standby at Nicosia (and later Akrotiri). MARSO sorties were almost always flown by night at very low level, and with no navigation or other external lights showing. The standard brief was to fly once, all the way around Cyprus at a range of about 20 miles from the coast; that would, typically, take about two hours if there were no 'distractions'. We were usually given the start point, which could be anywhere on the coast depending on the intelligence the HQ had at the time, and whether we were to fly clockwise or anti-clockwise.

"Our task was to search on radar for any suspicious-looking small vessels, but in particular for the small fishing boats called caïques. These were known to be regularly smuggling weapons and ammunition from Greece to Cyprus in support of the EOKA terrorists. EOKA, a Greek Cypriot nationalist guerrilla organisation, fought a bloody campaign with the twin aims of ending British rule in Cyprus and for the subsequent union with Greece (ENOSIS). When we found any surface contacts we illuminated them with powerful flares, photographed them, and if necessary called in the Royal Navy who were always on patrol, to intercept, stop and search them.

"Cyprus, especially the capital Nicosia, was a very dangerous place for British troops, on or off duty. One day, when we had some free time, four of us signallers decided to go for a walk around the central shopping area in Nicosia, known then as Murder Mile (I believe its proper name was Ledra Street). It was mandatory to wear uniform and carry arms off base. To this day I cannot remember what possessed us to take that walk. It certainly caught the attention of the ordinary Cypriots who watched us, but apart from that nothing untoward occurred.

"Early one morning, while we were resting from a night operational flight, our ten-man crew looked on as a large tented camp was erected, in just a few short hours, on open ground close to the runways at Nicosia. We then watched in astonishment as a stream of transport aircraft, mostly Hastings, landed on the airfield parking on every available space including some of the taxiways. We continued to watch as hundreds of fully armed British troops disembarked and occupied the tented camp. Hours later all those aircraft took off in quick succession and disappeared from sight. At the time we (the Shackleton crew) didn't know where they were going but word quickly spread that they were going to aid King Hussein of Jordan. Another persistent rumour was that the entire force of RAF aircraft present was meant to be merely a show of intent. According to that rumour the crews should, before crossing into Jordanian airspace, have been ordered to return to Nicosia. But, for whatever reason, the recall signal was never sent so the crews obediently continued to Amman and landed there.

"On the expectation that the large British task force would shortly be returning to Nicosia, our 38 Squadron Shackleton detachment was ordered to decamp and move south, across the central Troodos mountains, to the RAF's newly built airfield at Akrotiri. For the remainder of my tour with 38 Squadron most, but not all, of our operational missions were flown from Akrotiri where there were some inevitable initial operational teething troubles. One night, after completing a circuit of Cyprus flying at 500 feet above the sea to increase our radar coverage, we located several large contacts on the surface about 60 miles due south of the Akrotiri peninsula. This was further out than we or the smugglers normally went. It was near the end of a boring flight during which we had found nothing suspicious or interesting, so the captain decided we might as well investigate. We closed in, descended to 300 feet, and illuminated the contacts by launching several high-powered flares. The ship recognition expert on board our Shackleton shouted out on the intercom, 'It looks like the American 6th Fleet'. Another crew member watching from the nose compartment through binoculars added, 'Bloody hell, their guns are tracking us – let's get out of here!' We did.

"When we landed, a senior RAF officer was waiting at the aircraft. He told us that the Americans had officially complained at what we had done. Then he added, 'Apparently the US 6th Fleet are on a secret mission to Lebanon but they hadn't bothered to tell us they were in our area.' I suppose that would have been some consolation to our relatives had we been shot down.

"On the squadron's regular detachments to Cyprus, for MARSO operations, crews usually stayed for two weeks at a time before returning to Malta. On their return flight many crew members carried a box. This contained a gross of contraceptives (144 packets of three) the supply for married personnel based on Malta who rarely had the opportunity to leave the island. For religious reasons, contraceptives were not on sale in Malta. The RAF Police, not the local customs officers, always searched our luggage on landing at Luqa from Cyprus, but they never seemed to find the sealed boxes of condoms. Presumably by mutual agreement, they were concealed in piles of our soiled flying clothing under-garments – and no-one would wish to search through those.

"On the evening of 5 December 1958 38 Squadron was called out again on another SAR mission, this time for a missing target-towing Meteor of 728 Squadron Fleet Air Arm. Just a few minutes after the Meteor had taken off from the Royal Naval Air Station Hal Far, on Malta, radar and radio contact with it was lost. A search and rescue mission was immediately launched and the standby Shackleton at Luqa 'Playmate 10', was scrambled. Air traffic control at Hal Far reported that the Meteor had been on a local area flying sortie, so the search was concentrated on the sea area up to 100 miles from the coast at Hal Far, while land-based search parties started scouring the area around Hal Far. It was 0430 hours the following day 6 December, when our crew were called from our beds to join the search. After briefing in Quarry Operations, the underground complex at a distant corner of Luqa airfield, we took off at 0630 hours in WR964 using the call sign 'Playmate 11'. Following a formal handover in the search area we relieved 'Playmate 10', and that aircraft returned to base.

"We flew for just over ten hours looking for any trace of the missing Meteor while gradually widening the search area; my logbook records that we found nothing. In ideal daylight conditions we would expect to see a survivor afloat in a small dinghy within a range of three or four miles, depending on the sea state. However, if the downed airman was able to fire off his emergency flares, or was able to erect the antenna on his emergency radio beacon we would have been able to detect him from a much greater range. Three of the Shackleton's five air signallers kept a visual look out in the nose position and beam positions near the rear of the aircraft. The other two signallers manned the radar and radios. The two pilots also kept a sharp look out but their view downwards from the cockpit was limited. Had we located a survivor we had the option of dropping a larger life raft, containing more survival aids. We would certainly have homed in the RAF's high-speed motor launches which were searching nearer the coast. Although the search continued for two more days, as far as I am aware, nothing was ever found of the missing Meteor."

The aircraft lost was Meteor T.7 WS106 which had taken off on an air test. As Tony says, neither the aircraft nor its pilot Lt J V Bernard, were ever found.

"We sometimes played jokes on a new pilot. Towards the end of a very long sortie, when the auto-pilot was flying the aircraft and all ten crew members were getting bored and soporific, a group of three or four air signallers would rush from their usual off-watch gathering point near the galley in the centre of the aircraft, towards the Elsan. This unexpected rearward change in the aircraft's centre of gravity usually caused the auto-pilot's safety mechanism to trip out, whereupon the aircraft would suddenly pitch nose up and everyone, especially the new pilot, would suddenly wake up in some alarm. What fun! 'Sorry, Captain,' one of the signallers would call out on the intercom in response to the pilot's polite request to know what was going on, 'Had to rush to the toilet. Didn't have time to warn you!' The pilots' revenge for this could be very unpleasant. When a crew member was known to be seated on the Elsan an unscrupulous pilot, seeking retribution, would deliberately disengage the auto-pilot. He then gently started easing the aircraft's control column backwards and forwards, causing the aircraft to rock on its fore and aft axis – causing the fluid in the Elsan to start swilling about under the force of gravity. The pilot knew when to stop because, even above the roar of the four mighty Griffon engines, he could hear the howls of anguish as the foul liquid came into contact with the unfortunate crew member's rear parts.

"There was an even more alarming story current on 38 Squadron when I was there, although I cannot vouch for its authenticity. A crew member while sitting on the Elsan found another way to frighten the pilots – and the rest of the crew as well. The Elsan was mounted at right angles to the direction of flight thus, when sitting on it you had your back to the port side airframe and were more or less facing the rear entrance door. Along the port fuselage wall were the control cables, running through metal guides, that were directly connected to the rudders and elevators (no power-operated controls in those days). It is said that this particular crew member, while seated on the Elsan, reached behind his head and with both hands grabbed one of the control cables at random, and pulled down hard. This caused the aircraft to lurch violently. Very nasty.

"During my flying career I was involved in three near mid-air collisions – that's the three I know of! The first happened in the middle of the night while our crew was flying from Cyprus back to our own base in Malta. We took off on 25 July 1958 at 0145 hours local time from Nicosia, then the only operational RAF airfield in Cyprus. We were flying at 1,000 feet above the sea – but in cloud. The captain could have decided to climb above the cloud but, for whatever reason, he chose not to. About halfway through the trip most of the crew were asleep. We knew we were north of Crete because the central mountains (with peaks up to 8,000 feet) showed up clearly on our radar equipment. I was sitting at the rear of the aircraft, by the window at the port beam. There was nothing to do, and because of the cloud, nothing to see outside except the reflection from our port wingtip navigation light. All of a sudden, I heard a tremendous roar – from outside our aircraft. The inside of a Shackleton in flight was one of the noisiest environments I have ever experienced, and so for me to hear any noise from outside the aircraft, especially when I was wearing my flying helmet, meant that it must have been exceedingly loud. Almost immediately we flew through, what the captain later described as, air turbulence. Nothing unusual about that – it happened all the time at low level over the sea – but it was not usually accompanied by a loud noise. I asked on the inter-com if anyone had heard the noise, but no-one had or, to be more precise, no-one would admit to having heard it.

"After landing at Luqa one or two of my fellow signallers admitted to me that they too had heard the noise and felt the associated turbulence. They thought, like me, that it had sounded like another Shackleton. 'Better keep quiet about that, sergeant,' said the senior navigator, having overheard our conversation. So I did. Nevertheless, I checked on the squadron's flying programme and saw that another of our Shackletons had flown (in the opposite direction to us) from Malta to Nic-

38 Squadron MR.2 WL794 over Grand Harbour, Valletta. (Adrian Balch collection)

osia that night, and could have been north of Crete at about the same time as we were. A week later, when he'd returned to Malta a signaller friend, who had been on that aircraft, told me their crew had been flying in cloud at 1,000 feet. They had all heard what they thought was another Shackleton passing close by in the opposite direction, and they too had experienced some unexpected air turbulence. Thus, each aircraft had been close enough to hear the other, and each had flown through the other's wake turbulence. How close was that to disaster?"

My Final Week on 38 Squadron

"Wg Cdr Joe Saunders was OC 38 Squadron throughout my time on the squadron and Flt Lt 'Happy' Hanmore was my regular captain. However the 50-plus signallers on the squadron regularly flew with other crews simply to fill gaps left by courses, training, leave, sickness, etc. On Monday 18 January 1960 our regular crew set out from Malta on a straightforward transit flight to Gibraltar for a few days in Mk.2 WL744. Little did I know that it would be the start of my final overseas exercise with 38 Squadron, my last few flights as an air signaller, and one of my last days as a sergeant. The trip took seven hours 30 minutes, and was interesting only because the navigators could not find the Rock! To be fair it was a very murky day, but there was real cause for concern as the top of the Rock of Gibraltar is 1,398 feet above sea level. We had been flying over the Mediterranean Sea for several hours at 500 feet above the waves, and in aircrew parlance, the Rock has a greater rate of climb than a Shackleton. The signaller operating the HF radio had been in routine Morse code contact with the flight watch service every half hour for several hours. The pilots in the meantime were trying and failing, for what later turned out to be a complete power outage on the airfield, to contact Gibraltar Tower on the VHF radio.

"Eventually the captain instructed all crew members to man the portholes down each side of the aircraft, and the visual bombing position in the nose, exhorting everyone to keep a sharp lookout. I left the galley, where I had just finished disposing of the remnants of our in-flight meals and packing all the utensils securely away for landing, and moved to my assigned port beam position. I peered anxiously into the thick haze when suddenly, through the gloom, I saw low-lying land on the port side. 'Port Beam here, captain,' I called on the intercom. 'What's our heading?' '270 degrees,' replied the captain. 'Why do you ask?' 'There's low-lying land on the port beam; I estimate the range about two nautical miles,' I replied and added, 'It must be the North African coastline.' 'Nonsense', broke in the navigator from his darkened operating position near the front of the aircraft. He sounded outraged that a mere signaller should make such a suggestion. 'It can't possibly be North Africa.' 'Well it's definitely land,' I persisted. 'If we're heading due west, this land off the port beam can't be anywhere but North Africa, can it? Gibraltar must be either dead ahead, or even out to starboard.' There was a stunned silence on the intercom. After a few seconds, but it seemed a lot longer to me, the captain called urgently for climb power and we zoomed to about 3,000 feet. An almost empty

Mk.2 had quite a respectable rate of climb. There was a much clearer view from up there, and very soon the signaller on the starboard beam reported that he could see the familiar outline of the Rock of Gibraltar off our side and slightly behind us. We had flown at 500 feet above the sea, through the gap which was 15 kilometres at the narrowest point, between Tarifa near Algeciras on the southern coast of Spain, and Tangier plus Mount Sidi Moussa in Ceuta on the African coast. Mount Sidi Moussa and the Rock of Gibraltar are the two peaked rocks called by the Ancient Greeks 'The Pillars of Hercules'. If we had been right on track for Gibraltar we would have found it the hard way! We flew a left-hand turn, the long way round, back towards Gibraltar and landed a short time later. The curious thing is that no-one ever mentioned the incident, either then or later. No thank yous. I felt rather hurt about that.

"That evening our officers did whatever officers do on detachment duty, and we five signallers plus the flight engineer went off, on foot, to a nightclub in La Linea (just across the border into Spain). From what I remember we enjoyed some Flamenco dancing, some belly dancing, lots of wine, and…perhaps fortunately, I forget the rest. We must have got back by midnight because the foot crossing at the international border closed exactly at midnight every night. Late revellers were forced to stay overnight in Spain – which was expensive for a variety of reasons.

"The fortunate aircrew on 38 Squadron were always expected to do some shopping for the less fortunate ground crew who rarely had the opportunity to leave Malta during the whole of their 30-month tour of duty. My list was fairly typical but I can't, after all this time, remember whether or not I had time to collect all the money owed to me! As usual alcohol featured large on the list, as did 6,000 Senior Service cigarettes (they were certainly not for me because I've never been a smoker). It must have been a legal duty-free trade because we were always met on return to Malta, from Gibraltar, by Maltese customs officials. I've no idea who two sets of castanets, costing a total of five shillings (25p) were for nor the ten pairs of Perlon nylon stockings; at that time I had no idea what Perlon was.

"Day two of our Gibraltar exercise was free for doing touristy things, such as recovering from the late night and a hangover, and visiting the top of the Rock, and the caves inside the rock. My flying logbook for day three shows that we flew a ten-hour navigation exercise, but I can remember nothing about it. Day four was for shopping. On day five, Friday, we flew back to Malta. The flight took just over six hours so it must have been a direct transit, with no diversions along the way. As we taxied into our squadron dispersal at Luqa the captain told us on the intercom that the squadron commander, Wg Cdr Joe Saunders, was waiting. 'I wonder what he wants?' we all thought. I am sure that in the back of our minds, or at least in the back of the minds of the captain and navigators, the suspicion was that the boss had somehow heard about our non-standard arrival at Gibraltar. However, when we climbed down from the aircraft he came straight over to me. 'Welcome back, Cunnane,' he said cheerfully, holding out his hand to be shaken, 'You'd better go straight to the sergeants' mess and start packing. You're posted to Jurby (Isle of Man) for officer training. You fly out on Sunday. Congratulations.' There was not even time for me to arrange farewell drinks for my squadron pals, nor for them to arrange a farewell party for me! So it was that, barely 36 hours later, at 0620 hours on Sunday 24 January 1960, I flew out of Luqa as a passenger to Lyneham in a Hastings."

Ray Curtis – AEO

"My squadron was 38, where I joined an almost all SNCO crew – only the captain, a flying officer and the second navigator, a pilot officer were commissioned. There were two all SNCO crews on the station, one on 38 Squadron commanded by Flt Sgt Howard Croft, and one on 37 Squadron commanded by Flt Sgt Dickie Worthing.

"I suppose Malta was the most interesting tour, because the Enosis/EOKA problem arose in Cyprus when I was there. Greek army colonel Grivas, thought that Cyprus should be united with mainland Greece. He resorted to terrorist activity on Cyprus to achieve his aims – chucking grenades at British soldiers walking down the main street in Nicosia, and mining roads to blow up Ferret scout cars, stuff like that. To cut off the EOKA terrorists' supply of arms by sea from mainland Greece, the sea around Cyprus was divided into sectors. These were patrolled by a frigate or a minesweeper. Shackletons from Malta flew around the island at night illuminating with 1.75-inch photo flares any radar contact not burning lights. They then reported them to the in-area Royal Navy ship, who would then intercept, board and search for arms. These MARSO patrols were mounted from Malta. This involved fitting the Shacks with an overload fuel tank in the bomb bay. This was a large cylindrical tank which took up most of the bomb-bay space. We would take off from Malta in time to reach Cyprus at dusk, taking up to six hours. We would fly around the island once which took another six hours depending on the number of radar contacts investigated, and then it was a six-hour transit back to Malta. The longest MARSO I ever did was 17 hours. Eventually, to cut down on transit time, we were detached to El Adem, Libya to carry out MARSOs from there, and finally they based us on Cyprus at Nicosia. From there we were able to fly around the island twice on each trip. We had one hairy incident when flying from El Adem. We returned to El Adem at dawn, after 12 hours flying, to find the airfield shrouded in ground fog – yes, fog in the desert. It stretched from ground level up to about 1,000 feet, which meant the pilots could not have visual with the runway on the final stages of their approach. Our nearest diversion was Idris, which was over three hours flying away. After three attempts at getting into El Adem we diverted, landing at Idris three hours 35 minutes later. When the fuel tanks were dipped we had only just made it.

"While I was on 38 Squadron Princess Margaret made a visit to Kenya, flying into Nairobi and then joining the Royal Yacht at Mombasa. We detached two Shacks to Entebbe, at the top of Lake Victoria to provide SAR cover. We flew from Malta to Kano in northern Nigeria, passing over Timbuktu, night-stopped and then flew across Africa to Entebbe. On arrival we found there was no accommodation in the Lake Victoria Hotel because it had all been taken by Bristol, the aircraft manufacturer. At that time the Bristol Britannia was having icing problems with its engines at high altitude, so they had a Britannia, crew and associated boffins based at Entebbe where they were carrying out high-level icing trials. All of our Shack detachment, aircrew and ground crew, were billeted with the local expats of the colonial service.

"Also, while I was on Malta, the invasion of Egypt by Britain, France and the Israelis took place – Operation Musketeer. Colonel Nasser, the Egyptian president, had nationalised the Suez Canal. As a result, we had Valiant bombers coming in to Luqa. They were en route to carrying out bombing raids on Port Said and other Suez Canal targets, and had black and yellow stripes painted on their wings (to identify them to our forces as friend not foe). I can't remember our Shackletons having striped wings, although a few apparently did. Our task was to patrol off the Egyptian coast looking for E-boats (torpedo boats) which might come out and attack our capital ships sitting off shore. I don't think any E-boats were ever found – that was a bit of duff intelligence – or the E-boats stayed at their moorings. We also dropped medical supplies to the carrier HMS *Theseus*, which had been turned into a hospital ship. My tour on Malta finished in March 1958 when I was posted to 2 Air Navigation School at Thorney Island, via the air electronics course at Hullavington."

Mike Evans – engineering officer

"I was sent to Luqa to join 38 Squadron as the engineer officer; the first one commissioned. I was thrown in after only one week of experience at Ballykelly to acquaint me with the aircraft. As an ex-apprentice ('Brat') engine fitter, I fortunately knew a little about piston engines. However, just about every other ground crew member of the squadron, and the aircrew who had completed a long course, knew far more about the aircraft than me. It was a daunting time. Fortunately the B Flight commander Mo Short, who was responsible for the ground crew, was also an ex-Brat and was supportive. That tour, November 1961 to May '64 included a tour of the Caribbean, an Aden run via Nairobi and El Adem, and an extended detachment to Akrotiri (because the Turks were about to invade Cyprus). It was the era of 'gulping' where the Griffons expelled their lubricating oil all over the wing, which meant they had to be shut down."

Brian Howett – airframe

"I was on 39 (Canberra) Squadron at Luqa from 1957 to 1960. One day, when one of 38 Squadron's Shacks lowered its radar scanner a hydraulic pipe burst. This jettisoned all the hydraulic fluid, so there was none left to raise the scanner again. This had happened once before in Cyprus, and apparently, the aircraft broke in

Mike Beane and 38 Squadron's crew 7. (Rod Saar)

ing no wind. The wind calculations taken every half hour, or sooner if the pilots noted a change in the wind direction, all then enabled the navigator to calculate the MPP (most probable position) of the aircraft.

"We carried out three Operation Pipe sorties, but did not come across any Soviet vessels with tracking equipment in action, or indeed visible. A crew from 42 Squadron based at Khormaksar, took over from us and was fortunate enough to photograph the Soviet tracking equipment. From a navigation point of view the sortie could be very satisfying when after 15 hours, and approaching the coast of Kenya near Mombasa, we switched on our radar to get a coastal fix to find we were only five miles out on our dead reckoning navigation.

"Mombasa in 1963 was idyllic – no tourism! Nyelli beach was a long golden sandy beach full of land crabs, bordered by smart villas with swimming pools. I bought from a local on the beach, some shells and a piece of coral (which I still have) for a shilling. In those days most businesses and shops in Kenya were run by Asians, on the pavement outside were local street and market sellers, from whom I bought the odd piece of local wood carving. In our colonial-style hotel the most wonderful food was served, especially exotic fruits for breakfast.

"When we returned to Malta, we transited via Nairobi and had a great view of Mount Kilimanjaro. The short flight to Nairobi would only take one hour 20 minutes and as we had a full fuel load, we did not want to have to circle for hours to burn off fuel to get down to a safe landing weight. Mombasa did not have any equipment to remove the fuel, so we had to empty a large quantity of it onto the grass verges there before we flew into Nairobi – not a very proud moment. The following day

21 June we flew on to Khartoum in the Sudan, where we refuelled and just after midday flew on to El Adem. On the following day we flew back to Luqa.

"In November 1963 we went to Gibraltar for the annual spanex (Moontiger 2) exercise with the Spanish navy. It was during a guest night in the officers' mess that we received the shocking news that President Kennedy had been assassinated. The news was passed with disbelief from person to person around the dining tables. Even though that same year had seen the Cuban crisis which came so close to starting World War 3 when the Soviets sent missile systems to Cuba, it was still a moment that you will never forget.

"On these trips away from base we often loaded up with duty-free spirits as Malta was not a duty-free location. Whilst in Gib I recall a particularly lively Pimm's party, being worse for wear and crawling up the officers' mess stairs to my room. Officers could behave like this, but if you were an airman and caught drunk on the base you were in trouble. Apart from anti-submarine exercises we spent our Gibraltar time with navigation exercises flying to the Canary Islands, and volcanic outcrops in the South Atlantic.

"Gibraltar had a reputation for being problematic and dangerous in turbulent weather due to the wind shear caused by the sharp outcrop of rock close to the runway – in addition, the runway ends in the sea at both ends. At that time the side of the Rock closest to the runway still sported large black marks from aircraft which had crashed into it in wartime. On one occasion we made two attempts to land at Gibraltar early in the morning, it was dark and very stormy with very strong cross winds. Fg Off Mike Beane was captain, and Flt Lt John Postlethwaite was co-pilot. On our second attempt we hit strong turbulence, and lost 300 to 400 feet on finals as we were getting close to the ground. We lost some bits of the aircraft, and the inside was a mess with galley items strewn all over the place (apart from ten crew we also had half a dozen ground crew on board). Both pilots struggled to maintain control of the aircraft, and made another overshoot.

"Mike Beane wisely decided to abandon any further attempts to land and we diverted to an American air base at Port Lyautey, Morocco. On seeing us land, the Americans at the airfield could not believe that aircraft like the Shackleton were still on operational duty. They all came out to meet us armed with cameras and were also astonished to see 16 people leave the aircraft. As this sortie had been the closest in my flying career to having a fatal aircraft accident, it remains very clear in my mind.

"On one occasion when returning to Malta in March 1963 we had to divert to Decimomannu, Sardinia due to bad weather. In the evening our crew let their hair down somewhat, as usual. The following morning we hung around the aircraft waiting for clearance to return to Malta. We were not the only Shackleton crew that had diverted there and parked next to us was another Shackleton from England. Their captain was not amused about our very casual behaviour and liveliness in the mess the evening before.

"Winter in the Med could produce sudden bad storms, whilst in the summer the sea could be like glass and a submarine could be spotted even when below the surface. The Sirocco wind could blow over the sea from the Libyan desert bringing a lot of heat and sand dust. When flying at our normal operational height of 1,000 feet we could clearly see sea turtles and porpoises, which were a common sight in the Med. On 26 October 1963 we acted as SAR escort to Belvedere helicopters flying from Brindisi to Souda, and then on to El Adem; they were ultimately on their way to Aden.

"On 27 December 1963 crew seven was the SAR crew, and that morning we were told to get airborne soonest and fly to Cyprus; my friend Fg Off Mike Beane was the captain. My room in the officers' mess was on the first floor next door to Mike's and it was still early morning when he rushed into my room to tell me to pack a few clothes and get to operations as fast as possible. The Greek Cypriots and Turkish Cypriots were fighting each other. We took off and flew straight to the sea area between Northern Cyprus and Turkey, spending about seven hours looking for possible movements by the Turkish navy. We saw no unusual activity and later landed at Akrotiri.

"We were based out of both Nicosia and Akrotiri, and initially our role was to patrol the Aegean Sea around the Greek islands, and along the coast of Turkey to monitor activities of both the Greek and the Turkish navies. This became a regular detachment from Malta until I left the squadron in September 1964. Three weeks in Cyprus were followed by a rest week in Malta. No.38 Squadron provided 24-hour monitoring of naval activity north of Cyprus; 12-hour sorties were carried out every other day by each crew. With radar ranging out to 100 miles, flying at 1,000 to 2,000 feet our task was to identify all military shipping in the area; at night we flew without lights! Astonishingly we discovered that RAF HQ at 'Happy Valley' (Episkopi) was also tasking Hastings transport aircraft to carry out the same job as us at the same time – with only 1,000 feet separation, also without lights and in the same area as the Shackletons. The group captain operations was a bomber man, and clearly did not have the faintest idea of the Shackleton's capabilities. He ignored the fact that we had long-range radar designed to detect surface vessels, and dismissed the representations of the captains of the 38 Squadron Shackleton crews who wanted to explain our maritime capability. They also explained the hazards of tasking aircraft in the same area at night, without navigation lights and with only 1,000-feet separation. He was putting our lives at risk. It was sheer incompetence and arrogance which seemed to be ignored in a peacetime environment. In the end the MOD sent out an air commodore to sort this man out.

"At some point during 1964 the Turkish navy put to sea in large numbers. This could either have been an intended invasion of Cyprus, or a bit of political sabre rattling. To assess the threat we were tasked to fly at low level into the Bay of Iskenderun, where much of the Turkish navy was based, and to report on the shipping at anchor. One morning after doing a low-level recce into the Bay of

Iskenderun we were attacked by two Turkish F-86 Sabres – endeavouring to fright-en us off they actually fired across our bows. We went down to 100 feet, hugging the sea, and flew back to Cyprus as fast as possible. Episkopi HQ did not believe that the Turkish air force had fired at us until we had our photos developed which clearly showed the F-86s at work. It had been assumed that a fellow NATO member would not take this kind of action; once again the British underestimated the Turks (remember Gallipoli). Shortly afterwards I was promoted to first navigator and changed crews. Crew seven had been a great crew and was classified as the best crew on the squadron in competitions. To my surprise, in December 2015 I received a shiny campaign medal for my service in Cyprus 1963/64; 51 years had gone by!

"On our non-flying days, being largely restricted to the base, we would play squash and tennis. Once in a while, wearing our uniforms, we had a meal out in the evening. In Nicosia the taxi drivers would take us to the invisible dividing line between the Greek and the Turkish areas dropping us off there, and going no further. As time went on we came under curfew, and had to be back on base by 2300 hours. Once when visiting a nightclub in Limassol we were warned by the RAF police to leave on time and not break the curfew. As a lark we had swapped our uniform jackets with our NCO fellow crewmen, but this was not obvious to the RAF police. After a second warning we all left the nightclub and caught two taxis to return to base. However only the taxi I was in, with some colleagues, made it back to base – they had been persuaded by me not to go back to the nightclub. The other crew members, including our captain Mike Beane, returned to the night-club. They were promptly chased by the RAF police and although they tried to hide in the dancers' dressing rooms they were soon arrested. Returning under guard to Akrotiri they were also accused of impersonation. The swapped uniform jackets meant they did not have the right F1250 identification cards on them. The end result was that Mike Beane was given a reprimand by AOC NEAF – which will not have helped his career. We worked hard, but in true RAF tradition we also played hard; in wartime this bit of high spirits would have been ignored.

"Malta was a great place for bachelors, with school teachers, nurses or daughters of serving Brit-ish personnel making for a good

Fg Off Beane takes his Shack down low for a look at St Paul's Bay, Malta. (Rod Saar)

social life. In the summer, if not flying, we would go down to Tigni Beach in Sliema; a private beach for service personnel – although it was a bit rocky with no sand. You could get a packed lunch from the mess, and go off somewhere remote for a picnic with a girlfriend. The life of a young bachelor living in the officers' mess was carefree – apart from your flying role you had few responsibilities. Although you did not realise it at the time, it was in many ways an idyllic existence. From time to time when on SAR standby in the officers' mess I broke the rules. I had a casual girlfriend who was a BEA air hostess, who, when she arrived in Malta, would ring me up from the Phoenicia Hotel in Valletta. Although I was often on standby duty, I would take her out to supper. I would tell the mess receptionist where I was going and to contact me if we got called out so that I could hurry back. It never happened, I did not get caught out, but it was a bit risky.

"For some reason the bachelors on 38 Squadron had a bad reputation as far as women were concerned but I do not think it was deserved."

203 Squadron

The third and final Shackleton unit to be based in Malta, was 203 Squadron arriving at Luqa on 1 February 1969. No. 203 Squadron could trace its ancestry back to May 1914 when it formed as the Eastchurch squadron of the RNAS. In 1915 it became 3 Squadron RNAS, flying a variety of fighter types including the Bristol Scout, Sopwith Pup and Sopwith Camel, continuing as a fighter unit (with a short break in 1920) until 1923 when it disbanded.

It re-formed in 1929 as a flying-boat squadron, but by 1940 it had adopted a bombing role with Blenheims, then successively changing to the Maryland, Baltimore, Wellington and Liberator, operating in both the Middle and Far East theatres. By 1946 it had switched to the MR role at Leuchars, where it took on Lancaster GR.3s, and then moved to St. Eval the following year. Next came a 1952 move to Topcliffe and a switch to the Lockheed Neptune, before disbanding again in 1956. No.203 Squadron re-formed at Ballykelly, with Shackleton MR.1As on 1 November 1958, switching to MR.2s in 1962, then MR.3s in 1966, thus becoming the sole RAF MR.3 unit to be based outside the UK.

Keith Jarvis – pilot
"After I finished my tour on 42 Squadron I stayed out in Malta and 203 Squadron came to me, rather than the other way round. The Malta tour was fascinating. We had neglected it as a maritime base for some time and, in the meantime, the Soviet fleet had built up its presence. We were very busy and, in addition to operating

An early Mk 3 Shack visiting Luqa. (Tony Cunnane)

from Cyprus and Gibraltar, we flew exercises out of the bases of our NATO/CEN-TO allies in France, Italy, Greece and Turkey. At the beginning of the tour we could also ring the changes by making fascinating inland navexes over the Libyan desert. All that, of course, came to an end with Colonel Gaddafi's coup in 1969.

"One of the brilliant things we had around the Mediterranean was this sort of trading scheme thing. There was a very easy supply of cured hams in Malta, but they couldn't get them easily in Cyprus (that was before the island separated). We were forever doing detachments to Cyprus as part of the coverage of the Mediterranean, since we were the only RAF maritime squadron in the area. It was generally thought to be a good idea, to boost the squadron funds, to buy a few hams out of them, fly them to Cyprus and sell them at a small profit. Of course, then in Cyprus we could buy up all the lovely fruit and vegetables they grew there, load up a pannier and fly it back to Malta, or better still Gibraltar, and sell it at a small profit. Then we could buy some more hams and do the whole thing all over again.

"One time we were coming back from Cyprus with a load of fruit in the bomb bay, and a strange smell started to come through the aircraft. We thought that perhaps the bomb-bay heating system had broken down and was causing trouble. The engineer got down, opened the viewing hatch to the bomb bay, and came to the conclusion that what we could smell was the result of us cooking a load of melons. The bomb-bay heating system was obviously not good at preserving fruit! I don't think we actually lost any money on the deal, but we wouldn't have been very popular with the squadron if we'd lost one load of fruit. I suspect we were quite a comfortably off squadron fund on the strength of all that, and it didn't discomfort anybody. It was the sort of thing that you were flexible enough to be able to do in those days; no questions were asked.

"Our CO was anxious that we should take cultural advantage of any of the detachments that we did as part of the NATO and CENTO set-up. We always took one more crew than we really needed, and if we went to Crete we'd go to Knossos and the war cemeteries there; we also went up to Larissa and the monasteries at Meteora. We also visited Turkey where we were able to visit Ephesus, and the beautifully preserved classical remains in the southern part of the country before the tourists arrived. So, as well as getting the job done, we saw an enormous amount of the Mediterranean culture too, it broadened our horizons and we thoroughly enjoyed it. Once while going to Knossos we gave a young Greek airman a lift so that he could visit his home for a day. He was on national service, so this was a pretty rare privilege for him. The whole village was waiting to greet us when we got there, and they were full of apologies for how poor the hospitality was that they showed us. But really, it was absolutely magnificent, the fruit, nuts, everything, and a certain amount of wine; it was a fabulous day out.

"I did a couple of the JASS exercises up at Ballykelly. We had an American lieutenant commander who brought a Lockheed P-3 Orion across. He was nominated to be the spokesman for one of the ground exercises where we went into simulators. His oratory was totally Donald Trump, several decades ahead of the time. He stood up and gave a magnificent briefing at the beginning of the exercise, and we all came out thinking 'Good God, that's wonderful! Can't wait to get on with this. What a splendid chap to have in charge'. Then we paused and thought 'Well, what exactly is it that we're going to do?' We all did our best to operate our simulators, but I think the directing staff finally had to call a halt to the whole thing, as the whole plot got tangled up; ships went in one direction, helicopters in another and so on. We retrieved it from that point. That was a fleeting experience of exercising with the Americans, generally they were very professional and wonderfully well-equipped compared with us.

"In the opposite extreme, we were always rather amazed with the French to see them wandering up the ladder into their Atlantique aircraft with great boxes of food, vin ordinaire, and goodness knows what else. I worked with them out in Canada on one of the Neatplay exercises. We'd picked up a snork or a periscope in very good conditions at very, very long range. We were homing in on it in the standard fashion, getting to about four or five miles, bomb doors open, running in, when suddenly there was this cry over the radio 'Cert sub! J'attaque!' An Atlantique appeared from a hole in the cloud about two miles ahead of us and got to the sub before we did. I suppose it was nine out of ten for élan, but about two out of ten for flight safety.

"One night, as we were flying in some pretty rough conditions overhead Rhodes, we were struck by lightning. In those sorts of conditions the Shackleton was quite an amazing sight, with blue rain running up the windscreen, and the props like eight great, blue Catherine wheels out there on the wings – very impressive to look at, but it wasn't wise to look at it for long. So the co-pilot and I did the right thing, turning up the cockpit lighting and focusing on the instruments. We were very glad we did. There was an almighty flash as lightning hit one of the homing aerials on the nose. Presumably it exited somewhere down the back end of the aeroplane. When we got back and inspected the aircraft the next day the aerial which was normally about 18 inches tall, was just a little stub like a molten candle about an inch high. That had been a very impressive sight, but the performance of the aeroplane wasn't affected at all. At certain times of the year, out there in the Med, you saw an awful lot of this heavy weather.

"I don't know what the height record for a Mk.3 Shackleton is, but towards the end of our time out in Malta on 203 Squadron I took one up to 25,000 feet. We were told to do an air test, which would include running both the Vipers for an extended period of time. We checked that the aircraft was equipped with oxygen, it was very light, and so we decided to keep climbing, and we cleared it with air traffic control. To begin with, that light aircraft with four Griffons and two Vipers going, climbed like the proverbial 'homesick angel'. It got a bit slow once we got up into the teens, but she was still just climbing when we got up to 25,000 feet, and because we were not pressurised, we thought that was where we would stop. We closed down one of the Vipers so that we could get a picture of the island without the jet-wake spoiling the view. That was it, no more climbing, we just had to slide gracefully sideways and downwards and immediately went into a descent. The controls became amazingly sloppy up there, although it was not very sharp on the controls at the best of times. We believed no one should have been able to get any higher than that – in a Mk.3 Shackleton of course!

"I thoroughly enjoyed my Shackleton flying, but I cannot allow myself to get misty-eyed about it. We would have to be blinkered not to realise that we were hunting sophisticated submarines with little more than World War 2 equipment. Our operators were able to get amazingly good results from what they had (and this often trapped the unwary opponent), but to the semi-permanently submerged (nuclear) submarine we could offer little threat. The aircraft preserved dated technology. The Griffon engine was a superb piece of design and workmanship, but we asked too much of it for too long. A water-methanol boosted take-off in a Mk.3 Phase III seemed almost an act of cruelty to the machinery, and also the men who sat through an initial climb rate of no more than a couple of hundred feet per minute. The Viper installation was, I am sure, quite literally a life saver – but while the wrinkles were sorted out, we still had to use water-meth and carry the weight of two useless jets. I can remember when we first took off with the Vipers, Old Fred exclaiming 'Christ, a thousand feet already?!' Nor was the airframe much more comfortable; hot in summer, cold in winter and a noise level you could feel. I think the story of the Shackleton operators needs to be told, but I fear that it might emerge as an indictment of post-war procurement as much as a story of those who flew it."

Andy White-Boycott – pilot

"No.38 Squadron had been disbanded in Malta, and the Soviets were threatening Czechoslovakia; suddenly we hadn't got much of a presence in the Mediterranean. It was decided that 203 Squadron at Ballykelly would be told to go to Malta at relatively short notice. A decision is made to send single men where possible to minimise family disruption – I was a bachelor. It was before lunch that I met my boss who told me I was posted to 203 in Malta. He said, 'Aren't you pleased?' and I said: 'No, for God's sake, I was a child there and have marvellous memories of the place, if I go back it will ruin everything.' He said: 'Don't be so stupid. Cheer up and we'll talk about it again after lunch. I'll see you in the bar.' All my friends told me not to be stupid, so I changed my mind, joined 203 Squadron and went with them to Malta.

"I had to convert at Ballykelly from the Mk.2 Shack, with a tail-wheel, to the Mk.3 with a nose-wheel, and in no time at all we were off to Malta. I much preferred the Mk.3. Yes it was heavier and it was underpowered but on the other hand, it had the Vipers which gave it an edge. I could fly and land the Mk.2 quite happily, but when I came back to it after the Mk.3, I found it bloody awful. Perhaps I didn't have enough time on it, but I really didn't like the tail dragger.

"I was new on 203 Squadron waiting for a crew, but not to worry. I'm good at admin so I'll look after the dogs on the passage to Malta! What? Six dogs, which had to be looked after in Gibraltar, suitably sedated. By the time we got to Gibraltar the next day, the sedation had worn off and we had these bloody dogs wandering up and down the aeroplane. One of them managed to get his head into one of

203 Squadron Mk.3 phase III WR989 K in June 1970. (Andy White-Boycott)

the photographs when we arrived.

"Malta was fantastic. We were in the sun, we had a job to do, a young squadron with two Canberra squadrons as competition, lots of bachelors, and it was a great time. The downside of it was that the rest of the Shackleton fleet was converting to Nimrods, so the MOTU/OCU had closed down and hardly anyone new was being posted in. I realised that as there was no-one moving on, I was to be a co-pilot for the duration, but that was a small price to pay for being in such a brilliant place. Day-to-day work there was totally different from Ballykelly. The squadron was not part of the station and we were not one of three similarly equipped squadrons. The morning brief in station HQ was not maritime-orientated and so we hardly ever went to it, we were doing our own thing. If we weren't flying we pitched up at seven in the morning, and in the summer we'd finish by about 13:00 or thereabouts. It was a glorious routine and, in the summer, you'd expect to be on the beach at Kalafrana where I had a ski boat – I was hoping to be on the water by two o'clock. It was work in the morning with the afternoons off. If you were flying, and we did a lot of flying, then you flew as required.

"There are lots of entries in my logbook showing aircraft going unserviceable, or being diverted to different places. You couldn't really anticipate an engine problem. Engines were over-speeding as a result of transmission unit failure; that was always a worry. We always did our pre-flights very thoroughly; typically I would look very carefully at the underside of the wings or fuselage. On many occasions, I'd find fatigue cracks. The ground crew would just drill out the end of the crack and we'd be all right.

"In the spring of 1970 elements of 203 Squadron deployed to Souda Bay, Crete, for Exercise Epic Battle. The Souda detachment became an annual event, within which the bizarre seemed commonplace, and marked the beginning of my association with the US Navy. We, with Gordon Fennell as captain, were the (base) ops crew for the exercise, thus I was well placed to liaise with our allies. This meant specifically the US Navy P-3A detachment, who were camping, literally, on the other side of the Souda Bay runway. Their arrival was followed by an open invitation to fly in a P-3 Orion. At such short notice other engagements ruled out all but me. I accepted and agreed to meet the VP5 Squadron crew on the 'ramp' (or in 'Britspeak', loading area or apron) the following morning at 06.00.

"On arrival I was impressed by the relaxed informality, I found it impossible to differentiate between ground and aircrew, or even to identify the officers. Thankfully, someone broke off to greet me, and to show me to my intended position in the starboard beam. Half an hour later, two further individuals loom out of the dark. I recognise Frank, the officer who issued the invitation, he is also the PPC (patrol plane commander – captain to me).

"'Hi, Andy – welcome aboard – say do those wings mean you're a pilot?'

"'Yes.'

"'Gee that's great – our 3P is off sick, so the 2P does tactics, and you're the 2P!'

"Not much of this brief exchange makes sense – what are 'P's' and where are the navigators and AEO? I dare not ask. It soon becomes clear that 'P's' are pilots and that the P-3A has a complement of three, one of whom doubles as a navigator. In addition, there are an engineer and an armourer (both from the flight line), and three sensor operators. Significantly the complement does not include a navigator, or an AEO!

"As yet I know nothing of the sortie – if the main brief was to have been at 06.00, we must surely be running late. After dumping his kit Frank summons all present for a brief, not in ops, but grouped around the P-3's rear door. It is succinct: weather good, flight time eight hours, operating area north of Crete, route out and back direct, call signs, emergency drills, the task – two CASEX (combined air-sea exercises) with Greek submarines, questions?

"I start forward for the co-pilot's position, proud yet apprehensive of my new responsibility as 2P. There are no wing spars to clamber over, no navigators to squeeze past, no hatches in the floor, no Very pistol or sextant to crack my head – so far so good. The pre-start checks have begun without me. Conducted off intercom, the checks are delayed as the engineer moves his seat back to allow me past, further delayed as he helps me move my seat forward, stopped completely as he fastens my harness, and deemed complete as the captain starts the engines without either of us. Frank gives me a chance to redeem myself when he tells me to 'call for taxi'. How can I? I have yet to find a microphone, let alone the intercom or radio. Again the engineer has to direct me to the hand mike, selector box and radio. Too late as Frank has made the call and acknowledged the directions. We are now making up lost time in a high-speed taxi for the runway. It's clear that a P-3 can be operated by one man.

"The pre-take-off brief includes my duties, '2P call airspeed', and 'Rotate at 80 knots'. I try to acknowledge on the newly found intercom, but am reminded that all flight-deck drills are conducted off intercom. Significantly, I am not asked to make the radio call for 'take-off', Frank is all too aware of my inability. Now, for the first time, I study the assortment of flight instruments. Time is short, we are already accelerating and I have yet to find the airspeed indicator (ASI). Thankfully a needle, bottom left, moves off the stops – it has to be airspeed.

"'Airspeed' I call, tentatively, and then as the needle passes 80 'Rotate' – this with more confidence. After the briefest glance at his ASI, Frank rotates and poses the next problem 'Gear Up'. Once again my eyes sweep the likely area around the throttle quadrant – no sign of the familiar three greens, or a lever marked 'gear', let alone 'undercarriage'. After the briefest pause the engineer's hand moves to the appropriate lever (surmounted by two imitation wheels!) and moves it up. There is no request to raise the flaps as Frank quietly makes his own selection. At this stage I would happily have jumped, presuming that I could unbuckle the harness, move the seat back and find a parachute.

"The brief transit to our operating area is interrupted by a foreign voice with our call sign, and that of our Greek playmate. I instinctively respond with 'Authenticate Whisky Bravo' while looking for the authentication table (there isn't one). Worse, the whole crew, most of whom are now on the flight deck, are looking at me with mounting curiosity. Fortunately the playmate responds with a single letter and skips over the embarrassment of requesting our authentication. I suspect that the submarine is anxious to get his set piece rendezvous message launched. It soon follows – slow and deliberate. Having mastered the radio I copy the message and acknowledge.

"'Yukon 245 degrees' calls our Greek.

"'What the hell is he on about?' asks Frank.

"'He wants a rendezvous. Come on to 245, if we fly down that bearing we should pass directly over him.'

"'How can you be so confident?'

"'I can't but the sub has got a bearing on one of our transmitters, and he is following the ATP format.'

"'What the hell is an ATP?'

"And so the MOPs (maritime operations) lecture starts. As it happens I find the CASEX manual and the criteria for our intended CASEX, in a flight bag. When it is opened on the radar crate at the back of the flight deck, the mysteries of NATO begin to unravel for the crew. It takes three attempts to get our first visual 'on top'. The first run is simply too rushed. The next opportunity is lost behind a windscreen of salt – the suggestion of spraying (washing) and wiping is deemed original. The third, after a long steady run in with a clean windscreen, is rewarded with an excited visual before the 'Dike' call (the submarine calls 'Dike' as the aircraft passes overhead. This allows the two participants to lock their relative navigation systems). The passive Jez sonobuoy on the datum yields little – in fact nothing. I venture to suggest that in a similar situation a Shackleton crew would lay an active sonobuoy pattern, and keep the submarine at periscope depth until confident of holding contact. 'Say that's a good idea, Andy – can you fix it?' The Greek is happy to oblige, and we are soon embarking on a productive active CASEX. I am not in a position to see how the data is handled, as their SSQ-47 'pinger' buoys are non-directional. Suddenly the Shackleton's directional active 1C sonobuoy, with its lighthouses and light table seem state of the art. Attack criteria is a long time coming.

"For me, the sortie just gets better and better, I know about CASEXs, I know about diesel submarines, I know the value of a visual lookout. I enjoy the enthusiasm, and mounting respect of my US colleagues. I am kept firmly attached to the radio for the remainder of our time on station. My reward is to fly the P-3 back to Souda for a couple of approaches before Frank makes the final landing.

"What do I make of my VP5 flight crew? I have enjoyed their hospitality and trust, but am surprised (appalled) at their ignorance of NATO procedures and diesel submarine capability. And why no navigators or AEOs?"

"Six years later I awake to find myself an exchange officer with the US Navy, serving as patrol plane commander with VP45 equipped with P-3Cs. The standard crew now includes two NFOs (naval flight officers, navigators by another name). I have come to understand why the USN uses national procedures in preference to NATO's. Of what relevance are NATO's procedures in the Pacific? I have learnt too, that USN ASW training concentrates on the SSN/SSBN-type threat; diesel submarines are a low priority. My USN colleagues view co-operation with friendly submarines on 'air-sub barriers' as an esoteric ASW opportunity for 'blue on blue'. My final six months with VP45 are to be a deployment to Sigonella, Sicily. With my new understanding of USN priorities, I returned to the Med determined to command a VP crew which was exemplary in its execution of NATO procedures.

"I completed a full tour on 203 Squadron, but clearly we knew we were going to be replaced by the Nimrod. Essentially, a completely new batch of people came out to form 203 (Nimrod) Squadron. In 1971 Dom Mintoff was the Maltese prime minister and he was going through an anti-British phase, and we were 'persona non grata'. We still operated the Shackletons out of Malta, but on a reduced scale and several of the aircraft moved to Cyprus. When the Nimrods arrived they went straight to Sigonella in Sicily as their operating base. Basically the transition from Shackleton to Nimrods was messy because we were having a tough time. The Shack aircraft were being flown back to Bitteswell and other places to be scrapped. It was an untidy end. Eventually, most of us then went off to enjoy another life on Nimrods.

"The whole thing about flying the Shackleton was that it was enormous fun. It was a crew of people who largely got on very easily with each other. As a squadron we were very stable – no-one left Malta and no-one came out. Everything in the aeroplane revolved around being effective against submarines, which we practised endlessly. We would get a radar contact at 14 miles, ten miles, five miles, whatever and then go to 'action stations' and run in on the radar target, dropping sonobuoys, depth charges or torpedoes. It was a dance, a beautifully choreographed dance, and at night the drama was enhanced by all the pyrotechnics going off. The illuminants were shot out of the side of the aircraft (24 of them in rapid succession), and really lit up the sea but gave a treacherous shadow or tilt to the horizon. The pilots could get disorientated if they weren't ready for it. The bomb aimer would pick out the target, which was usually a splash target (which looked like a submarine snorting), and was towed by a high-speed launch. On gaining a radar contact the captain would make the decision to either keep the radar on and close with the target, or switch the radar off and close with the target 'blind'.

"When we turned the radar off (blind homing), we'd turn it back on at three or four miles. A submarine could detect our radar, and assess the signal strength and rate of bearing change. A strong signal would be a 'danger level racket', and a steady bearing would indicate that we were closing in. A blind homing denied him these danger signals. As soon as the radar was back on he would know for sure that we were running in for an attack. If he had been foolish enough to stay on the surface he had very little time to evade. Radar homing was the basis of pretty well everything and, as you ran in, all sorts of things were going on in the aircraft. The radar scanner went down to the 'attack' position, which was something like 12 feet below its retracted position. This gave a better arc of view as the wing lowered in a steep turn, and the radar operator was in effect driving the aeroplane. At a certain stage the bomb doors had to be opened. It was great as the depth charges or torpedoes were dropped and the illuminants and photo-flashes went off, followed by sonobuoys and their markers of smoke and lights. Great choreography, there was a lot going on, along with a terrific smell of cordite.

"On one occasion the radar got stuck in the attack position, due to a self-induced hydraulic failure when we had to use emergency air to blow the wheels down into the locked position. One of the side effects of that was having used the emergency air, you then found you couldn't reposition the flaps, and if the radar was up it started to go down. The solution was to attach a ditching rope to the scanner in its well, pull the bloody thing back up again and tie it up. There was some scope for embarrassment!

"It's hard to believe now but when we needed to call the tower for take-off, landing or approach, we'd use UHF or VHF, but once we'd left the airfield we'd just forget about the radio. We had a radio operator behind us but everything he did was on HF and probably long-wave as well. Under certain circumstances this required an aerial to be trailed below the aircraft, unless you were going down to low level, in which case you certainly needed to wind it back in again, otherwise it hit the sea. The navigators used drift meters, which had a rubber eyepiece. Our jape was to blacken said eyepiece with boot polish or something similar; the unsuspecting navigator or other crew member would get a black eye. Another game, especially during an instrument rating when many of the crew got bored, was to run up and down the fuselage to upset the trim. In the tail, where some of the sound-proofing material had been removed (to reduce weight), it had exposed some of the control wires. These were given a tweak, which would certainly upset the pilot up the front.

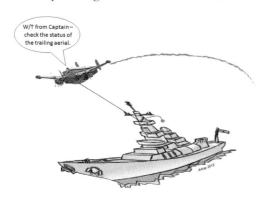

W/T from Captain—
check the status of
the trailing aerial.

"Going back to the engines. On one occasion either number one or number two wouldn't start. As we weren't at a Shackleton base there were no facilities. What to do? The next thing we knew the flight engineer was out on the wing, armed with a big hammer, lifting the engine's cowling. He seemed to be making some well-aimed blows at

Trailing aerial. (Rob Knotts)

the starter motor, and after that it started! There was another method of starting a reluctant engine, and I'm not really sure if this was fact or not. You would wind a rope around the prop boss and attach it to the back of a Land Rover which would then be driven at 90 degrees to the engine centreline, and the bloody thing started. I am not sure whether we were simply talking about how we might do it but, on the other hand, the engineers were great guys.

"During things like instrument ratings the examiner would always fail an engine on you, and then wait to see how long it took you to realise that No.3 wasn't doing its stuff. This wasn't always easy to spot because you could cut the fuel off, but the constant-speed system kept the prop going at the same speed. When you put the power back on you waited to see which way the aircraft was yawing. We had lost power somewhere, so then you had to look to see whether it was No.3 or No.4. Then you'd put No.3 up – nothing happened, so you'd put No.4 up – you started to yaw. Then you knew it was No.3 that was out. The examiner would have put his hand up behind us and given a signal of three fingers or four (or whatever), as a sign to the engineer to cut the fuel to the appropriate engine. We tried to see what his hand signal was but it usually took me by surprise. The Viper engine on the Mk.3s was a bit of an embarrassment really. It got so hot you could only leave it on full power for five minutes or so."

By 1971 the clock was ticking on the Shackleton fleet and the aircraft were getting very tired. In September that year severe damage, due to rat infestation, was discovered on MR.3 WR986, and deemed uneconomical to repair, so it was scrapped on site.

In October 1971, 203 Squadron finally re-equipped with the Nimrod MR.1. It remained at Luqa as the only Nimrod squadron to be based overseas, an indication of the importance still being placed on maintaining an MR presence in the Mediterranean to counter the growth of the Soviet Black Sea fleet. The squadron was finally disbanded there on 31 December 1977 and, like so many other Coastal squadrons, has not been re-formed since then.

RAF Luqa continued to exist as a staging post until its final closure on 31 March 1979. This followed a UK government decision not to renew the lease, as the new payments demanded by the Maltese government were considered to be excessive. During the final years 8 Squadron from Lossiemouth had occasional deployments to the island, thus continuing an RAF presence. The RAF facilities have since been absorbed into what is now a substantial international airport on the site.

CHAPTER SIX

'INTO THE REMOTE PLACES' – RAF KHORMAKSAR, ADEN

RAF Khormaksar was first used in late 1917 when 31 Squadron detached there from India to form the Aden Flight with a few Henry Farman F27s. They were joined the following year by 114 Squadron also with F27s plus some BE.2es. Following a period of inactivity, the station came back into use in 1927, and thereafter became increasingly busy with a variety of squadrons employed on colonial policing duties. Wartime use included convoy patrols and anti-submarine work by 203 Squadron, using Blenheim IVfs, 8 Squadron Vickers Vincents, and 621 Squadron with Wellingtons on MR work.

After the war on-going operations against dissident tribes in the region ensured that Khormaksar had a major role to play, and it quickly became one of the largest stations in the RAF. No. 8 Squadron continued to be a major player with Tempests, then Vampires, Venoms and finally Hunters. Three-quarters of Middle East Command aircraft were based at Khormaksar, which was a joint user airfield as it was also Aden's civil airport. The RAF also provided airfield, navigational, meteorological and communications facilities to the civil airlines. Shackletons from UK-based squadrons were detached there from time to time, but a permanent presence was established in August 1957 when 37 Squadron and its MR.2s moved in from Malta.

On 18 January 1963, the colony of Aden was incorporated into the Federation of Arab Emirates of the South, against the wishes of North Yemen. The city became the State of Aden and the Federation was renamed the Federation of South Arabia (FSA).

Bill Tyack – navigator
"Colonial policing came to be one of our major roles. Bomber Command Lincolns were available to support ground forces in the Arabian Peninsula up until 1956, but that year the task was passed to Coastal Command. After working up in the new role 42 Squadron

Aden, with the crater at the top of the photograph and RAF Khormaksar bottom right. *(Dave McCandless)*

No. 37 Squadron MR.2 WL752 over Aden Protectorate. (Bill Tyack)

sent a detachment to Khormaksar, where they flew their first operational mission on 13 January 1957. From then on there was a permanent Shackleton presence in the area until 1971. No.37 Squadron was based there from August 1957 until September 1967. Other squadrons sent detachments to the region throughout the period, operating at various times out of Bahrain, Masirah and Salalah in Oman, and Sharjah in the Trucial States. The tasks were many and various: photo reconnaissance, communications relay, air observation, vehicle convoy escort, supply dropping, leaflet raids, and coastal reconnaissance to interdict gun running. However the aircraft were ultimately there to provide a 'big stick' in the form of more offensive tasks, such as bombing and strafing with the 20-mm nose guns. Some aircraft also carried a Bren gun in the starboard beam lookout position. Fifteen 1,000-lb bombs or 52 x 20-lb bombs (or an equivalent mixed load) could be carried at a time.

"By September 1957 the Shackletons had dropped over 530 x 1,000-lb bombs, and the focus of attention shifted from Aden to the Oman. Operations were centred on the Jebel Akhdar; routine targets were the dams and water systems needed to irrigate the tribesmen's crops, but specific attacks were also made under the direction of forward air controllers. This campaign lasted from August 1957 until February 1959. During this period Shackletons flew 429 sorties dropping 1,500 tons of bombs and firing 700,000 rounds of 20-mm ammunition. There were further short-term bombing operations in 1960, 1961 and 1962. During 1964 operations became focused on the Radfan, with Shackletons mainly undertaking harassing operations by night, dropping small bombs and flares. Things were relatively quiet after this and 37 Squadron was disbanded in 1967. However, a permanent detachment, mainly sustained by the MR.3 squadrons from Kinloss and St. Mawgan, was based in Sharjah until late 1971 (see Chapter Seven). From there the crews flew anti-gun-running patrols, and practised medium-level bombing with 1,000-lb bombs. The coastal patrols (Operation Bronze) flew from the Straits of Hormuz south along the Omani coast at 100 feet above the beach and back again, conducting a visual search for signs of suspicious activity, which would be radioed to the Trucial Oman Scouts. I clocked up many hours in the nose-gunner's seat, which was the ideal lookout position, and a sighting by my crew resulted in a capture by the Trucial Scouts."

Above: 37 Squadron MR.2 WL744 B over Isfahan, Iran in 1965.
(Neville May)

Below: Briefing at Isfahan with Iranian officers and 37 Squadron in
1965. (Neville May)

Ray Carran – pilot

"Two crews were deployed from Gib to Aden on 21 May '64 to reinforce 37 Squadron's four aircraft and crews. Our mission was to carry out night-bombing ops up country, using a load of 15 x 1,000-lb bombs. These targets were where 'dissident tribesmen' were holed up, and the plan was to knock them out, or kill them, or at least interrupt their sleep so they would be easier targets for the Khormaksar Hunters and the ground troops. This seemed to be working until a political decision was made that, '1,000-lb bombs were inhumane', and we were to replace our load with 60 x 60-lb anti-personnel bombs. These bombs were a lump of coiled wire wrapped around an explosive device, set up to explode four feet above the ground (via a proximity fuse), and scatter shrapnel out to a distance of 600 yards. So much for being humane!"

Neville May – pilot

"Shackletons were used for observation of Hunter sorties as well as bombing operations. Air cover for the Dhala convoy (by Hunters as well as Shackletons) kept the lifeline open for the troops up-country and was quite interesting: flying down the gorge in a slow aircraft with dissidents firing from the hillsides (thankfully ineffectually) as the Shack went by.

"In September 1965 two Shackletons were detached to work with the rescue control centres at Tehran and Isfahan during Exercise Nejat I, a CENTO (Central Treaty Organisation) search and rescue exercise held in Iran. The aim of the exercise was to develop, exercise and increase the search and rescue capabilities of the

CENTO nations, with the participation of 37 Squadron and the RAF NEAF mountain rescue team from Akrotiri. A regular destination was Eastleigh, Nairobi, where the Shackleton's capacious bomb bay was loaded with panniers of York hams, steak and other scarce delectables, which had to be extremely quickly unloaded and distributed after landing at Khormaksar!

"In March 1964 a 37 Shackleton took a Leeds University volcanological team on an often very, low-level aerial survey of volcanos, especially the Red Sea's Jazirat and Jabal Al-Zubair islands. The Leeds team had studied Jebel Shamsan and explained that at some time in history the whole complete Aden volcano crater had filled with lava. Then it had exploded, probably dwarfing the cataclysmic 1883 Krakatoa event, and creating the gap in the eastern side wall of the volcano now occupied by the Crater township."

Above: Jebel Shamsan from a Shack in 1965. (Neville May)
Below: Bert Fuller, pilot (centre), Hugh Mackie air signaller (behind Bert) and Horse Freer signaller (with moustache), Khormaksar January '66. (Peter Kendall)

Peter Kendall – navigator

"Following my first tour as a navigator on 210 Squadron at Ballykelly, after re-mustering from air signaller in 1960, in August 1965 I found myself settling into life on 37 Squadron in Aden and continuing to fly the Shackleton Mk.2. I joined the crew of Flt Lt Bert Fuller, a very experienced pilot having been trained in Rhodesia toward the end of World War 2. Norman Tregaskis also joined Bert's crew, shortly after me, as co-pilot. My first month as second navigator was spent familiarising myself on medium-level bombing techniques, getting to know my way around the various desert patrols especially in and around the Wadi Hadhramaut area, and coming to terms with the overall security situation.

"Just before Christmas 1965,

after taking over my flat on the Ma'alla Straight, in preparation for the arrival of my family, a car just ahead of me exploded and burst into flames – all hell was let loose and the British Army (the 24th Infantry Brigade I think) were, as always, in control in seconds. The story was that a grenade had been thrown from the car but had been thrown back into it, killing all the occupants.

"In late April 1966 when Bert left for dear old 'Blighty', Trevor Davies took over as captain, handing over to Abe Lincoln a month or so after that. Abe, a New Zealander, had followed me out from 210 Squadron and was joined by Rod Hellen as AEO and Roger Denny as second nav.

"Just before Bert left in 1966, we were involved in leaflet drops, a frequent requirement as part of our internal security (IS) duties. We spent quite a bit of our time operating out of Salalah, Masirah Island and Sharjah. One of our 'one-off' tasks whilst operating from Salalah was to provide top cover to a group of American civilian oil company men, moving a 56-ton oil rig that had been off-loaded on the beach at Salalah, and needed to be transported up the escarpment north of Salalah, thence through the sand dunes to the site chosen to search for oil. The rig was on a sort of low-loader and accompanied by some caterpillar tractor earth-moving units to get the stuff through dunes and, moving dangerously slowly, especially up the Jabal al Qara escarpment, it was an easy prey for any rebel group in the vicinity. Unfortunately, our Shackleton was u/s on day two so Dakota KN452 from the comms squadron based in Khormaksar was flown up by Peter Norris to fill the gap, so to speak. I have two and a half hours on it included in the 44 hours and 50 minutes flown in May '66 recorded in my logbook! We were told later that no oil was discovered on that occasion and all the equipment was left to rust in the warm desert sunshine.

"Bert was still in the left-hand seat when we took WL795 out as a replacement aircraft to the Majunga detachment in April '66, flying WL961 back to Mombasa for an overnight stay before stocking up with fillet steaks, fresh vegetables and eggs in the bomb-bay panniers and returning to Aden. Ras Sharma, an AEO on the squadron, had a relative in Mombasa who ensured we received top quality provisions delivered on time and at competitive prices. Fu-

Fifty-six-ton oil rig climbing a pass in the Jabal al Qara. (Peter Kendall)

ture aircraft change-overs for essential servicing were done in Mombasa, so the guys stuck in Majunga and doing the Beira Patrols could have a spot of R and R, 37's Squadron fund could keep topped up, and its members enjoyed a spot of fresh food for a change. OC 37 Sqn

Vintage Marshall's towing tractor, Majunga. (Peter Kendall)

Ldr Derek Blunden, a navigator, along with a few other personnel were instrumental in setting up the Majunga detachment following Ian Smith's UDI being implemented. The 37 Squadron aircraft were soon augmented by detachments from UK-based Shackleton squadrons. Majunga is situated in the mangrove swamp area on the north coast of Madagascar and was not the healthiest place to be based, dysentery becoming something of a problem. The story goes that most of the guys used the lavatories just before lunchtime because at that time all the flies were in the kitchens! Aircraft parking was very restricted on the airfield and our ground crews used a vintage single-cylinder Marshall tractor (made in Gainsborough, Lincolnshire) to manoeuvre the Shacks in and out of the dispersal area.

"A good deal of our airborne time on 37 was spent patrolling the Persian Gulf from Sharjah, usually taking off around 08.00 hours and flying between six and nine hours on average. Anti-gun running and anti-immigration patrols were common, working with Royal Navy minesweepers to do any follow-up operations. We did the occasional maritime exercises with the Royal Navy both in the Gulf area and off East Africa and on one exercise, worked with an American fleet around the Straits of Hormuz.

"In October 1966 we had a break and took part in an SAR exercise Nejat II based in Shiraz in Persia. We only had one short sortie to fly and had the opportunity to take in the beautiful parks in the city of Shiraz, visit Persepolis, and enjoy a trip up to Tehran in a C-130 courtesy of the Iranian air force. Even in those days one could sense the anti-Shah feelings rumbling amongst the Iranian people. Despite water shortage (no rain for seven years) the grass around public statues of the Shah were being watered regularly and there was evidence of acute shortages of basic commodities. We were constantly being pestered for shoes!

"In May '66 another 'one-off' sortie was a combined operation to the north-east of Khormaksar involving 78 Squadron Wessex helicopters, 8 Squadron Hunters, a forward air controller and ourselves armed with anti-personnel bombs. The rebels were spotted, but because of the possibility of their being women and children amongst them acting as human shields, the air controller had no option but to call off the attack. We had to ditch our weapons in the sea and we heard later that two helicopters had been damaged by small-arms fire, one hit in the fuel tank and one hit in the gearbox, resulting in two federal soldiers on board being killed.

"In December 1966 we were called out on SAR to find a downed Army Sioux helicopter in the Radfan area to the north of Aden. The wreck was located and a recovery team dispatched. Unfortunately, the deceased pilot had been through Arab rebel hands reinforcing to us the need to take great care of our 'goolie chits'!

"We were issued with a Smith and Wesson 8-mm pistol and did evening security patrols around our multistorey flats throughout each night, on a well-organised rota basis, essentially to deter booby trap bombs being planted under our private cars. We also patrolled around our respective messes on 'film nights' when most members' attentions were concentrated on watching the films. One evening during a film we heard the scream of mortars heading toward the mess – everyone ducked as they hit the deck – the mortars had been intended to hit the station power station near the camp entrance but had overshot and exploded harmlessly on the station sports field adjacent to the mess. The story goes that when everyone ducked not a drink was spilt.

"The security situation began to deteriorate rapidly during early 1967, our children were taken to their schools in armed convoys and in May that year all families were evacuated back to the UK. Sadly many of the crew members serving on 37 Squadron, some on our crew, were subsequently killed in accidents during December 1967 and April 1968 back in the UK.

"My last flight before leaving Aden was on 22 August 1967 when we flew a night illumination sortie dropping sticks of 4.5 recce flares. The area was north-west of Aden along the then Yemen border. Sqn Ldr James was the pilot captain and we were passed ranges and bearings from an upward-beamed light set up in the mountains at a pre-determined position. The system worked well and we carried out a number of runs during the eight-hour sortie, being able to clearly see the rebels caught in the lit-up sky and suffering very accurate tracer machine-gun fire from the federal army units below us. We knew where to expect any AA fire so gave those areas a wide berth.

"All in all, a fascinating albeit challenging tour. The esprit de corps was very good too, despite the difficult, extremely hot and humid (not to mention noisy) working conditions. The ground crews, many on unaccompanied tours lasting up to a year, did a remarkable job ensuring we had a serviceable aircraft, armed up and fuelled at all times under the control and guidance of Mr Breedon, a well-seasoned warrant officer very experienced on the Shackletons. There were a number of splendid characters on the squadron at the time including Frank 'Nick' Nicholls, a pilot and the A Flight commander with whom we often flew. Geoff Greenstreet, a navigator and B Flight commander, Bob Nairn AEO and OC Squadron Fund,

Master Signaller Stanley 'Horse' Freer, Viz Nagan air signaller, plus many others.

"I returned to the UK just a few days before the squadron finally left on 7 September 1967. I joined 120 Squadron at Kinloss and was soon back to Sharjah on MARDET, the second time in 1969 as a navigator captain, finishing my career flying in the 'old grey lady' which had started as a fifth signaller back in 1958 on 42 Squadron at St. Eval."

Chris Dance – engines

"I was posted to 37 Squadron Khormaksar in December 1965. The squadron was short of manpower and needed engine and airframe tradesmen. It was not an easy life at Khormaksar because of the 24-hour guards. Plus, if you lived out in Ma'alla there were regular street patrols.

"The squadron itself didn't have a single role. The pilots had to do mandatory flying to keep their hours up, and we were also involved in preventing gun running; one of our aircraft was based at Sharjah most of the time. The squadron had the search and rescue role, but was also involved in the Radfan operations carrying out bombing runs to support the army. In 1965 the problem of the Rhodesian oil blockade arose, and 37 Squadron was the first squadron sent to Majunga, Madagascar. No.37 Squadron only had four aircraft; Shackleton Mk.2 phase II (no insulation or luxury galleys like the later 8 Squadron Lossiemouth Shackletons had).

"All aircraft faults had to be fixed on the squadron. During the Radfan operations the Shack, because it was so slow and low flying, was very vulnerable to any tribesmen's ground fire – they were pretty accurate, those tribesmen with their 'blunderbusses'. I distinctly remember one aircraft coming back with bullet holes near the navigator's position – the Hunters were a lot faster of course, so much harder to hit. Squadron armourers were kept very busy loading bombs and guns. Tribesmen attacked the squadron at Khormaksar with mortars, and they reported that all the Shackletons had been grounded. To prove this statement wrong, fabric patches

were put over the shrapnel holes, and searches made to recover pieces of shrapnel from inside the fuselage. The aircraft flew over Aden the following morning! [see also pages 196-97.]

"The Shack was not very reliable. On landing the flight engineer would rou-

37 Squadron at dispersal, Majunga. (George Masters via Dave McCandless)

tinely fill pages of the F700 with snags; the majority regarding airframes and engines. The engine snags were mainly magneto drops, oil leaks and problems with the props. Propeller translation units routinely had to be 'exercised' during flight, in order to prevent possible propeller overspeed.

"There was an aircraft, flown by Flt Lt Nicholls (a very good captain), which had an engine fire going into Nairobi; he managed to save the aircraft. He didn't dive to put the fire out, but stalled and starved the fire of oxygen [see Malcolm Elliott and Norman Lindsay's accounts on pages 190-191]. The No.1 engine had broken up; the crank shaft had come through the side of the engine casing – a major disaster. Manpower was a problem and more tradesmen were sent from Khormaksar. No.1 engine was changed and a new bulkhead fitted. The aircraft also needed a full primary inspection, which involved all trades. Following this work a compass swing was required. However, Nairobi civil airport authority did not want a dirty Shackleton on display. They didn't mind shiny Britannias, but they didn't want this old Shack anywhere to be seen. In the end the aircraft was flight tested and the compass calibrated in the air.

"After the air tests it was time to return to Aden. On the return flight the aircraft started to lose oil pressure on No.1 engine – the one that had been changed. The captain said that if the oil pressure fell any lower he would have to shut it down, which was done and the prop feathered. Shortly after that oil was sighted leaking back from No.3 engine's propeller, so the captain shut down that engine as well. The aircraft was now flying on two engines. This situation necessitated getting flight clearance to fly over Ethiopia. The flight clearance never came, so the captain told us to look out for flak. On the approach to Khormaksar fire engines and ambulances were alerted; fortunately the aircraft landed without incident. An investigation was carried out to find out what had gone wrong. It was found that No.1 engine's low oil pressure was only indicating an instrument fault. The oil pressure pipeline connector to the rear bulkhead had been wire locked, but not tightened. It was a technical error by the instrument fitters loaned by another unit. The oil leak from No.3 engine propeller was found to be because the inter-shaft seal had completely come adrift. In future, to prevent this happening again, the split pin (which locked the seal) was always fitted with the head of the split pin on the inside of the inter-shaft seal.

"Engine faults were mainly mag drops (indicating loss of power), but what was always feared was a mag rise, which could be very dangerous. Amongst other faults were oil leaks and coolant pump leaks. One aircraft had a fuel tank leak; this necessitated getting the aircraft into a hangar for a fuel tank change. It was a big task for a first-line squadron. The fuel tank change was carried out in a hangar called the overseas hangar. We asked why we couldn't get in the hangar before a stated time, and were told it was because the sea tide affected opening the doors. The land the hangar stood on was reclaimed from the sea, so when the tide was out the hangar doors could be opened, but when the tide came in the doors were jammed.

All available manpower, regardless of trade, was involved in the fuel tank change and subsequent fuel flow checks. Squadron aircraft stood outside all the time, so you can imagine the condition they were in. Aircraft wash facilities were not always available, besides which aircraft could not always be spared just for a wash.

"One incident that happened after landing and taxying to dispersal, was when a Hunter brake parachute was picked up by the propellers; this caused a lot of damage to the propellers and a bomb-bay door. A new bomb-bay door had to be sent out from the UK; this was another big task for an already very busy squadron. Doing all the out-of-phase servicing items (items which did not fit in with scheduled maintenance), added to the other regular tasks. Every 100 hours engine tappets had to be checked, and spark plug changes were sometimes awkward, especially the ones on the inner-engine blocks.

"The squadron disbanded in September 1967. The four aircraft were flown back to the UK via Tehran, Akrotiri and Malta. For the return flights some faults which did not affect aircraft safety had to be 'carried' (accepted). Our first stop in the UK was St. Mawgan; the green grass of Cornwall was a delight to see after about two years in Aden. Here tool inventories etc. were handed over, and after a night's stop the aircraft were flown to Shawbury where they were eventually scrapped.

"The skill and dedication of the aircrew on 37 Squadron could not be faulted. The ground crews also worked hard, often in trying circumstances, plus the 24-hour guard duties about every three days, which did not help. Ground crew on an unaccompanied one-year tour would volunteer for permanent detachments to escape the guard duty. Married personnel on two-year tours, living off the camp, had the worry of leaving their families in Ma'alla when they went on detachments.

"After saying farewell to the crews at Shawbury, my new posting was Linton-on-Ouse. My family were in married quarters at Dishforth. I travelled by train from Crewe to Thirsk, then on to York. A lady sitting opposite me on the train from York asked if I had been on holiday as I was very tanned. I said that I was returning from a tour in Aden. 'Is that in the South of France?' she asked!"

37 Squadron 1965 Ma'ala married quarters. (Neville May)

Malcolm Elliott – engines
"I was with 37 Squadron in Aden from 1964 to 1966; the COs while I was there were Sqn Ldr Ian Balderstone, a pilot and then Sqn Ldr Blunden MBE, a navigator. The engineering officer was Flt Lt Barry Wiggins, and there was a pilot named Ivor Gibbs. At about 2300 hours one night we

launched Ivor Gibbs and his crew for them to search for a yacht sailing from Dji-bouti to Aden. At that time HMS *Victorious* was sailing around the area (their Buccaneers were doing 'bolters' at Khormaksar) and when Ivor landed in the early hours I said to him, as a joke, why didn't he do a few approaches on the *Victorious*. His reply was 'I did 100+ deck landings during the war' – Korean I guess. I think he had been on a service exchange with the US Navy, and had flown a lot of hours in piston-engined Skyraiders, which he said were a very good aircraft, flying at 500 feet and hundreds of miles from the carrier. However, they didn't find the yacht, apparently it hadn't left Djibouti!

"In July 1966 Flt Lt Nick Nicholls and his 37 Squadron crew were beset with a persistent engine fire on a flight from Majunga back to Khormaksar, and were forced to divert to Djibouti. Nicholls was awarded a Green Endorsement for his skill in handling the situation. The subsequent report says that following the engine fire breaking out, he: 'Initiated a Mayday call and began to descend to look for a crash-landing area and reducing airspeed to avoid fanning the flames to greater intensity. The engine fire died down and Flt Lt Nicholls, considering the distance, facilities and favourable winds, decided to divert to Djibouti. However, the pro-pellers of the failed engine un-feathered themselves and continued to windmill, making it impossible to climb (the aircraft) to safety height. He therefore decided to divert to Nairobi, the only possible alternative, which itself offered the hazard of high elevation and high ground en route. To compromise between the dangers of shredding the wind milling propellers and overheating the operating engines, he reduced the speed to 105 knots, with take-off flaps set, and also reduced the RPM on the three live engines. He then flew varying courses calculated to avoid high ground with the aircraft gradually losing altitude. From the start of the incident it took more than three and a half hours to reach Nairobi, and this at night and IMC.'

"I had taken over the ground equipment inventory at short notice from a chap who was being casevac'd home (casualty evacuation). As time went by more and more ground equipment was sent to Majunga. I had a 'great' time trying to hand it over in turn to my successor. Actually it wasn't too bad because I was able to write off bits and pieces that had long been lost, or relocated. There was a Besson-neau canvas hangar on the inventory, which I couldn't find. Apparently it had been blown out to sea and lost some years before my time, but had never been written off. A lot of the ground equipment went down to Majunga, which we knew was unlikely to be returned, especially as it was being used by other squadrons. I man-aged to write most of it off, but not the Bessonneau hangar. Eventually, before I came home, I got it off the inventory, by converting it from 'hangars airframe' to 'hangers coat' and handing in a metal coat hanger. Implausible, but true!

Navigation instrument fitter **Norman Lindsay** *was one of three 37 Squadron ground crew onboard Flt Lt Nicholls's aircraft in the incident described above.*

"The ground crew were Chf Tech Danny 'Taff' Thomas, J/T Norris 'Nodge' Myers and me. We had flown down by Argosy to do an engine change. Danny and Nodge were engine fitters and I was nav inst. Why a 'Fairy' (nav inst) for an engine change you might well ask? Because Danny asked me if I'd like to 'volunteer' to help out is the answer. Having heard numerous tales of Majunga I was more than curious to see for myself. The job went well and the test runs were fine, so it was time to go 'home'. After a period of little rest all of us were quite tired, so after take-off we adopted the usual ground crew positions and slept.

"It was sometime later when I was fast asleep in the port-beam seat, when one of the siggies, Harry Patterson I think, shook me awake, and told me to go to my ditching position. I could tell by his face that it wasn't just because he wanted the seat for himself. I moved forward to the galley where Danny and Nodge were both kneeling on the bottom bunk looking out. I joined them to see what was so interesting, and was greeted by the sight of No.1 engine on fire with flames streaming from it.

"On arrival at Embakasi everyone gathered around No.1 engine as Danny and Nodge removed a couple of panels, which resulted in many metallic bits and pieces landing with a clatter on the ground. As there was nothing to be done to rectify the damage, 'Nick' Nicholls, the captain, decided we should head off in search of accommodation and get some rest. This involved stopping at a pleasant watering hole where the boss bought the first round, and several more followed before all of us finally got our heads down around five o'clock in the morning. Later that day we returned to the airfield to have a look around in daylight, only to find that members of the Britannia detachment based there had moved the Shack to a remote corner out of public view, because they were embarrassed. They were left in no doubt as to what we thought of their 'embarrassment'. The next two or three days were spent savouring the delights of Nairobi's Spread Eagle Hotel before heading back to Aden courtesy of East African Airways.

"As usual, official RAF reports tend to understate the severity of the situation, and technical reports are, by their nature, factual. The situation faced by Nick and his crew was very serious and potentially fatal. An unextinguished engine fire could have led to the ignition of hundreds of gallons of high-octane aviation fuel contained in the wings. If the fire had not blown itself out, Nick and his crew would have been forced to crash land, in very poor weather conditions, in a hostile terrain. The un-feathered propeller on the failed engine was also potentially disastrous.

"The variable-pitch propellers, as fitted to the Shackleton, were designed to be controlled by engine oil pressure and the increase pitch/feather line ran in the 'V' of the engine casing. In this incident, a connecting rod had snapped and punched through the casing severing the coarse pitch/feather line. With no pressure in this line the prop went to 'super fine' pitch causing a massive overspeed. This greatly increases the drag, and reduces the performance and handling of an aircraft with asymmetric power. In this case the windmilling propeller was on the No.1 engine, and the drag caused would present significant handling problems. In reducing the airspeed to an absolute minimum, and nursing the remaining three engines, Nick demonstrated exceptional skills in safely landing the aircraft at Nairobi. I still have the plaque presented to him by his crew. It simply says: 'To Nick – 29 July 1966 – Thanks'."

Alec Audley – wireless

"Around April 1966, I was summoned to the administration wing at Kinloss, and informed I was to be posted to 131 MU (Maintenance Unit) at Khormaksar in August. This was not welcome news as Claire, our first daughter, had been born ten months earlier, and Aden was in turmoil due to the activities of the Nasser-backed rebels. The National Liberation Front (NLF), and the Front for the Liberation of Occupied South Yemen (FLOSY), both wanted the British out of Aden and South Arabia. Still as the saying goes, 'If you can't take a joke you shouldn't have joined up'. The next two and half months were spent vacating our semi-detached hiring in Nairn. We then moved my wife Helen and Claire to a surplus married quarter, close to her parents and mine, at Castle Bromwich, Birmingham. This was the airfield where Spitfires and Lancasters were once built and tested. I joined 131 MU in mid-August, and was immediately confronted by 300 sonobuoys sitting in the sand, in vertical racks, outside the workshops. I immediately declared these supposedly serviceable sonobuoys as unserviceable. They were in need of a clean, a protected environment and immediate attention was required to bring them to a serviceable state. We formed a team of four, two working a day shift and two an evening shift, on alternate weeks. We brought all the buoys inside the workshop and commenced servicing them – they were sand encrusted. Luckily there were no immediate demands for them from 37 Squadron. An immediate perk of moving to shift work was the team's release from the regular weekly armed guard duties. These were necessary because of the NLF and FLOSY terrorist activities, which included throwing grenades at military vehicles and firing grenades into Khormaksar, trying to hit the power station.

"Serviceable sonobuoys were soon available, so we could meet 37 Squadron's demands. In November/December 1966, there was also a need for a Sonics specialist to join a 37 Squadron detachment at Sharjah when an exercise was called. Courtesy of 84 Squadron I found myself in a Beverley, along with a consignment of sonobuoys, transported to Sharjah. On arrival the sonobuoys and I were transported to a bunker at Sharjah bomb dump. I immediately started preparing the buoys and carrying out first-line checks on them. Because of the number of buoys we had brought this was a lengthy process. Staff at the bomb dump ceased work at 1300 hours, so they gave me the keys and asked me to lock the place up when I had finished. By the time I had finished it had been a very long day, getting up very early in Khormaksar to catch the Beverley flight, the flight itself and then carrying out the buoy preparation straight away. On reaching my allocated air-con-

No. 37 Squadron MR.2 C arrives at Sharjah. (Dave McCandless))

ditioned accommodation, I could have gone to sleep standing up!

"The following morning the detached Shackleton was being prepared for an upcoming night sortie. This meant I had to service the airborne sonics, as its calibration test function was not working correctly. A quick tweak of the modulation levels had it working as it should. In the evening the Shackleton, with the sonobuoys loaded, aircrew aboard and all four engines running, was ready for the night exercise to rendezvous with a submarine at sea in the Gulf. Then there was a shout of 'Radio' from the aircraft, the intercom was not working, and if it could not be immediately fixed the submarine rendezvous was going to be missed. I scrambled aboard, and headed for the floor underneath the navigator's table, removed the floor cover, gave the relevant black box a quick thump, and the intercom sprang into life. Cover replaced I made a quick exit from the aircraft, which then quickly taxied across the sand to the runway and took off into the night.

"On my return to Aden, Geordie Russell, a sonics colleague from Kinloss, joined the team. With the impending closure of all the stations in Aden, we set about preparing the sonics section for its move from Khormaksar to Sharjah. Geordie, who would be going to Sharjah, organised everything, preparing drawings for the required horizontal sonobuoy racks to be manufactured at Sharjah, and sorting all the sonics section equipment that would be transported there. My year's tour in the desert sun was coming to an end, and I was looking forward to returning to Helen and my young family. Kathryn, our second daughter, had been born in February 1967 whilst I was away. Coastal Command does not easily let go of its personnel, and my next posting was to Mountbatten Marine Craft Unit adjacent to Plymouth. Thus, my close association with the 10,000 rivets flying in close formation came to an end."

Simon Morrison – air radio

"I loved flying in the Shackleton whenever the chance arose, which was not often. When a 37 Squadron Shackleton was detailed to participate in an exercise in the Far East, I was assigned from 131 MU sonics bay to ensure the sonobuoys were kept in fine fettle. You can't imagine how crest-fallen I felt while at Changi when a rather vexed aircraft captain summoned me to his office. They had known from intelligence that a submarine was nearby, but all six sonobuoys they dropped that day had failed to detect anything at all. Having told me that he would ensure an adverse report was recorded, I spent a restless night worried sick, what could I possibly have done wrong?

"The following day, to my great relief, he approached with a huge grin and slapped me on the back saying, 'Don't look so worried corporal, it wasn't your fault, nav re-checked the coastal charts last night and found the sea depth was only 30 feet in that area'. Now the hydrophone detector extended below surface on a 60-foot-long cable before it rotated to sweep for submarines, so little wonder their monitor said no rotation, each hydrophone having been embedded in mud! The crew had a good laugh and from then on it was a great trip, and the captain even invited me to fly the 'plane for an hour on the last leg back to Aden. They turned out to be a really friendly crew and that was the nicest apology I ever had.

"The radio bay had about 50 blokes. During my two-year tour one was killed by a grenade and two were shot in the back of head. We worked from 7 a.m. to 1 p.m. and my afternoons were spent at a desert air strip at Bir Fahdl, five miles north-west of Khormaksar, flying gliders. Luckily IEDs (improvised explosive devices) were less advanced back then. On 21 February 1965 I was startled by an explosion which popped open all the inspection panels on the T.21 two-seater, just prior to take-off. I jumped out to see the bomb had luckily blown skywards so there were no casualties other than our ear drums, and the rear windscreen was blown out of Bill Harrop's Fiat. A grenade bounced off Terry McAlinden's shoulder one day on his way home. The Land Rover he was in was passing through Sheik Othman, and the driver, Ben Braine REME (Royal Electrical and Mechanical Engineers), stuck his foot down to distance themselves before the grenade went off, injuring several Arabs passing by. Nice quiet Aden!"[7]

Dave McCandless – engines

"I was in Aden from February 1966 until the end of 37 Squadron in July/August '67. I was part of the ground crew that flew the four aircraft back to Shawbury via Tehran, Persia as it was in those days, to be scrapped. I didn't have my family with me there (my new wife was still in Majunga, Madagascar), however, Chris Dance and his wife Mary were out there during the troubles. Families in Ma'alla were being grenaded and shot at, and then in March 1967 were repatriated in Operation CallFam – leaving Ma'alla a ghost town.

"I had just about acclimatised when I was sent on detachment with one of our Shacks for two weeks at Salalah. For the most part it was idyllic. When we were off shift there were no guard duties and we had a ride to the beach with an Arab bodyguard, to take a swim in the crystal waters of the bay on most days. However, one day our relaxation was broken by the news that a sandstorm was not only forecast and on its way, but was imminent. So, caught a little off guard, we franti-

7. www.radfanhunters.co.uk and Sandy McMillan

cally rushed about, dressed only in our shorts, to blank off the engines and make sure that the aircraft were turned into wind. Then it hit us, the sand stinging our exposed faces, legs, midriffs and backs as we finished blanking off the aircraft before blindly rushing into the line hut to weather out the storm.

"Then .... BANG!! followed by another BANG!! against the line hut. When we looked out of the window we could not believe our eyes; two empty 45-gallon oil drums being tossed around in the swirling gale. As we were taking this in, another drum headed our way in full flight, landing short and rolling towards us. The wind had suddenly changed direction and was picking up empty oil drums from the station POL (petrol, oil and lubricants) store. Initially in a downwind direction relative to us, it had now changed to obliquely upwind. If it kept changing direction, it might eventually blow its 'missiles' full astern into our aircraft.

"Then some brave person made the decision that we would have to go out into the stinging, swirling sand – where visibility was down to ten yards – and deflect these 'missiles' away from the aircraft (Health and Safety read no further as what happened next was beyond belief). Six of us donned our shirts and masked our faces, leaving the hut armed with crew room cricket bats, a dustbin lid and a couple of brooms. As two lookouts manned the cabbed tractor, which had been parked side-on and directly behind the aircraft for maximum protection, the other four sheltered behind it. Then two (including me) ran to the left and two to the right, depending on the shout from the cab. One oil drum hit the tractor and lodged under it, whilst we managed to deflect another one on the left from hitting the tailplane, but it continued on, hitting the main undercarriage wheel before bouncing off into the distance. Meanwhile the team on the right had deflected two drums that flew their way. Through good fortune, and a bit of skill, none of the drums struck the aircraft. We all survived unscathed, although we were much redder from the sand-blasting. Lawrence of Arabia – eat your heart out!

Aden Wing Hunters formating on a 42 Squadron MR.2. (Bob Lyall)

"The terrorists up country hated the Shacks. Whilst the Hunters came and went in a matter of minutes and everyone simply took shelter in the caves, the Shacks could stay on station for hours. They would poke their heads out only to get bombed with one of the 22 bombs on board. Also, because the Hunters had to go in low, some of the terrorists used to perch on the mountaintops and shoot down onto them with rifles. A number of times I was dragged off Shacks (as I had worked on Hunters), to change an engine because a bullet hole had been found on the top of the fuselage after a flight.

"I was on the pan when nine bombs came raining down on the airfield, fired from homemade drainpipe bombs situated on the causeway. The Six Day War had been and gone; though there was a heightened state of tension. Our wives and dependants had been sent back to the UK, and living-out personnel had been brought on to camp. The natives were definitely restless. It was a quiet Sunday morning, and the only flying on 37 Squadron's programme was 'manders' for one of the aircrews. As not much was involved it was thought OK to allow an armourer sergeant (me!) to be NCO i/c Duty Crew, with a couple of responsible adults (i.e. corporal fitter and a corporal rigger) on hand to show me where to put my 'X' in the F700. The duty crew went out on to the pan to do whatever they had to do (I believe there was an engine run involved). I was left in charge of the squadron office (probably the first time I had been in there) with the red telephone to ops up at Strike Wing HQ.

"I was idly reading through the list of punishments on offer for any false entries made into the F700 when I heard a bang, followed by a dull thump. 'What the f***!', only to be stopped nano seconds later by a louder (much louder) bang, followed by a thunderous thump. This was accompanied by the sound as if all the cats in Khormaksar were doing a clog dance on the hangar roof. I ran out of the office, through the hangar, and out onto the pan, only just avoiding 'Death by Land Rover' as the squadron vehicle came hurtling into the hangar. The ashen-faced duty crew were clinging on like KD limpets (would my demise have been attributed to 'friendly fire'?) We all piled into the office where the crew talked excitedly, and loudly, about being shelled/bombed etc, all the time puffing nervously on their fags (even the non-smokers). Just then the Tannoy came to life and a voice told us the camp was under attack and all personnel should take cover.

"I showed my leadership qualities by promptly diving under the office table. About ten minutes later the red 'phone rang. By this time the lads had calmed down a bit (although I was still under the table). I gingerly reached up and brought the handset down to my ear. 'Hello,' I squeaked nervously, expecting an Arab voice to call on me to surrender (I already had a rather grubby white hankie ready). A voice on the other end, which I recognised as the squadron CO, asked, 'Is there damage to any of our aircraft? Are they airworthy, if not how long to get them ready to fly?' 'Err, I don't know, I haven't been to look yet' was my brave retort. There was an icy silence for a second or two, I realised I had not given the proper reply, 'Damn it!' I thought, there goes my BEM (British Empire Medal).

"'Why haven't you checked the aircraft for damage?' he demanded. Quick as a flash I had my answer. 'We were ordered to take cover Sir, we haven't been given the all clear' (a master stroke, I think you will agree under the circumstances. Who says that plumbers are slow witted?) A longer, icier silence, was finally broken by a 'humph', then the 'phone was put down, none too gently. 'Cowardice in the Face of the Enemy, Dereliction of Duty, Lack of Moral Fibre, Conduct to the Detriment of Good Order and Discipline', this was the sub text of that 'humph'. For weeks afterwards I checked my mail for any attached white feathers.

"Some five minutes after this conversation the door of the office opened, and in strolled the skipper (a Kiwi flight lieutenant) of the aircraft due to go on 'manders'. He was probably surprised to see all the duty crew in the office, with the NCO i/c cowering under the table, however, being an officer and a gentleman, he didn't comment. It transpired that he had no knowledge of the attack as he had been driving in from his quarters and hadn't heard the explosions or the Tannoy! 'I thought it was a bit quiet this morning', he remarked! He then asked if any of the duty crew had been wounded during the attack, which is more than the squadron commander ever did.

"The flight lieutenant sauntered out onto the pan 'to view any damage', with the fitters and riggers trailing after him. Eventually all the duty crew left the office except for me – I had come out from under the table by then. As time went on more members of the squadron arrived, so I relinquished my command of the duty crew, and slunk back to the familiar territory of the squadron armoury. I believe that there was a fair amount of shrapnel damage. The whole station turned out to patch the holes in the Shacks with fabric and dope (after sniffing for petrol). We then loaded the bomb bay with 1,000-lb bombs to go on a mission into the Yemen – to demonstrate that the terrorists' mission to destroy the dreaded Shacks had failed. It was being declared as a resounding success on the Yemen radio. So that was the Khormaksar mortar attack of 1967, not just under fire, but also under the table. In passing, it may well be that the mortars had been supplied by the British to the South Yemeni army!

"I was also out there during the crater massacre when Col Mad Mitch's men were slaughtered and handed back days later as, what the high commissioner disgustingly referred to, a 'peace offering'."

Nick Von Berg – 8 Squadron Venom pilot

"I was flown into the Eastern Aden Protectorate as air liaison officer with a wireless-equipped Land Rover to join a force which was to support a Sheikh loyal to the Raj. He was being threatened by a neighbouring Sheikh. The Levies were commanded by a colonel who was assisted by a rather pompous subaltern from a cavalry regiment. I brought a bottle of whisky for the colonel and a case of lager. Our pompous friend, stating that the El Aden Protectorate was dry, had nothing to share as a sundowner, so I offered him some of my grog, which he took a taste to!

"On reaching our destination and camped on a tall building, we were visited by a pair from the squadron who enquired how things were going. I told them all

was OK, but that there
was a 'Pongo drinking
all my grog!' The reply
was to be expected,
'Tough Nick, we'll
have a cold one on
your account when we
get back'. My reply
was unprintable. As
luck would have it the
station commander
was in the ops room
when they were being
debriefed, and when
he asked if they had

An 8 Squadron air liaison officer and his wireless-equipped Land Rover.
(Peter Goodwin)

contacted me they relayed what I had said. He then enquired if there was a Shackleton going up that way the following day. Having been assured that there was, he
said to tell the dispatcher to draw a case of beer on my account, and have it dropped
to me. The following day the sound of four Griffon engines announced the arrival
of a member of the 'Kipper Fleet'. I retrieved the package and on opening it there
was a note 'Dear Nick please return the package and the parachute – you may drink
the beer!' The subaltern said: 'Do you mean to say you chaps in the RAF just call
up on the radio when you run out of grog?' 'Yes Old Boy, we're organised!'"

Roger Ward – airframe

"In March 1966 I was posted to 37 Squadron at Khormaksar. This was probably
due to my Shack experience, although it was my first time on Mk.2s. I had a great
time and made many friends whilst on the squadron, many of whom I am still in
touch with, including Norman Lindsay and Davy Hamilton. While I was there I
did a long detachment to Sharjah, and also a short trip to Bahrain to fix a Shack
with a tail-wheel problem.

"Social life for the Shack ground crew, like most service personnel, depended
on alcohol. Besides the NAAFI, and clubs on camp, there were favourite pubs in
the local towns. Khormaksar had the Camel Club which was right next door to
Hunter Block, my billet, where most of the night time 'socialising' was done. There
was very little off camp at that time, due to security problems, The Rock Hotel was
an exception, but I was only there three or four times. Aden had good beaches at
Telegraph Bay, Elephant Bay and The Lido, and was a good place for snorkelling.

"Khormaksar had the worst airmen's mess (mess being the best term for it). In
the months I was there from 1 March '67 to the closure I think I only ate there
twice – except for toast and butter! Usually we survived on meals at the Camel
Club, down town at Khormaksar shops, or from our bearers, Seth and Ali, who

did a roaring trade in cheese banjos. There was great good-natured rivalry in the Camel Club between 37 Squadron Shackleton personnel and the 8 Squadron Hunter mob. I always thought it was poetic justice that 8 Squadron became the last RAF squadron to operate Shackletons.

"Towards the end before the close-down, I was on a 24-hour guard shift near the 43 and 208 Squadrons' Hunter Wing hangar. Sneaking a cigarette behind some sand-filled barrels with another guard, we heard 'Buzzzz ding...tinkle! Buzzzz ding...tinkle tinkle', we were being shot at. It was from such a long range that the bullets were hitting the hangar roof and rolling down, so by that time it was not worth making a fuss, we ducked down and finished our smoke. 24-hour guard duty came around about every seven days. Besides frisking locals entering the camp, we would find ourselves wandering around the tarmac, bored, with a big heavy rifle or 'riding shotgun' on a garbage truck driven by locals, picking up slops from the different messes. We would then escort the truck to the dump in Little Aden. I'm not sure that being in the cab of a truck with a weapon the size of a .303 rifle and five rounds of ammunition would be much of deterrent to an attack!

"Power cuts on the camp were common, usually only affecting the airmen's quarters, clubs and facilities, and leaving the officers' mess and tennis courts flood-lit. That was until a riot and mutiny in the barrack blocks around the Camel Club rectified the problem, and power was restored. It was no fun in +30°C with no fans, air conditioning or places to go to cool down or to eat and drink. Aden was originally a two-year posting, but I was only there for a few months before they closed the place down. I don't regret being posted there, it was bit rough but a good experience.

"When the squadron disbanded in September 1967, the parade was a fairly casual although sad affair. The Khormaksar clothing store had been one of the first places to close so most were dressed in scruff order. As we marched past the guard room we all chanted: 'I'll give you a song it won't take long, all coppers are

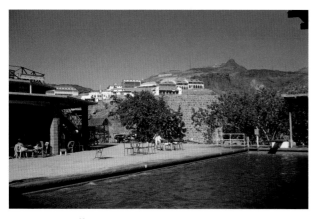

Steamer Point officers' club, Command HQ and hospital on the hill.
(Neville May)

b*****ds'...and contin-ued out of the gate. Most of us ground crew were posted to the Hunter Wing, 8 and 43 Squad-rons, who had been our main rivals at 37. It was quite a hectic time as the Hunters were always in action. Shortly before Khormaksar closed in November 1967, I was posted to Muharraq, Bah-rain, onto the 215 Squadron Argosy detachment. Known as 'Whistling Wheelbarrows', nothing ever seemed to go wrong with Argosies, they never seemed to break down airframe wise. It was just A/Fs (after flight), B/Fs (before flight) and replenishments etc."

Keith McDonald – pilot

"One very unpopular flying task was border patrol of the 'Empty Quarter' desert. This was a prohibited area to prevent gun-runners and smugglers. In the cool season it was simply boring, but in the hot season visibility was poor because of dust in the air, so we had to fly at low level. In turn that meant bumpy conditions and heat. The temperature in the aircraft was driven further up by the equipment, and the sun beating in. It sometimes exceeded 50°C. Flights lasted ten hours. Opening the windows just increased the noise and dust.

"For months not a thing was to be seen then suddenly we spotted a camel train. We dropped leaflets on them telling them to stay where they were, and the army would come and investigate them. They simply waved and pressed on, so we put a burst of cannon fire across their bows. They instantly leapt off their camels and legged it across the desert. But of course there was no protection, nowhere to run to, and after covering about 200 yards it evidently occurred to them too. So they dug down into the sand.

"We called up the army but as it was going to take them a good four hours to get there we just had to be patient. Eventually they came into sight. They were having a terrible time, as their trucks kept sinking into the sand; this necessitated furious digging if they were going to make it before nightfall – or ever. Finally they made it and surrounded the camel train. Having got the camels unloaded, they called us and asked if we knew what the loads were. Astonishingly we did not! It turned out that the camel train had spent two weeks heading from the coast to a salt hole in the desert. Having loaded up they were now on the two-week return trip. They did not appreciate our cannon fire as times were hard, and they were only going to get today's equivalent of 50p a bag. Apart from a stern ticking off about being in a prohibited area and as they were not carrying anything illegal or suspicious, they were allowed to continue. Everybody was so surprised by this revelation that we all forgot to ask the obvious question – why take salt to the coast which is littered with salt pans producing umpteen tons a day of the stuff?" [8]

Sandy McMillan – navigator

"It's about 06.00 on Friday, 20 July 1961, and just getting light. I park outside 37 Squadron's HQ, a cluster of long low buildings, and go in to meet the crew for today's sortie. Keith McDonald is my captain, a friend and flying colleague for the past five years; we best-manned each other at our weddings, and I'm a horribly inadequate godfather to his first child. We trained together on Lancasters at Kinloss,

8. www.radfanhunters.co.uk and Sandy McMillan

and then served in Shackletons on 206 Squadron in Cornwall – a fairish cry here from jolting up and down over stormy Atlantic wastes in search of Soviet submarines or lost mariners. At ease with each other's company, we have an enjoyable friendship and professional partnership.

"Peter is the co-pilot, and Rick the second navigator. Dodd the AEO and two of the signallers, Bas and Josh, are also about and Mike the engineer has just arrived. We've been crewed together for a month or so, have come to trust and respect one another's competence and are melding into the mutually reliant group that forms a good operational crew. Keith, Peter, Rick and I are officers and the others NCOs, but rank disappears in the air and we call one another by abbreviated roles – 'cap', 'eng', 'nav', 'sig'.

"A cheerful young Arab is circulating; this is Mohammed, always called 'Chico', who enterprisingly runs an unofficial snack bar for the squadron. He has a rusty fridge and a ramshackle table in one of the corridors, provides cold drinks and Nescafé, and makes delicious sandwiches with fresh local vegetables and rolls, and the strong cheese that's flown in from Kenya. 'Steem, Bebsi, cheese-tomato?', he offers us. 'Stim' is an Aden-produced range of soft drinks; they also make Pepsi under licence, but there's no 'p' in the Arabic alphabet. The squadron's catchphrase for 'Excellent!' is 'Very cheese-tomato!'

"Our tactical function in the Aden Protectorate is colonial policing, a term betraying many underlying attitudes. This 'uses operations which are psychological in intent to maintain or restore order within an area which is dissident or potentially so' (from the training manual I wrote for 37). 'It will be seen that air policing, aimed as it is at the preservation of peace, must be designed to avoid conflict, rather than seek it… all possible non-violent approaches are tried before resorting to the use of force.' Well, yes; but I'm less comfortable with this now.

"South Arabia, like Gaul, is divided into three parts: the vast and barren Empty Quarter, or Rub' al Khali, where we sometimes hunt for gun-running camel trains, and which we flippantly call the GAFA (the Great Arabian F*** All); then the coastal strip that runs from Oman in the north, turns the corner at Aden on the southern tip, and extends north-west to Jordan in the Red Sea. Our final operational area is sandwiched between the two, and is a great 'V' of mountains, rainy, green and fertile in the Yemeni west, dry, barren and almost impenetrable in the Aden Protectorate east. This is where we and 8 Squadron's Hunters attempt to subdue rebellious up-country tribes' people. In the protectorate there's no shortage of people who are 'agin the Guv'mint' for reasons varying from general cussedness and a tradition of arms, to a preference for levying their own customs duties on passing travellers. There are also people with an honest desire for independence from what they see as colonial occupation, but we in our Hunters and Shackletons don't know this then. We're told that the up-country political advisers have identified recalcitrants who are rejecting the benefits of British advice and its civilising influence. They must be taught lessons by destroying their property, while at the same time going to great lengths to avoid actually hurting or, God forbid, killing anybody.

"So we drop leaflets on these allegedly frightful baddies telling them that they must be good chaps, or 'government will not be responsible for its actions'. This splendid euphemism means 'Come in number 7, your time is up – or we'll huff and we'll puff and we'll knock your house down'. In both the Shackletons and the Hunters we have become adept at finding tiny villages, and even individual houses, in the harsh and confusing mountains and wadis of the protectorate. We've also got quite good at using rockets, or bombs, to modify the stone and mud buildings. Not every aircraft finds the right target, and not every target is actually struck; we mostly manage, thanks to directions from the political advisers on the ground. None of us thinks to question the underlying premise that military force will convince people to change their attitudes and actions. Nor the corollary, that if this doesn't work first time round then an application of greater force will persuade them to say 'Ah, I see that I was wrong all along'. These propositions now seem debatable.

"In the ops room this morning the briefer isn't the irascible wingco ops (known for mysterious reasons as 'Bubbles'), but the less abrasive squadron leader. He takes us through the form bravo that orders the operation. I start to fill in the ops bombing form that details who we are, what explosive devices we're carrying, and how they're disposed in the bomb bay. The met man tells us what he thinks the weather will be: an informed guess, since there are few local reporting stations. Sandstorms are an occasional hazard but he thinks they're unlikely today.

"Today's target is a village called Farar Al Ulya in the Wadi Sarar. We know it

No. 37 Squadron bombing up at Khormaksar. (Sandy McMillan)

well; we were there last week, and yesterday, to deliver its mail – a fluttering cascade of leaflets warning people to leave their houses lest ill befall them from the actions for which government declines to be responsible. It's near Al Qara, a spectacular village on a pinnacle, to which we've also delivered leaflets and bombs. We've been told that it's the home of Mohammed Aidrus, a serious dissident who needs to be taught a particularly sharp lesson. It's many years before I discover that Mohammed Aidrus is actually a member of the ruling family of Lower Yafa, and one of the founders of the South Arabian League. The league is a political, mainly peaceful, movement and is almost the start of the pressure for independence that later builds so strongly. It all ends in the bloody internecine battle between NLF and FLOSY, as British forces give up and escape; but that's all a long way ahead of us today.

"Nobody in our crew this morning knows that Mohammed Aidrus has been deputy ruler of Lower Yafa, being forced into the mountains because he refused to be docile and compliant. In 1960s Aden, as elsewhere, one man's terrorist is another's freedom fighter. We also don't appreciate that we're about to attack Muslim property on a Friday, the holiest day of Islam's week. For us, this morning presents a series of fairly demanding technical tasks: put a fully armed and serviceable Shackleton over a tiny village, that looks very like many others, and then destroy as much as may be with 15 1,000-lb bombs. Our view is apolitical, and focused on working together as a professional crew to do what we're told as well as we possibly can – the justification of military men everywhere. I have many close Arab friends, so have an extra perspective which is largely ignored by my crew and squadron colleagues. I've contrived to compartmentalise this so that I can continue to work professionally. It will be some years before the conflict between what I believe and what I'm doing forces me to resign.

"I'm first navigator, so can pull rank on Rick to oblige him to do the first transit navigation: his job is to get us within visual contact of Farar Al Ulya, not that easy in this ill-mapped and confusing terrain. I'll be bomb aimer today for the first seven bombs of the strike, relishing some demanding technical challenges. Rick will aim the other eight bombs; I pull his leg gently with 'Well, you need the practice' and he gives me two fingers. Finding Khormaksar again at the end of the sortie isn't difficult – we just keep going southwards until the land comes to a point. We chat briefly about the route; it's quite a short transit time, we flew it yesterday and the maps, such as they are, are already marked up, so no worries.

"Now we're walking out to the aircraft, slightly delayed by several small annoyances – a slow fuel bowser, late delivery of the rations box, a re-check to make sure one of yesterday's unserviceabilities has been fixed. The morning sun glitters off the sand and flashes from the windscreens of parked aircraft and passing vehicles; the day is warming fast. Ground crew and servicing vehicles cluster round our aircraft. WR959 is a Mk.2; 16 years old and came to 37 Squadron in October last year. It has just come back from a major service at Eastleigh, Nairobi. The cavernous bomb bay and pair of 20-mm cannon are ideal for 37's colonial policing role.

Shacks vibrate drummingly in the air and are noisy enough for 'Shackleton high-tone deafness' to be a recognised medical condition.

"The inside is a cramped corridor of scuffed metal, sharp edges and obstructions, cluttered with equipment and projections to stab, cut or bark the unwary. Modern air travellers might find it claustrophobic. It smells of a blend of glycol, engine oil, aviation fuel, hot aluminium, worn leather and young men, with just a soupçon of Elsan fluid. But Shacks are robust and solid, their four Rolls-Royce Griffons are a great comfort, and aircrew regard them with exasperated affection, trusting them to get everybody home, deafened, but safe. Keith and I had got used to the greater comfort and lower noise of the later Mk.3 aircraft on 206 Squadron, so returning to Mk.2s is a slight come-down for us.

"Keith is already walking round inspecting '959 in the pre-flight ritual of 'kicking the tyres' to check that we've got everything that we should have, and nothing we shouldn't. I climb the ladder into the back of the aircraft, and negotiate the obstacles down the long tunnel with the certainty of practice – left foot just here, side-step past Bas unloading the ration box in the galley, left hand grasps rack, vault over the main spar, duck roof projection. I stow helmet and nav bag on the navigation table, move further forward past the engineer's position and between the two raised pilot seats, dropping down into the nose to check the bomb-aimer's panel. All bomb selector switches off, jettison bars and clips in place; clamber back to the nav's position to check that his console is similarly safe, and his changeover switch set to 'bomb aimer'. Back through the aircraft, repeating the entry acrobatics in reverse, and walk under the open bomb doors to check the bomb load.

"The armourers who bombed up the aircraft at first light are waiting for me. I'm squadron weapons leader, so have a lot to do with these seasoned professionals. I've started a campaign to improve our bombing results and safety procedures, writing manuals and training people, and the ground crew are vital to this. I've been encouraging bomb aimers and armourers to get together more often to share problems and solutions, so relationships and standards are improving. I was astonished to turn up in a New Year Honours List a couple of years later. It was only a Queen's Commendation, which is as far down as you can get without actually falling off the list, but it's nice that people noticed what I was doing.

"The corporal armourer and I work through the bomb bay checking that the 15 thousand-pounders are on the allocated stations, and that they feel secure and aligned. Now I have to go back inside the aircraft again to check the camera in its floor housing aft of the door; yes, it's aligned for vertical shots, the circuits operate, the magazine is loaded, two test exposures fire OK. So I close the camera hatch knowing that we should now get high-quality photographs every time I click the switch. Now to repeat the obstacle-course back to the nose, so that I can work through the checks on bomb sight and bomb-dropping mechanisms. Lights flash when they should, the distributor arm rattles over, Connell pre-selector works, the bomb release checks out on test. Everything works, and the drum switch is back on 'safe except for jettison'. Nearly finished, with one more trip back through the aircraft and out to the armourer in the bomb bay. Together we pull the safety pins from their tail fuses thus arming the bombs, and I take charge of the pins to prove we've done it. 15,000 pounds of high explosive is now live and primed, enough to create a respectably large hole in the dispersal and make a number of eyes water. The corporal's responsibility now ends, and mine begins. He wishes me luck and sets off for his well-earned 'cuppa char'.

"One final time for the obstacle race. Keith passes me as I get back to the nav station, 'All safety pins out, bombing equipment and camera checked and serviceable' I formally say. 'OK', he says and makes for the left-hand pilot's seat. I settle into my seat beside Rick, who is checking through his instruments and gear, put on my helmet and plug in the intercom. This is noisy with the familiar litany of pre-start checks as the pilots and engineer work through their lists and make us ready for today's tasks. It's already very hot inside and everyone is stripped to shorts, desert boots and flying helmets. We're supposed to wear our flying suits, but authority sensibly turns a blind eye when people don't; heat exhaustion is not a desirable condition for operational crews. The two pilots' windows stay open until just before take-off, as does the rear door, but it makes little difference to the increasing heat. We're all darkly tanned, for none of us has heard of skin cancer and the aim on any overseas posting is to 'get yer knees brown' as soon as may be. We're also mostly slim, another effect of the heat; I'm a stone down on my, already light, UK weight and will stay that way until the end of my tour.

"Now the four Griffons are bellowing and we're taxiing, but the delays have lost us the coolest hour at the start of the morning and put us into the danger zone for

MR.2 WR959 F of 37 Squadron over Aden harbour, 10 March 1962. (Sandy McMillan)

engine temperatures. Everything has got much hotter in the 20 minutes since we first got into the aircraft. Ahead of me Mike, the engineer, raises his left arm to check something on his panel, and I see water running like a tap off the point of his elbow. There's a squadron competition for hottest Shack on the ground, currently held by another crew at more than 125°F. On the taxiway we're parallel to the runway and as we are pointing downwind the engines are breathing their own exhausts, so Keith, Peter and Mike are anxiously monitoring cylinder head temperatures. If we are forced to wait too long while others take off ahead of us we could start to melt Rolls-Royce's finest products. Luckily there's only one Aden Airways DC-3 in front of us and he's away quickly, so we're unimpeded.

"As we approach the end of the runway Keith seeks to save time and cool down people and machines. He tells Peter he doesn't want to pause to line up and hold at the end of the runway while we wait for clearance. 'Khormaksar, 959 requests rolling take-off', Peter says, and the tower comes back '959 clear for rolling take-off'. Bas slams and locks the rear door. We turn off the perimeter track onto the runway, Keith lines her up and opens the throttles full, punching everybody hard with the acceleration that always exhilarates me. '959 rolling', Peter says; the tower responds '959 roger'. All our 10,000 rivets thunder down runway 08 Left, and climb out eastwards over the sea.

"Immediately, the temperature inside mercifully drops as draughts blow through the leaky old aircraft; suddenly it's bearable! Wheels are up and flaps are in, power is back to normal climb, and we're turning port. 'Heading please nav', says Keith, and Rick responds '018 captain'; we straighten out on course and start climbing to the 8,000 feet above sea level that we'll need as our safety height for bombing. As the target area is about 60 miles away our transit time is less than half an hour. I unplug my intercom, grin at Rick, pick up a marked route map and go forward into the nose.

"We're over the sands of the coastal plain; Sheikh Othman and the road to Lahej are on our left, and we're just inland with the beach and coastal track on our right. I plug in my intercom again and relax; nothing to do for a bit except keep an eye on the terrain and be ready to help Rick if we start drifting off track. After five minutes or so the coast has curved away from us to the east, and I can see the cotton plantations of the Abyan delta and the villages down it to Zingibar. Jan and I were there not long ago, after an exhilaratingly hairy drive at speed along the beach with Sharif Hussein and a big party of retainers. Ahead is the abrupt division between the sand and the foothills of the mountains that rise up steeply across our track. As we pass over the join we level out at operational altitude.

"Most of our intercom speech is curt and business-like, with quite long silences, but today Rick says '18 minutes to target captain'. Then he says, 'Something hidden – go and find it – go and look behind the ranges! – something lost behind the ranges! – lost and waiting for you. Go!' A baffled engineer says 'Do what?' I cut in with, 'Don't you like Kipling?' Peter says 'He wouldn't know – he's never Kippled' which prompts Bas into, 'Ah, the old jokes are the best'. 'Enough, enough,' warns Keith, and we fall silent.

"A little later I spot a village we know and say 'Nav I've got Sarar on the port side, a bit too close. We're about two miles port of track.' 'Roger' responds Rick. He goes quiet while he calculates, then 'New heading 030 captain'; '030' confirms Keith and the Shackleton turns. We track over the mountains and steep wadis for a little longer. We're so close that I switch on the bombsight and make ready to run in. There's always a friendly contest between Keith and me to be first to spot the target, and today he wins with 'Target is visual – lining up'. Now I'm about to start directing us, so I say 'Bomb aimer, first run for target photographs and wind finding. Nav, stand by with WFA [wind finding attachment, a device that calculates local wind direction and speed from an accurately timed circuit]. Captain, stand by for timed WFA run.' Both acknowledge, so I start sighting for the run.

"Farar Al Ulya is a typical mountain village of about 20 mud and stone houses, crammed close together and perched on a mountain ridge – stray too far from your back door and you'll fall a couple of hundred feet. People build defensively here-abouts, preferring to look down on anyone approaching; it's also easier to shoot downhill than up. Such villages are hard to infiltrate from below; however it didn't occur to the founders that somebody might be able to command even greater height! The ground falls away steeply into the wadis below, and the slopes have been la-boriously terraced into long narrow fields a few yards wide for the villagers' crops. It's around 150 feet long by 50 wide, about one-sixth of a football pitch, so not an entirely easy target from 4,000 feet above. A few yards undershoot or overshoot, or a few yards left or right, and the bomb will explode deep in the wadis under the village; it's much easier to miss than to hit.

"There's nobody to be seen in the village, for they've responded to yesterday's leaflets by climbing up to the nearest mountaintops for a grandstand view of our efforts. They don't seem to have bothered to take their weapons either, for there are none of the little sparkles of muzzle-flash that we often see. Aircraft occasion-ally come back with neat little holes from ancient Martini-Henry rifles. One startled navigator realised he had narrowly avoided emasculation when he found a spent round embedded in his seat cushion. Wg Cdr Bubbles sometimes threatens us with rumours that the tribes have acquired Egyptian anti-aircraft weapons, but we've met nothing larger than .303 calibre so far. We don't know at the time that Stephen Day, the political officer for Lower Yafa, who commissioned today's strike, is on one of the mountaintops watching with interest while we deliver his message to the unruly tribesmen.

"There's little danger in our operations, other than the normal hazards of flying with things that go bang. No Shackleton was ever lost in the Aden Protectorate. Keith, flying with Alan another bomb aimer, came close one day. The aircraft had an unsuspected electrical fault in the bomb-bay electrics. Turning in for their first run over a mountain peak close to the target, Alan called 'Bomb doors open'. As

No. 37 Squadron Shackleton carrying out medium-level bombing practice. (Peter Kendall)

the doors parted, and the fault kicked in, 15 1,000-pounders were jettisoned in a single salvo. Freed of the weight the aircraft leapt crazily, seconds later there was a huge flash and huge explosion that threw it around the sky. The safety height for 1,000-pounders was 2,790 feet, and 15 had gone off on the peak just a few hundred feet below peppering the aircraft with stones and shrapnel. It was a quiet and thoughtful crew that returned to Khormaksar. As luck would have it, we heard later that the unintended jettison caused a landslide that engulfed a hostile camel train. 'It's an ill wind that blows nobody any landslides,' observed Alan.

"Today the houses have started to slide under the graticule of the bomb sight, and I now have effective control; 'Left, left, left, left…steady,' I say as I fire the camera for some 'before' shots, and Keith steers to respond. 'Steady… steady…right… steady…steady…On top…Now!' Back at the nav station Rick starts the WFA and his stopwatch as Keith takes us into an accurate left-hand circuit. I can shut up and let him expertly get on with it, waiting for the target to swing into view again some four minutes later, when I talk us on until I can again say 'On top, now!' Rick stops the WFA and stopwatch and starts calculating the wind velocity over the target, while Keith takes us into a wider orbit to stay in visual contact.

"I'm propped face down on my elbows on the worn leather of the thinly padded floor. The Mk.14A bombsight in front of me looks forward through the V-shaped Perspex sighting panel, and the banks of switches and bomb-control gear are on my right. The vital bit of the bombsight is the collimator head (looking rather like a modern xenon overhead desk lamp) which projects a sighting cross of yellow light (the graticule) down onto a gyro-stabilised reflector glass. The aircraft's airspeed, altitude, and nose up/nose-down attitude go into the sight automatically. The bomb aimer adds the target height (to give the distance the bombs will fall), the aerodynamic characteristics of the bombs, and the wind speed and direction over the target (hence the WFA fiddle of a moment ago). Now the fore-and-aft line of the graticule should track in the same direction as the aircraft is travelling, and its cross-line should show exactly where a bomb will strike. None of this will be right unless the ground crew instrument fitter levelled the sight accurately at the last service, so we depend on his skill.

"'Co-ordination between the members of the bombing team – pilot, navigator, bomb aimer, and instrument section – must be of a high standard' says my manual, adding 'Personal idiosyncrasies count highly in bombing teams'. Keith, Rick, the 37 Squadron ground crew and I are good at this; on the actual bomb run Keith and I are attuned. He knows how fast to turn when I say 'Left, left…steady', moderating to a tiny alteration for 'Left, left steady'; we depend on his ability to hold a heavy aircraft straight and level for minutes while the turbulence buffets us. We trust one another, and our results are good and improving. Some crews never quite manage to reach this pitch: the bomb aimer doesn't quite have the judgement (the 'eye'), the pilot struggles to keep the Shackleton stable and responsive, the navigator's winds aren't entirely… But we do all right.

"Bombs theoretically obey a complicated formula with lots of variables, but apparently behave rather oddly to the eye. They seem to fall straight down below the aircraft for most of their drop, but then look as if they're racing ahead as they get near the ground. If I lean forward I can see some of this happening. However the bombsight is in the way, and mustn't be nudged or jarred even slightly, or we'll go home as failures. It's hard to call the strike accurately, so one of the signallers often goes back to the tail cone to observe results.

"Rick gives me the local wind velocity from the WFA circuit and I set it on the sight. 'Stand by for live run' I say, and hear Keith acknowledge with 'Roger, live run, turning on'. Down in the galley helpful Josh asks, 'Want a tail observer bomb aimer?' 'Yes please' I say, and a moment or so later Josh says 'Tail cone, intercom' as he checks in. He has crawled into a tail cone consisting entirely of clear Perspex, and this can give a sudden unnerving shock of having 'no visible means of support'. For a second or two one feels suspended in space, and vertigo has given many of us a queasy shudder – but it's a superb viewpoint.

"Keith has taken us some way out so as to give plenty of time for adjustments, and we're now swinging onto an attack heading as the jagged mountains slide under me in the turn.

No. 37 Squadron border patrol Hadramaut 1965. (Neville May)

Though he can see the target ahead it will shortly go out of his sight under the nose. He calls 'Running in…running in', I acknowledge and say 'Target sighted, bomb doors open'. I hear the whining growl as the doors start to part, and the draught past me increases. I flick the selector switch for the bomb on station 1, front right of the bomb bay – we're dropping singly today. A stick of four or five might increase our chances of getting at least one thousand-pounder onto the hilltop, but the village is so narrow that any line error would waste all of them.

"I watch the little group of brown houses start to slide in under the graticule. We're pretty well aligned already, though the aircraft is bouncing a bit; 'Steady… steady…right…steady,' to get a tiny starboard correction, 'Steady…'. The bomb release is sweaty in my hand and I'm concentrating hard. 'Steady, steady, steady'. At the last second, just as I press the release, the aircraft judders and the target slips infuriatingly off the right-hand side of the graticule. 'Number one bomb gone, bomb doors closed, switches off…probably a miss,' I say. A moment later Josh confirms from the tail cone, 'Overshoot, 100 yards port – tough titty'.

"We turn away for a second run, and something similar happens with the bomb from station 5 on the other side of the bay: the aircraft bumps at the last minute despite all Keith's efforts, and this one is an undershoot and 150 yards starboard. Now our blood is up and we're determined to get a hit. We line up early and settle into the groove; everything goes smoothly and as I press the switch I think 'Good one!' There's a pause while we hold our breaths, I crane to watch the bomb racing over the ground dead in line with the village but lose sight of it before the burst. Up comes Josh from the tail cone: 'Cheese-tomato! Direct hit, Bomb aimer, dead lucky.' 'Actually, we rely on skill' I say, and somebody blows a raspberry on the intercom. As we go past the village on the downwind leg for another run we can see that the bomb has damaged several houses. 'Reckon you posted that one through Mohammed Aidrus's roof,' says Peter.

"At an evening party some years later, in one of those uninventable coincidences, I'm chatting to my Bedu companion and we establish by chance that his house was one of those I knocked down. I needn't be worried as he's very amused and highly complimentary, retelling the story to everyone in the room. 'Most of those pilots weren't very good,' he said. 'We'd sit on the hills and watch them missing. Lakin Saiyid Sandy…wallah, hu azim!' (But Mr Sandy, by God he was wonderful!)

"The sortie continues, with pauses to level the bombsight. As thousand-pounders leave us and fuel is burned up '959 gets steadily lighter, and her flying attitude changes. When this happens her nose goes up, though she continues to fly straight and level or as much as Shacks ever do. They actually tend to hunt gently around a specific heading and altitude, being directionally and aerodynamically unstable. If we didn't do anything about these attitude changes then we'd get increasing overshoot errors and so every so often we take time out for a levelling run.

"The morning goes on. I get another direct hit and a couple of very near misses out of my other four bombs. Then it's all change. Peter and Keith swap seats,

Rick comes into the nose and I go back towards the nav station, pausing in the gangway to stretch muscles cramped by long concentration and an awkward posture.

"I wander back to the galley for a coffee. It's an unlikely rehearsal room, but Dodd is back here practising his trumpet. 'Cherry Pink and Apple Blossom White' is mostly submerged in the uproar of four Griffons, so nobody can hear him. He also avoids the usual complaints from neighbours in his mess. Peter and Rick start methodically 'disposing' of the remaining eight 1,000-pounders. Rick gets one direct hit, a couple of honourable near misses, and one large undershoot which people jeer at!

"When the final bomb has gone we fly one last overhead for an 'after' photograph. It's plain that we've knocked the village about considerably, and even Rick's major undershoot has coincidentally taken out a tower that was on a nearby hilltop. The near misses have also wiped out many of the terraces, so that fields, crops and the old walls have all fallen a couple of hundred feet into the wadis. The villagers will have to work long and hard to rebuild their terracing by hand – no machine could get here, let alone work on those near vertical slopes. At the time, it doesn't occur to us that this may mean people will starve, unless they can find another source of food. We're conscious of having done what the briefing required of us very efficiently, and were probably feeling rather smug.

"'Heading 190, 24 minutes to base,' I tell Peter. We turn for home and I write 'off task' in the nav log. We are all starting to think about lunch, and perhaps a bottle or two of Carlsberg in the mess bars. In 20 minutes we're calling for clearance to re-join Khormaksar's circuit, then letting down across Aden harbour and over the ships at anchor, to round out over the end of 08L touching down with a screech of tyres. I log the time, and 'landed'. Immediately the Shackleton starts to heat up again, and by the time we're turning into dispersal everybody's running with sweat and eager to shut down and get out. The marshaller lines us up on the pan, Peter locks the brakes on and opens the bomb doors. Two ground crew duck under the wings and chock the wheels.

"We complete our after-flight checks, switch our equipment off and start packing away our gear into flight bags. One by one the Griffons run down; we're pulling off our helmets into a silence that seems very loud, and clambering out of our seats. Josh has opened the back door and the ladder is in place. '959's long corridor is full of everyone queuing to get out into the fresher air, and the chance of a breeze, even if it's almost as hot outside.

"Somebody arrives from the photographic section and takes charge of the camera magazine for immediate processing. Later that evening Keith and I will stroll into ops to delightedly discover that the photographs show how very successful we've been, but for now we can put '959 to bed and debrief our sortie. By the time we've stowed our gear away and told our story it's just on 2 p.m. Aden time and the light is glaring. Keith, Rick, Peter and I could just make it to the Jungle Bar in the mess for a couple of cold beers, and we debate the temptation briefly.

"And here I'll leave us, momentarily irresolute in the sunlight, and return those 58 years. It's a challenge for the 86-year-old to try to re-inhabit the 28-year-old, and become aware of his perceptions and feelings, for I'm very aware that all autobiography is a confabulation. 'Old men forget…but he'll remember with advantages what feats he did that day', says Shakespeare's Henry V, and some of these stories have been re-told many times. I know about some of the inaccuracies – '959 wasn't our call sign, but neither Keith nor I can remember what it was! Perhaps some of the minor events didn't happen on that day, but on another. And we can't recall whether we went for a beer or not. But there must be other errors I don't know about, and other omissions that would make a difference to 'the truth' of this story.

"If I could sit down with that young man and buy him a Carlsberg, would we have anything to say to one another? I'm much more aware of him than he ever was of me, for at his age 'When I'm 86…' is unimaginable. He was an honourable young man; ignorant and unquestioning, but believing that he and his companions were doing an honest and necessary job in as humane a way as they might. His story is inevitably one of technicalities, of levelling settings, wind speeds and terminal velocities, of concentrating hard to get the best from mechanisms that were inherently inaccurate, and often unreliable. It's also one of trusting and being trusted, of a close-knit team where people respected one another's abilities. There were many things to enjoy, and it now seems to me that we had an easy and pleasant life with many diversions and pleasures, making friends from both British and Arab communities. Some of those friendships still endure and I value them."[9]

> *The 1966 Defence White Paper stated that South Arabia should become independent by 1968 and that all British forces should be withdrawn from the region by then. Anti-British feeling mounted as departure came near, and all service families were repatriated from May 1967. The final withdrawal date was set for 29 November 1967 with 37 Squadron disbanding on 7 September (it has not re-formed since). With a ceasefire in place, and the docks and the airfield perimeter guarded by Royal Marine commandos, the remaining troops and civilians were evacuated by the Royal Navy. The last RAF aircraft (Hunter FR.10s of 1416 Flight), left on 28 November and flew up to Muharraq to become part of 8 Squadron which had already left.*
>
> *By the end of the following day all British forces had quit Aden. RAF Khormaksar was no more, and today is simply Aden International Airport. Aden itself became the capital of the People's Republic of South Yemen, later renamed the People's Democratic Republic of Yemen.*

---

9. www.radfanhunters.co.uk and Sandy McMillan

CHAPTER SEVEN

'FROM THE LAND TO THE SKY'[10] – RAF SHARJAH, TRUCIAL STATES

Sharjah control tower. (Peter Kendall)

A very basic airfield existed at Sharjah in the 1920s, but it really started life in 1932 as a landing ground for Imperial Airways Handley Page HP.42 services to India, with RAF aircraft starting to use it the following year. Throughout World War 2 it was used as a base for anti-submarine patrols, and as No.44 Staging Post; its geographic location ensured it remained an important station in the post-war period. Among the squadrons based here were 84 and 244, with Blenheims. The station was little used in the immediate post-war period, but unrest in the region brought a detachment of 6 Squadron, with Vampires, in 1952, later followed by 8 and 249 Squadrons with Venoms, then 8 and 208 Squadrons with Hunters.

Shackletons were first deployed from 228 Squadron to Sharjah from 1957 to 1959 to help tackle political unrest in neighbouring Oman. Aircraft from 37 Squadron at Khormaksar arrived briefly in 1967 before the unit disbanded, to be replaced by the maritime detachment (MARDET) operated by UK-based squadrons in rotation (see also Volume 1). This continued until November 1970 when Ballykelly's 210 Squadron was relocated to Sharjah, remaining there until it too disbanded almost exactly a year later.

MARDET

Mike Norris – navigator

"I finished my first tour on Shacks in the UK in October 1969 having volunteered for a job in Sharjah. I was there for a year and enjoyed the tour. This was largely because there was a continuous Shackleton detachment, MARDET, manned initially by Kinloss, later by Ballykelly. I had a lot of fun with many old friends and

---

10. 'Min Al-Barr Ila Al-Sama'

made a good few new ones. I returned home via Jeddah and Malta with Kim French and crew from 210 Squadron. This trip was the first to fly through Saudi air space for a long time, and someone at Coastal Command HQ with a sense of humour gave us the call sign 'Mosus' (Moses?!)

"During my time on Shacks I suffered 18 engine failures of differing types while flying a total of 257 sorties, a failure rate of 7%. At the time I didn't bat an eyelid although I now wonder why we didn't take a look at the way we were operating the engines. Despite limitations it is indisputable that the Shackleton served the RAF well. Maintained by exceptional engineers, handled with respect, and operated by professional crews it produced results far beyond reasonable expectations. I have many happy memories, but I also remember with sadness colleagues who lost their lives doing the same job that gave me such satisfaction."

Peter Kendall – navigator

"After arriving back in the UK during the autumn of 1967, from my two-year tour on 37 Squadron at Khormaksar, I joined Andy Blake and crew one on 120 Squadron at Kinloss in mid-October '67. I soon became au fait with the Mk.3 Phase III version of the Shackleton. It was a slightly more comfortable version of the Mk.2, the main differences being the tricycle undercarriage, the addition of the wing-tip tanks, the ability to jettison fuel and the addition of the two Bristol Siddeley Viper 203 jet engines situated under each of the outboard engine nacelles. So, after a couple of months' flying on the 3s, I was off on my first of two MARDET detachments back to the Middle East, arriving at Sharjah in March '68 for a three-month stay.

"Most of the MARDET flying was surface surveillance, anti-gun running/smuggling and illegal immigration being the main tasks. Other tasks included coastal reconnaissance and beach photography, some internal security work and of course SAR. It is perhaps interesting to note that in the mid to late 1960s, after the withdrawal of the Shackleton squadrons from both the Mediterranean (Gibraltar and Malta), and the Middle East (Aden), there was no effective permanent British SAR air cover between that provided by the St. Mawgan squadrons in Cornwall, and the single 205 Squadron Shackleton Mk.2 on continual SAR detachment from Changi to Gan. MARDET helped redress this shortfall, and may well have been an important factor in the final decision to establish a permanent Shackleton force at Sharjah at that time.

"The first detachment, whilst enjoyable, was basically uneventful – 'duty carried out' one might say. Sqn Ldr Parry Evans was officer commanding MARDET on my second, and last detachment, from March to June 1969. I had taken over as captain of crew 1 from Andy Blake earlier that year, and on arrival at Sharjah we continued the usual patrols in the Gulf area.

"Whilst on a shipping surveillance sortie on 10 April '69 we were diverted to locate a ditched Sikorsky S.62 helicopter of World Wide Helicopters, which had

HI 2 OMARDETSHRAF OO75 F/L KENDALL IOA

World Wide Helicopters' ditched S.62 from the SAR Shack 10 April 1969. (Peter Kendall)

been operating somewhere east of Qatar in the south-western area of the Gulf. Fortunately the downed aircraft was soon located in the very shallow and flat calm waters just east of Qatar. It was roughly where HQ said it would be. It can be been seen from the photograph that, despite having deployed their life raft, the helicopter crew preferred it would seem, to stay on board the ditched chopper out of the fierce heat of the desert sun. A Wessex from the SAR Flight at Muharraq, Bahrain, was soon on the scene to pick the crew up and we, after providing some communication support, resumed our patrol around the Gulf.

"The following day, 11 April, we were doing our stint as first SAR standby crew when we were called out to search for a missing single-seat Piper Pawnee light aircraft. It had last been heard of somewhere west of Abu Dhabi, not too far from the coast. The apparently undamaged aircraft was spotted, and we had some problems I seem to remember, letting the pilot of the Pawnee know what was happening. So one of our crew dispatched our written message in some kind of canister fashioned out of a flare cartridge, and dropped it through the flame-float ejection tube! The pilot was subsequently rescued by land forces.

"Both these SAR incidents were pretty straight forward and not in any way dramatic, but nevertheless all personnel involved were successfully picked up and 'mission accomplished'. Certainly the two events were a rewarding change from what, on some sorties, could become a somewhat tedious routine. There were many hundreds of Arab dhows operating in the Gulf area. Occasionally one or two were spotted trying to hide in coves, or with an unusual number of people on board, or sometimes both. Royal Navy minesweepers were on hand and should it be considered necessary, could be called in to investigate the vessel further. One such dhow which we spotted hiding in a cove on 25 April was absolutely jam-packed with possible illegal immigrants, and so was intercepted by the navy. It was all interesting stuff.

"Unfortunately one member of our crew, a master signaller, had to return home for personal reasons, so we continued operating with a crew of nine for most of the time. A few weeks after returning from the Gulf area to Kinloss, we found ourselves in Bodø, north Norway – a somewhat cooler environment, shadowing the Soviet Fleet rather than the more flimsy wooden Arabian dhows!"

Bill Tyack – navigator

"When Britain withdrew from Aden in 1967 37 Shackleton Squadron, based at Khormaksar, was disbanded. Thereafter the maritime air presence in the Arabian Peninsula and Persian/Arabian Gulf was provided by Shackleton detachments from UK squadrons based at Sharjah. Sharjah, on the eastern coast of the Gulf 80 miles south of the strategically important Straits of Hormuz, was one of seven Trucial States that became the United Arab Emirates in 1971. British treaties with the Trucial States dated back to 1820, and the British military presence provided the states with a measure of protection against the territorial ambitions of large neighbouring countries such as Iran and Saudi Arabia.

Bill Tyack and Dave McAllister in a 42 Squadron MR.3 Phase III c.1969. (Bill Tyack)

"Our 42 Squadron crew was detached from St. Mawgan to Sharjah during the summer of 1969 and was captained by Dave 'Bog-H' Baugh. We collected Mk.3 XF701 from Kinloss and flew out to Sharjah via night stops in Gibraltar and Luqa, and a refuelling stop at El Adem in Libya. In the hot conditions after taking off from El Adem we had to use both Viper jets to help drag our fully loaded aircraft up to the minimum flight level on Egyptian airways of 10,000 feet; we then needed to burn one Viper continuously to maintain that level.

"Sharjah in the 1960s was a desert sheikhdom with few roads and almost no infrastructure. Sharjah town, the capital, consisted of a 19th century fort and a couple of rows of buildings along the creek. Local tribesmen visited the bazaar dressed in flowing robes with khanjars (curved Omani daggers) in their belts, and antique muskets over their shoulders. It was just before the AK-47 became the weapon of choice for everyone in the region. There was sufficient local atmosphere to satisfy those romantic souls who had grown up reading about Wilfred Thesiger, who had undertaken his famous crossings of the Empty Quarter only some 20 years earlier, T E Lawrence and Gertrude Bell.

"The Shackleton detachment shared the airfield with a permanent detachment of Hunter FR.10s from 8 Squadron, based at Muharraq in Bahrain, and Wessex helicopters of 78 Squadron. Of course it was an all-male station, apart from a lady from one of the charities who ran a canteen. She lived in her own secure compound in the officers' mess. It was rumoured that shortly after her arrival she was admonished for hanging her washing out to dry because it was feared that this would excite the troops! Entertainment on base was limited to sports such as soccer and tennis, despite the sweltering heat, and the occasional film night in the messes. To relieve the boredom some of the more senior aircrew officers (Ken Maynard and Tony Hinds were the ringleaders) and who were familiar with North Yorkshire from tours at Topcliffe, Leeming and Acklington, used to celebrate market days. It turned out that each day of the week was the market day in at least one North Yorkshire town. The significance of this was that, in those days, the pubs were open all day on market day. Someone would announce, 'Today it is market day in Ripon', and the worthies would settle down after lunch with a crate of beer and tell tall stories to one another. Expeditions further afield were limited by a lack of transport. However, one trip that was memorable for the wrong reasons, was a fishing trip in an Arab dhow. I felt fine on the journey out to the fishing spot, but once the engine had stopped the dhow started to wallow in the swell. I was soon leaning over the side to delighted cries of 'Ground bait!' from my companions. For the remainder of the 12-hour trip I lay comatose and increasingly dehydrated – there was no shade and I could not even keep water down – while my friends enjoyed their sport. That trip taught me more about the challenges of survival at sea than any sea-survival course.

"The Shackleton detachment had three main tasks; Operation Bronze, Operation Turquoise, and also to practise the capability for ground-support operations in a counter-insurgency role. We would also fly occasional sorties to exercise with Royal Navy ships in the area. Every sortie was tasked to check that the Sharjah flag was still flying on the Greater Tunb and Lesser Tunb Islands in the eastern Persian Gulf. These were specks of land totalling some 12 square kilometres in area, with a small population of Arab fisher folk. They lay 17 miles south of the Iranian Qeshm Island, and about 44 miles from the Trucial coastline. Ownership of the islands had been disputed between Iran and the Arabian sheiks for centuries; in the 1960s they were under the control of Sharjah, but claimed by Iran. The first Hunter sortie of the day overflew the Tunbs to 'show the flag' and check that the Iranians had not invaded during the night. Later Shackleton overflights reinforced the protect-ing power's presence. In late November 1971, two days before the British treaties with the sheikhdoms lapsed and the United Arab Emirates was formed, Iranian forces invaded the Tunbs and ejected the Arab population.

"Operation Bronze was a maritime surveillance of the Gulf, using a radar/visual search to report vessels of in-terest to the British Forces Gulf headquarters in Bahrain.

Kinloss Wing MR.3s at Sharjah in 1968. WR983 E centre. Note that D has its Vipers running. (Ray Deacon collection)

Bronze was one circuit of the Gulf, and a Double Bronze was two circuits. These were rather tedious. Visibility was poor, especially in the heavily polluted northern part of the Gulf, while the heat and humidity flying at 1,000 feet were debilitating. We flew with urns of squash, that started out ice-cold, and each member of the crew took turns at supplying everyone else with a constant supply of drink.

"Operation Turquoise was much more interesting, a visual search of the Omani coastline to interdict arms smuggling. In the late '60s two Marxist groups, the PFLOAG (Popular Front for the Liberation of the Occupied Arabian Gulf) in Dhofar Province to the south, and the NDFLO (National Democratic Front for the Liberation of Oman) in the north were fighting the Sultan's forces. Britain provided military support to the Sultan that ultimately led to the defeat of the rebels in 1976. Meanwhile the rebels were supported by the usual suspects – China, Iraq, Soviet Union and Yemen – and were receiving arms shipments via small boats landing at remote spots on the coastline. We undertook our reconnaissance by flying through the Straits of Hormuz, and then descending to fly at 100 feet along the shore looking for suspicious boats or signs of landing. With two pilots, nose gunner, bomb aimer, tail and two beam lookouts we could bring seven pairs of eyes to bear on the task. Flying as far south as fuel would allow, we then returned the same way but flying about a mile out to sea. Anything suspicious was reported by HF radio to the Trucial Oman Scouts, a local para-military force raised by the British. The scouts were able to intercept a group of arms smugglers as a result of a report from our crew.

"British military support to the Sultan took several forms, which included special forces, RAF Regiment field squadrons and RAF pilots flying Omani Strikemaster aircraft in the close-support role. The Shackletons were held in reserve as a 'big stick'. The MR.3 could carry 12 x 1,000-lb bombs, while the MR.2 could carry 15. Although we did not drop any weapons in anger during my detachment, all navigators had to qualify at bomb-aiming from medium level (around 12,000 feet). To this end the aircraft were fitted with a variant of the World War 2 Mk.XIV bombsight. We did find a bullet hole in our aircraft after one sortie, but we judged that this had more likely originated from a wedding celebration rather than a hostile act!

"Apart from one or two ports, such as Muscat, there was virtually no sign of human habitation – it was a wild and beautiful coastline. We would spot a couple of fishermen launching a small boat, or a single man standing in the water casting a net apparently miles from anywhere. Every so often we passed a 'Beau Geste'-style fort, many of which were originally built by the Portuguese in the 16th century, with armed warriors patrolling the ramparts. It was astonishing to think that at the same time as Neil Armstrong was making the first footprints on the moon (20 July 1969), we were looking for footprints in the sand on the coast of Arabia. Looking back, this was a fascinating few months for me when I was part of a short chapter in Britain's long involvement in the Gulf. It gave me glimpses of a way of life that has all but disappeared as a result of the oil money and tourism that have flooded into the region."

Nev Feist Sharjah 1967.
(Nev Feist)

THE START OF THREE-MONTH DETACHMENTS, OR TAKING THE LINER ROUTE FROM KINLOSS TO SHARJAH

Nev Feist – navigator

"In the mid-sixties Harold Wilson and the Labour government decided to pull the armed forces back to Fortress Britain and closed down all the overseas bases, military schools, hospitals and all that sort of thing. The military all returned to the UK, however we still had defence arrangements so Coastal Command Shackletons started doing three-month detachments; three months away, two or three months at home, and that went on for five years.

"You may remember that 30-odd years ago Iraq was threatening to invade Kuwait, the Shah of Persia had invaded the Tunb and Abu Musa islands just inside the Arabian Gulf, and the Congolese warring tribes were duffing each other up after the Belgians had cut and run (*plus ça change, plus c'est la même chose* or, as they say over there – the more things change, the more they stay the same). As we had defence arrangements with the Trucial Gulf States, it was decided that the might of the RAF (Shackletons and Hunters) and army would sort the Gulf problems out.

"Our heavy ground equipment went on ahead through the Suez Canal. There it stayed for years as the June 1967 Arab/Israeli war caught the cargo ship part way through the canal. Our 206 Squadron crew 6 flew the first aircraft out, with the others following at intervals of a few days. We set off northwards from Kinloss to follow the longest route from A to B that could possibly be dreamt up. We chugged slowly through the Pentland Firth, Minches and the Irish Sea en route to Gib (nine hours), then on to Sal in the Portuguese Cape Verde Islands off West Africa (eight hours five minutes). On the way to Sal we heard on the radio of the war going on in the Congo around Kinshasa (the capital of one of the warring parties, Brazzaville just over the river being the other capital). Needless to say, we were planned to route through Kinshasa.

"Now it happened that we had our CO on board. He told us all sternly that we should not take any notice of the media reports, as HQ 18 Group would have their finger on the pulse and would see us right. So after Sal, we chugged on to Ascension Island (eight hours 35 minutes) listening to the news; the next day we were destined for Kinshasa. The news was bad, with the British embassy in Kinshasa having been burnt down, Europeans being killed, and Simbas and mercenaries running around – and we thought that we might be destined for the pot! The CO read the riot act over the intercom, saying that there would be a signal waiting for us at Ascension if there was a problem with Kinshasa. Needless to say there wasn't, yet the CO refused to signal our concerns about clarifying the situation, saying that there would probably be a signal for us the next morning. Yes, you guessed it, the next morning

dawned and no sig-
nal, so in near revolt,
off we went in an
easterly direction to
meet our destiny.

"We were well on
our way to Kinshasa
when someone at
HQ realised that
there was one of the
old grey bombers
swanning across the
Southern Atlantic to
a most uncertain

No. 206 Squadron crew six and flight commander ops (John Forteath, back row third from right) doing a bit of bundoo bashing near Sharjah in 1967. (Nev Feist)

fate. We received a flash signal to divert to Luanda, which was then the capital of Portuguese Angola (nine hours 15 minutes). Luanda was not exactly in a settled situation, with heavily armed Portuguese conscript soldiers everywhere. After dumping our kit in the hotel, we all went off on a remarkably cheap night out. This was thanks to the very beneficial exchange rate between the Portuguese and the local Angolan Escudos.

"The next day we flew over many miles of jungle to Nairobi (eight hours 15 minutes) for a two-day sojourn including a safari – well, we had earned it hadn't we? As the heat and high altitude did nothing for the poor old Shack, we had to take off from Nairobi at around two o'clock in the morning. After 20 minutes or-biting the airfield, gaining a few feet running up and down wind, and trying to maintain altitude on the turns, we reached 2,000 feet above the airfield. So we decided to set off as we weren't going to get any higher. ATC then cleared us via an NDB (non-directional beacon) which was situated on a hill higher than us! I remember that Claude, the captain, said that it was like flying whilst sitting on the edge of a razor blade. He had all the ground crew sitting in the aisle behind the nav's and sensor's seats, and no one was allowed to move around for a couple of hours until the centre of gravity moved forward a bit. We flew up to Masirah (ten hours 20 minutes), and the last leg to Sharjah (two hours 15 minutes) after an epic eight-day transit.

"Iraq thought better of taking us on (with not a single American in sight), and the Shah pulled his troops out of the islands, leaving us to fly those terribly hot and boring Bronzes, Turquoises and other colours I can't remember. Shortly after arriving at Sharjah, we ambled down to Aden, South Yemen (from which we were withdrawing), to give some support to the Arab forts on the border with Marxist North Yemen, as FLOSY were infiltrating at night through the passes. As the Shack Mk.3 engines were none too reliable we wanted to go flying loaded for bear (rifles, Stens, Brens, etc.); ready to fight our way home if there was a forced-landing. But

'I think that Stan Swanson the flight engineer has had enough and is off, followed rapidly by the rest of us.' (Nev Feist)

the CO wouldn't agree to our forming a Kipper Fleet Army.

"During the night flights we dropped flares to light up our attacks on the forts, and tracer fire lit up the area beneath us. We also covered the 'Retreat from Riyan', up the coast from Aden. We had a bomb bay full of fragmentation bombs, loaded 20-mm cannons, and about six feet of paper giving the rules of engagement. However, nothing untoward happened, apart from the magnificent sight of a salvo of 48 jettisoned frag bombs as they hit the sea at the end of the operation – no one lands with those old World War 2 exudation encrusted leftovers.

"Claude Fryer the captain of 206 Squadron crew six in 1967, had joined the RAF in 1943, and flew Spitfires in Iraq before changing onto jets. At that time Sharjah was a weekend jolly; it was little more than a fort into which everyone retired at night time. He had also buzzed down many of the valleys in the back country. One day we were on the Jebajib bombing range, and after the navs had taken turns at missing the target ring of barrels with the 25-lb practice bombs, the AEOps had a go at gunnery against an old tanker on the range – needless to say they didn't hit it. Claude was getting fed up with this and got the gunner to level his guns and fire when ordered. We then came round and made a shallow diving pass (à la Spitfire), with the result that the tanker was well and truly shot-up.

"One of Claude's other old tactics during an ASW detection was to get up to about 4,000 feet with the radar set to stand-by. The subs couldn't see us up there, but snorting subs showed up wonderfully. Having gained a visual contact, Claude would pull back the RPM to produce a disking effect of the props which basically presented four solid surfaces to the air. We then fell out

'Oh no, not again eng.' Crew 6 at Sharjah in 1967. Looks like a proper job. (Nev Feist)

of the sky at a huge rate of descent, probably out of the sun if I remember our Claude's thinking in those days. It's no wonder that we were made a select crew!"

Nev's captain Claude Fryer now takes up the story of that challenging eight-day trip to Sharjah from the pilot's point of view.

Claude Fryer – pilot

"The Shackleton Mk.3 Phase III with Viper fit was in service by the mid-sixties and pilots soon became aware that the AUW of 108,000 lbs had certainly made a great difference in performance. The Griffons now had to work at higher power settings to maintain operational cruising speeds. However the 2,200 up to 2,400 rpm range was prohibited, and so 2,400 rpm became the norm for hours on end. In August 1967 we flew out to Sharjah, and subsequently to Aden to cover the evacuation of Riyan. We did this heavily laden with anti-personnel bombs. The flight out (described above) was rather circuitous as befitted this overweight beast.

"I had previously flown out of Nairobi (Embakasi – 5,500 feet above sea level), when serving with 120 Squadron en route to Cape Town for 'Capex 63', during which the SAAF lost a Shackleton which crashed in the mountains in extreme weather. Then I was flying WR989 which was a Phase II fit and our 'tank'. But I digress, having arrived at the aircraft in good time I found the ground crew busy working on the starboard Viper door. It appeared to be totally inoperative, and no way could it be repaired at Nairobi. Of course this rendered the engine inoperative. I was of the opinion that we should defuel to a reasonable level, and then fly downhill to Mombasa to refuel at sea level, and then continue. [As Nev has said, the heat and high altitude meant that a Shackleton at maximum take-off weight would really need both Vipers in order to take off.] It appeared that there would be a considerable delay in finding an empty tanker to take our excess fuel, probably not until later in the day. The flight engineer and I retired to the aircraft to study his

SAC Colin Bell marshalling MR.2 WR987 Z of 210 Squadron at Sharjah 1971. (Mike Speake)

charts. We knew the single Viper would have a reduced output at altitude. We also knew that there was controversy about the combined use of water-meth and Vipers. We calculated that the aircraft could just scrape off the ground using the full length of the runway – but this was certainly not recommended!

"At this point we were joined by the CO, who having listened to our conclusions, confirmed that he would be prepared to carry out the take-off if I demurred. I could now see myself reporting to the air attaché at the high commission for a flight home. I asked the CO to review his decision, but without success, and I then made the most stupid and dangerous decision I have ever made and which, even today I strongly regret – I decided to take off. I taxied out to the extreme end of the runway, it was dark and there was no wind. With checks complete, I called for high gear water-meth and the one remaining Viper to full power. With temps and pressures OK I released the brakes – nothing happened! Then there was a gentle movement to a slow walking pace which eventually improved to a hurried stroll. Already the illuminated 1,000-foot runway marker had slowly passed by. We must have been well past halfway before the ASI registered 60 knots, and all the time the thought that we did have 13,500 feet available coloured my judgement. At 120 knots the red barrier lights at the end of the runway were approaching rapidly, but I was determined that the nose-wheel would remain on the ground until the last moment. At 130 knots I gently eased back, we came off, the red lights shot underneath, the undercarriage was up in a flash and the stick shakers were working overtime. My backside was off the seat as we staggered into the blackness of the National Game Reserve. We were at zero feet on the altimeter for at least a mile or two, and I could envisage a trail of headless giraffes in our wake.

"As the speed gradually built up, we gained some height and at 150 feet I selected flap in. This helped considerably and after what seemed like an age we reached 1,000 feet and I was able to select low gear. The tower called to say that they had scrambled the crash crew but recalled them as we appeared to lift off. The engineer then came forward and whispered in my ear 'Skipper, we were rolling for five minutes and eight seconds'! This really must be a record never to be repeated. After race-tracking over the airfield for half an hour, in a vain attempt to reach safety altitude, we set off on our route downhill towards the coast. ATC cleared us to an NDB which was on a hill higher than we were – well spotted first nav. Our three months spent in Sharjah was a continuation of training and medium-level bombing, with little else to report!"[11]

*As described in Volume 1, **Dave Lawrence** witnessed a similar dramatic departure from Nairobi's Eastleigh airfield while transiting through there en route to Majunga.*

---

11. Via Nev Feist.

"We saw for ourselves the problems that Mk.3s were having, when we bumped into a crew at Eastleigh; they were preparing to leave on their way home. Eastleigh is some 5,400 feet above mean sea level and both their Vipers were unserviceable and therefore just additional weight. We heard them set full power with little visible sign of movement, then disappear from view Griffons roaring. We saw nothing for some time, until the Shack climbed back into view in the far distance having taken full advantage of low-lying terrain to gain speed."

In November 1970, 210 Squadron arrived from Ballykelly to take over from MARDET. As Bill Tyack has said, a primary role of both MARDET and later the incumbent 210 Squadron, was to operate what were also referred to as 'Blue Turquoise' policing patrols which took them north to the Straits of Hormuz, then on to Masirah, Salalah and back to Sharjah. One aircraft was airborne at all times.

210 SQUADRON

Jerry Evans – navigator

"As I left MOTU, it was all starting to come to a close east of Suez, the Gulf and Singapore. Until the latter part of 1970 the Sharjah detachment had been handled by the UK squadrons on a rotation basis; each time going out there for three months. It was now decided to re-form 210 Squadron (also known as Gulf Flight). They would be based in Sharjah until November '71 – the final year of our Middle East presence. It was a small outfit with Dave Moule, a squadron leader, as the CO.

"Who was going to go? It was decided that the captain (normally the first pilot), the first navigator, the AEO, perhaps a couple of the senior signallers and the engineer, needed to be experienced people. The whole crews were going to be chosen from people at MOTU. Obviously the experienced half were the MOTU instructors to the less experienced students who were going through, or who had just gone through. That was how they constituted the crews to go out, and of course I was nobbled as one of the first navigators. We went out in October '70 and were there for a year. At that time we had two boys and we had our own little house just outside St. Mawgan, which was very nice. My wife knew all the neighbours and we were all good friends, and the kids were in junior schools. Going to Sharjah unaccompanied obviously wasn't something I wanted to do, but a lot of things depend on your personal situation I think. We also knew that we could be flown back for a free leave after six months, but we also had allocated leave to take if we wanted to. We could save this up, although they wouldn't fly you home. It soon became obvious that it was the easiest thing in the world to just buy yourself a ticket back – it wasn't expensive, so I flew back in the interim period. I actually came back three times, so I was there for four chunks of three months.

Two MR.2s and a Pembroke sweltering in the Sharjah heat. (Dave McCandless)

Jerry Evans doing some 'poling' for a change, 210 Squadron Sharjah '70-71. (Jerry Evans)

"When it all wrapped up it dictated my whole future career in the service – there were two obvious routes for me to take. One was to stay on the Shackleton which was going to take on the AEW role, as the Nimrod AEW was so long delayed. In fact it was delayed even further and finally cancelled by Margaret Thatcher because it was so late. So they formed 8 Squadron with Shackletons, which at first went to Kinloss before moving over to Lossiemouth. I didn't want to do that, I didn't want to change role completely. Obviously, I could have stayed in the role and gone onto the Nimrod, but I wanted to try something quite different. I asked: 'How about sending me to Germany, where I could do some light transport flying, that sort of thing?' When I look back, it sounded a bit unrealistic.

"When I was home on my third bit of leave from Sharjah, with only three of four months to go, I was amazed to receive a very long letter from my boss copying a signal to me. They'd obviously given great thought to what I'd asked for and said: 'We can't give Evans what he wants, there is no opportunity there. However, we note his previous request for where he wanted to go, and the station intelligence officer post at RAF Gibraltar is coming up, would he like it?' I liked it, so off I went to do a ground tour at Gibraltar. We had an extra year there and it was just wonderful, we loved the place.

"However, it meant that when I finished that tour and was due to go back into flying, I had no relevant operational background. The Shackleton MR role had finished, and I wasn't current in anything. The only way they could use my expertise was to teach, so I went to Finningley to instruct at the nav school."

SHACKLETONS DON'T BOTHER ME

Mike Speake – photographer

"In 1971 I got the shocking news that I had been selected for a nine-month unaccompanied tour to Muharraq, working on 8 and 208 Hunter squadrons. However,

No. 210 Squadron MR.2s at Sharjah. (Mike Speake)

this was short-lived as after a few weeks I got posted to 210 Squadron Shacks at Sharjah, the last tradesman to do so before disbandment. No. 210 Squadron had just three MR.2 Shacks, W, X and Z as far as I remember. They also had had the front cannons removed – toothless wonders I thought at the time. I will never forget the Argosy flight down to Sharjah as I had severe Bahrain Gut at the time, and there was just a urinal for our use. I didn't know if there was a proper toilet in the flight-deck area – maybe I should have asked. Anyway, we got to Sharjah and one of the airmen, whom I knew previously, met me with the squadron Land Rover. How I made it to the arrivals toilets I will never know, but the relief was beyond belief!

"After a couple of weeks or so there were just three photographers left at Sharjah, a ground photographer (who we didn't have much to do with), plus Dan and then me as the corporal on the squadron. Dan and I took turns to do the 'clikkie' B/Fs every morning and mid-afternoon, seeing the aircraft in and film downloads, then processing the films and printing. Amongst the ground equipment was a refrigeration unit, which had its large diameter hose pulled through the rear door of the aircraft. Unfortunately the cameras were right at the back of the fuselage, so you sweated buckets there when changing film magazines and tried not to drip sweat onto the camera glass platens.

"It was common knowledge that the daily sortie by a singleton 210 Shack was to check on the Soviet Kotlin-class destroyer,

No. 210 Squadron Shackleton MR.2 Sharjah, 20 June 1971. (Mike Speake)

OC Gulf and OC 210 Squadron puzzling about
something, Sharjah 1971. (Mike Speake)

which was anchored some way into the Gulf. Although our Shack flew in very low the ship would be waiting, and when the photos were developed you could see the ship's guns and missiles trained on the aircraft as it circled.

"I recall one incident when one of our aircraft landed one afternoon and the tail-wheel broke right off. It carried on taxiing off the runway. It then stopped for a make-shift trailer rig to eventually be attached to its rear for it to make a rather shame-faced journey back to the hangar pan. Over the next couple of weeks or so the riggers hoisted up the rear of the fuselage and repaired the undersides of the twin fins, which had been scraped away as the aircraft landed and taxied. Of course there was a lot of squadron mickey-taking, chiefly that the aircrew hadn't realised, at first, that the tail-wheel had broken off, it only dawning on them when the attitude of the aircraft seemed a bit more inclined than usual!

"We had a sometimes 'grumpy' engineering officer on the squadron. The lads thought up a wheeze to cheer him up on his birthday, with the aid of our cross-eyed Arab cleaner, Ali. He was a pleasant young man, and very obliging, but you never knew if he was talking to you or not. Anyway, the lads taught him to sing, 'You are my sunshine'. On the morning of the engineering officer's birthday Ali was propelled into his office and proceeded to sing, with a very quivery voice, his well-rehearsed song. After a few seconds of this we heard, 'Ali, f*** off out of my office!' Everyone outside burst into laughter as Ali beat a hasty retreat followed by the engineering officer who could do little else but join in our merriment.

"Eventually the end of November dawned. Harold Wilson had decreed that the Gulf stations would close (the only thing for which I am grateful to the Labour Party). Some of our ground crew transited back with our faithful old Shacks, while the rest of us piled into a VC10 and lorded it all the way back to a wintry UK. My wife Pat, our little daughter Coral and I met up on Swindon station to have an emotional and joyful reunion, and we then travelled on to London for the weekend. That was really ace. I got posted back to St. Mawgan yet again, but by this time the Nimrods had taken over and the Shacks were being withdrawn from service.

"A handful of MR.2s were converted to early warning versions to equip the newly re-formed 8 Squadron at Lossiemouth. The best memory I have of the Hunter-equipped 8 Squadron was its arrival at Sharjah for the last few weeks of the station's existence. We were all waiting on the line to see them fly in, and they did so in spectacular fashion, line abreast at zero feet and seemingly maximum speed, with the desert dust swirling up behind them with the jet-wash. Absolutely awesome!"

Dave Lawrence – pilot

"In March 1969, still as a co-pilot, I was posted to 206 Squadron at Kinloss. In early May the crew to which I was allocated (the captain was Carl Pallister) was rostered to go out to Sharjah to operate sorties for Operation Double Bronze. I only flew two of these flights, plus a medium-level bombing training sortie (of which I have no recollection, but that is what my logbook says!), before we were tasked to ferry a Shackleton WR973 back to Kinloss for servicing, and then ferry another Shackleton back to Sharjah. The route planned for us was Sharjah to Muharraq to El Adem, Libya, to Luqa, Malta, to Gibraltar to Kinloss. However, on the leg from Muharraq to El Adem, about halfway across Saudi Arabia, we had an engine failure. No.4 engine just stopped with no warning or any other indication; it turned out to be a structural failure in the magneto assembly which affected both magnetos. Anyway, we decided to divert to Jeddah, where we arrived safely. However this took the Saudis rather by surprise – they weren't expecting us. After a long time wondering what to do, they took all our passports and sent us to a hotel in Jeddah, where we stayed for ten days. When we left there was no indication in our passports, or anywhere else, that we had ever been in Saudi Arabia. The reason for the delay there was that it took that long for the RAF to get a replacement engine sent out and to install it. When this had been done we did a quick 15-minute air test, and the next day we continued on to El Adem and the rest of the route back to Kinloss."

The British withdrawal from Aden was quickly followed by a pull-out from the Persian Gulf. On 2 December 1971, Sharjah, together with Abu Dhabi, Dubai, Ajman, Umm Al Qawain and Fujairah joined in the Act of Union to form the United Arab Emirates. RAF Sharjah closed on 14 December and today the airfield has been considerably enlarged and developed as a civil airport. Little evidence remains of the RAF station, but the original control tower and adjacent buildings now house the Al Mahatta Museum, which includes a small collection of Gulf Aviation aircraft.

CHAPTER EIGHT

'STRIKE THE WATER'[12] – 35 SQUADRON SOUTH AFRICAN AIR FORCE

Three MR.3s awaiting delivery to the SAAF in 1957. (Adrian Balch)

On 2 February 1945 SAAF's 35 Squadron came into being by renumbering South African-manned 262 Squadron RAF, flying Catalina IVs from Congella (Durban), St. Lucia on the Natal coast and Langebaan on the West Cape coast. In April 1945 the squadron received the first of 16 Sunderland MR.5s which were initially used for ferrying South African troops home from Cairo. In the late 1940s, a Citizen's Force element within 35 Squadron operated Harvards, Spitfires, Oxfords and Venturas from Stamford Hill, Durban. By 1952 only the Harvards remained in that element and it became 5 (Citizen's Force) Squadron.

At the start of 1957, 35 Squadron SAAF was in its last months of operating Sunderlands from its base at Congella, in Durban harbour. In August, the first three of its eventual fleet of eight Shackleton MR.3s arrived, and the unit moved its headquarters to Ysterplaat near Cape Town. Because Ysterplaat's runway was not long enough, the aircraft were based at nearby D F Malan airport. Border patrol operations got underway in 1958, and continued for a total of 27 years.

During all that time only one aircraft was lost. On 8 August 1963, 1718 crashed at the Stenskloof dam near Rawsonville, in the Wemmershook Mountains near Cape Town, after hitting a hill off its planned route during bad weather. It had been on its way to join Exercise Capex with the Royal Navy off Port Elizabeth; all 13 on board lost their lives (see Appendix Three). RAF navigator **Peter Morris** of 120 Squadron was on detachment there at the time.

---

12. 'Shaya Amanzi'.

"We should have been flying at the same time as the SAAF Shackleton. Our CO took one look at the weather and he cancelled, because we couldn't have done anything as the sea state was so rough that you wouldn't see anything. So we cancelled, but the South Africans didn't, took off and we never heard anything of them again. A hurricane had passed through, and they reckoned the winds were 150 knots at 6,000 feet.

"As the crew who should have flown the previous day, we were called in first thing in the morning, and were first for search and rescue. We were sent out on the route that he should have taken to see if we could locate anything. I was getting winds of 80 knots, and we just couldn't believe the sea state, it was so high. We couldn't find anything at all; we did about 14 hours I think. The next day we did another search over the Cape Town bay in case he had gone that way, but again we didn't find anything. Our CO was asked to take over because he was more experienced in search and rescue than the South Africans were. He got the R/T tapes from air traffic control, listened very closely, and heard a very feint 'Mayday, Mayday' about 20 minutes after take-off, and they thought they must be in the hills. A helicopter was sent and they found the aircraft. It was upside down, the bomb doors were open, and they could see the sonobuoys, which were dayglow red; of course, the crew had all been killed. The exercise was called off after that and we came home."

In addition to its traditional MR role, 35 Squadron was also frequently called upon to carry out SAR duties. In 1962, the SAAF ordered 16 Buccaneer S.50 strike aircraft to replace the Canberras operated by 24 Squadron. Delivered by air in pairs, only 15 Buccaneers were to reach South Africa. En route, No. 417 was lost 500 miles south of the Canary Islands, after suffering a double-engine flame-out followed by a spin. The crew, Captain Jooste and Lieutenant de Klerk, ejected successfully. 35 Squadron navigator **Knoppies Coetzer** *took part in the SAR operation to find them.*

"On 27 October 1965 Shackleton 1722, from 35 Squadron Ysterplaat, took off from D F Malan airport, Cape Town at 1000 hours on its way to Air Force Station Rooikop near Walvisbay. The aircraft commander was Maj Pat Conway, and the co-pilot was Capt Johan Kruger. The navigators were Lt Henning Els, CO Bokkie van der Merwe, and myself CO Knoppies Coetzer. The electronics leader was Lt Wynand Bloemhof (he later saw the light and also became a navigator!) The mission was to fly to Bissau, in Portuguese Guinea, and to be on SAR standby for the ferry flights of the first eight Buccaneers that were acquired from Great Britain. The Buccaneer ferry flights were scheduled for 30 October, and the route to be covered by the SAR aircraft were the two legs from Ilha do Sol (Sal Island) to Ascension Island,

and then from Ascension Island to Luanda.

"Shackleton 1722 flew to Rooikop, refuelled and waited for nightfall before departing for Ascension Island at 22:00 that night. A second Shackleton was supposed to follow us, but it encountered various snags and it only joined us in the air, way out over the sea, due west of Bissau in the early morning of 1 November. Our late evening departure from Rooikop was carefully planned to arrive at Ascension Island just before sunrise on the 28th. The navigation entailed serious astro-fixing techniques, aided by the ADF (airborne direction finder) tuned to the 10 KW NDB installed on Ascension Island.

"Our cruising altitude to Ascension Island was 5,000 feet, which was 'full throttle height' for the Shackleton under those atmospheric conditions. On reaching our cruising altitude, I tuned in to the NDB on Ascension Island, call sign 'AW'. Lo and behold the ADF (automatic direction finder) needle jumped to the 12 o'clock position on the compass rose, as if the beacon was 100 nautical miles in front of us; it was in fact more than ten times that distance, a clear demonstration of sky waves at that time of night. Incidentally, the ATC tower call sign for Ascension Island was 'Wide Awake Tower'!

"The astro fixes became refined and soon we had three good star fixes, making the accuracy of the navigation better than five nautical miles. The NDB bearing from AW disappeared periodically as we flew into the skip distances of the sky waves, and then it was steady again, dead ahead of the aircraft. From 400 nautical miles out from Ascension the bearing was dead steady, and we could home in to the island. We landed on the 28th at 05:20 local time after a ten-hour 20-minute flight. The next leg, Ascension to Bissau was scheduled for the next day at 10:00.

"The bar and canteen on Ascension Island never closed, and meals and drinks were available 24 hours a day, seven days a week. In those days one South African rand was equal to US $ 1.14. You could buy a case of Bacardi rum, or a case of any whisky for ten rand from the American PX. The PX also stocked various electronic devices which were not available in South Africa. Also sporting equipment and household appliances which we would buy on the way back home. Of course, *Playboy* magazine was freely available!

"On 29 October at 10:00 we got airborne for the flight to Bissau. Again we transited at 5,000 feet for the same reasons as previously mentioned. The flight to Bissau was seven hours long and uneventful. However, we were all aware of the murderous ITCZ (Inter Tropical Convergence Zone) round about the equator; massive thunderstorms could occur with the tops of the cumulonimbus (Cb) clouds reaching 75,000 feet. In fact we were so far out to sea that there was no sign of any of these. The only turbulence that occurred was when Bokkie van der Merwe counted down the latitude before crossing the equator. On 'zero' captain Pat Conway induced a massive bump, sending some WOps flying out of their bunks in the galley, where they were sleeping off the effects of Ascension Island. It was the first time for most of us to cross the equator, unfortunately we did not have the fun and games experienced on board ship.

"The approach into Bissau was marked by a language barrier as the ATC was not informed of our arrival; eventually he said 'Shackle 722 please land', which we did. We were met by Commandant Wally Black, who was then staff officer operations at SAAF HQ. How he got to Bissau, I don't know to this day, but he was the head of the rescue co-ordination centre which was established there. We checked in to the hotel in the heat and humidity that we were unaccustomed to – together with a great thirst!

"Supper time in the hotel arrived, and we were in for a brand-new experience. The main course was white steak. When I cut into my steak the blood shot into my eye – I was quite peed off; a boerseun (Boer's son) does not eat raw meat! Language was a great problem because none of us could speak any Portuguese. I called the waiter over with the intention of telling him to put my steak back on the fire until it was done. I stabbed the steak with my fork, and with my other hand got out my Zippo lighter to show the man that the steak needed more fire. I flicked open the Zippo, and hit the flint. Sadly this was one of the rare occasions that the Zippo did not fire up. The waiter's face brightened up, and he disappeared, without taking my steak. He soon returned and handed me a small box of matches – my mates at the table fell off their chairs.

"The following day was 30 October 1965, the day of the Buccaneer ferry flights. We got up bright and early; one cannot sleep in that heat and humidity. At that time air conditioners were not an option because Bissau's electrical supply could not cope with the demand and was load shedding. I think Escom was also their service non-provider at that stage. After breakfast we started a bridge game in a well-ventilated area, with fans cooling down the surroundings. Lunch followed, and then the bridge game continued. Wally Black was in and out keeping us informed of the progress of the Buccaneers. The Buccaneers were flying in two four-ship formations an hour apart.

"At about 14:30, whilst the bridge game was very interesting, Wally came into the room. He announced that a Buccaneer had gone down and that we must scramble immediately. We laughed at his joke and continued with the game. He was serious, and proceeded to open a map across our bridge table, of the oceanic area to the west of Bissau. That was when we knew he was serious because nobody interrupts a 35 Squadron bridge game. We navigators had all our planning instruments and maps with us at the hotel, and we quickly prepared for the transit to the search area. We filed a flight plan with Wally, who did the liaison with ATC.

"At 16:00, Shackleton 1722 got airborne out of Bissau and proceeded to the search area. According to Wally Black's briefing, one of the accompanying Buccaneers had relayed the downed aircraft's crash position back to Sal Island oceanic control centre. They in their turn informed a Portuguese airliner from TAP (Transportes Aéreos Portugueses) who was overflying the area. The airline pilots picked up a distress signal on the emergency frequency, of 243 MHz, and saw a red flare

MR.3 1722 35 Squadron at Port Elizabeth, 11 July 1969. (Dave Becker via Adrian Balch)

in the area. They marked the position as best they could, and relayed the lat and long to us. We, in the Shackleton, immediately updated the position of the search area and proceeded towards it. Wynand Bloemhof was manning the SARAH (search and rescue automatic homing) onboard equipment; this was a primitive J-scope system giving a straight line on the cathode ray tube (CRT) running from left to right. Should a SARAH signal be received it produced a spike. The aircraft would then turn towards the spike. In those days the aircrew personal locator beacons were SARAH equipment, transmitting a carrier wave only on frequency 243 MHz, but with no speech facility. Therefore, there was no way we could talk to any downed airman.

"The transit time to the search area for the downed Buccaneer aircrew was four hours due west from Bissau. An hour before we reached the Buccaneer's last known position it was dark. We were at 1,500 feet AMSL, which is the normal operating altitude over the sea. With 30 minutes to go to the Buccaneer's position Wynand reported 'SARAH contact!' The signal strength was very weak, but it held until Wynand shouted 'On Top!' We marked the position on our maps, and estimated the accuracy as approximately one nautical mile. By now we knew the aircraft equipment accuracies well, and we could thus refine the doppler and GPI (ground position indicator) positions with greater accuracy.

"At the 'on top' call, we marked the position with flame floats and marine markers, which provided a flame for about four hours. After that call we never had SARAH contact with the downed aircrew again – both their SARAH locator beacon batteries were dead. We decided to drop a set of Lindholme equipment to the downed two-man crew; Lindholme consisted of three canisters: one containing fresh water, the centre one containing a ten-man dinghy and the last one containing rations. All three canisters were connected by a floating rope. We first made a pass illuminating the area with flares and the pilots saw the two one-man dinghies tied together. We carefully marked the position again. Then we turned in for the Lindholme drop. But the height was wrong, the speed was wrong and the pilot flying looked out to the illuminating flares – we almost joined the downed Buccaneer aircrew in the water! Fast reaction from Pat Conway – bless his soul – rescued the situation, and the Lindholme was successfully dropped.

"The ten-man dinghy deployed prematurely and its floor was damaged in the process. Luckily the Buccaneer crew managed to get hold of the joining rope and hauled themselves towards the dinghy. They were able to get their one-man dinghies inside it, and so could settle for the night. Having been able to only spend two and a half hours in the search area, we were just about on 'Bingo' (minimum) fuel by this time. We made sure that the area where the aircrew and dinghy was, was well marked with marine markers. We dropped a pattern with some of the markers having delayed ignitors to light up after certain time intervals. In the meantime, the second Shackleton was eventually on its way to the search area from Ascension Island.

"It was now almost 22:30 and we had to leave the Buccaneer aircrew to go back to Bissau, refuel and return when we were ready. We had VHF contact with the second Shackleton and briefed them about the situation. Accurate positions were given, and they estimated to be over the downed aircrew some two hours after our departure from the area. As stated previously, there was no way to inform the Buccaneer aircrew about the situation. We just hoped that they would be OK. We landed at Bissau on 31 October at 01:30, refuelled, got airborne again at 04:15 and proceeded back to the search area. Just before we got airborne our mates in the other Shackleton landed at Bissau. We told them to standby and we would call them if we needed them. There was no sense having two aircraft in the rescue area in the darkness.

"At 07:45 we were in the rescue area again, and saw all the marine markers, looking like a small village. We had to wait for half an hour for sunrise before we were able to see the dinghy with our 24 Squadron comrades Captain Jooste and Lieutenant de Klerk on board. As the visibility improved, we could see all the marine markers but no dinghy. Did they sink? The dinghy and the marine markers were supposed to have the same drift rate, but we all forgot that the floor of the dinghy had been damaged during the drop, and that had obviously changed its drift rate. Now we had to execute a brand-new search for the downed aircrew. We decided on a clover leaf-type search. This was where you started in the centre, and searched in the clover leaf pattern to a distance estimated to be the extreme distance the dinghy could have drifted. On our eighth and final turn (at the extreme of the clover leaf pattern) the co-pilot, Johan Kruger, spotted the dinghy below the starboard wingtip. He called 'Mark, Mark' and two flame floats were launched. After this we did not lose sight of the dinghy again.

"The WOps could turn out a mean breakfast in the small galley of the Shackleton and we had a feast on board. While one pilot, one navigator and one engineer worked, the rest ate. They then took over the work and the others could eat. I took up the prime place in the nose-gunner's position to keep the dinghy in sight and to take some pictures. Of course, by now, we had done many low passes next to the dinghy to confirm that both the crew were alive and well. At about 09:00 we made contact with the first of two C-130 Hercules that were on their way to the rescue area. They informed us that they were busy vectoring a 13,694-ton Dutch cargo and passenger ship, the SS *Randfontein*, to the rescue area. The C-130s were not sure where the dinghy was exactly, so we proceeded to the ship and overflew it in the direction of the dinghy rocking our wings. The *Randfontein* altered course, and we returned to the downed crew. At about 10:00 the ship was alongside the dinghy, and the aircrew pick-up was completed successfully.

"We returned to Bissau and landed at about 14:00. By this time, our crew had been awake for just on 32 hours, going non-stop. We joined the second Shackleton crew for a celebration at the hotel in Bissau. But the beer and the wine were warm, and we got 'pissed' quite quickly. The next day, 1 November, both our aircraft departed at about 14:30 for Ascension Island, arriving at 21:30. On our arrival, the 14 crew members of the remaining seven Buccaneers were waiting for us. When the Shackleton doors opened, and the ladders were in place, we could not get out. We were crowded by Buccaneer air and ground crew carrying crates, and crates of ice-cold beer. The party went from the aircraft, to the canteen, to the bar and we got to bed at about 21:00 on 2 November.

"The seven Buccaneers departed Ascension Island for Luanda at about 10:00 on 3 November; we had to wait at Ascension until the last Buccaneer was safe in Luanda. We finally departed Ascension Island at 21:20 for Rooikop, and landed there at 09:00 on 4 November. We refuelled, had a meal and then departed for Cape Town at 13:40; and landed at D F Malan airport at 18:00. The Buccaneers departed Luanda at 13:00 on 3 November, and landed at Waterkloof at 16:00.

"On 7 November 2015 we celebrated the 50th anniversary of the first landing of a Buccaneer on South African soil at Waterkloof, with a 24 Squadron get-together at the Hartbees Club. Incidentally, the presence of SAAF Buccaneers in Luanda was the first and last time that the Buccaneers were in Angolan airspace in a non-menacing role."[13]

During 1968 the SAAF Shackletons were modified locally to a Phase II standard that involved electronics and armaments modifications. The replacement of the fleet with more modern maritime patrol aircraft had been thwarted by an international arms embargo. The SAAF also embarked on a re-sparring programme to extend the service life of its fleet to some extent. Shackleton 1716 was the first to be re-sparred between 1973 and April

---

1976, with Shackleton 1717 following between September 1975 and October 1977. Ultimately, these two aircraft were the only ones in the fleet that had the modification, and the fleet began to shrink as both reducing spar life, and an increasing shortage of spare parts, led to permanent groundings.

Hartog 'Horace' Blok – navigator

"At 12.34 on 22 July 1983, the SAR crew was called to ops and told to be at the aircraft as soon as possible for a 13.30 take-off. At 13.33, laden with 3,600 gallons of fuel, we were airborne in Shack 1717, (call sign 'Rescue 403'). We transited through the bay to datum 67 nautical miles south of Cape Seal to search for a fishing vessel, the *Shin Huie*. We reached the area at 14.50 and commenced a clover leaf search, with a ten-mile radius and a one-mile track spacing. The weather in the area had a 2,000-foot cloud base with visibility of two to five miles, reducing to half a mile in rain showers. On the first leg radar reported a contact at 270 degrees and 18 miles. A homing to the mark was done but nothing was found, so the aircraft then resumed its search. When overhead the datum for the third time radar again reported a contact – a solid contact – at 360 degrees and 12 miles. The aircraft was turned onto the heading, and at 15.10 the *Shin Huie* was sighted. The trawler had been found with great difficulty as the sea was very rough, and the white paintwork of the vessel camouflaged it against the heavy seas. A marine marker and two flare floats were dropped to mark its position.

"Initially, we had been of the opinion that the vessel we had just located was transiting to the search area, as it appeared to be steaming into the wind and swell. However, on returning to the trawler a crew member was sighted aft frantically waving a red flare. We then knew that this was the vessel in distress. On subsequent flypasts more red flares were released from the ship which hinted at panic. Our aircraft commander, Capt Japie Horn, was rather surprised at their actions as the vessel appeared to be seaworthy.

"After ten minutes the vessel was side on to the swell, and being breached by very heavy seas. By now an oil slick surrounded the boat, and we were convinced that it was in trouble. We discussed a Lindholme drop, and were considering breaking procedure by dropping the gear upwind from the ship. We thought this would give the

Fishing vessel Shin Huie *with attendant rescue helicopter, 22 July 1983. (Hartog Blok)*

survivors a better chance of survival, as we suspected that the dinghy drift rate would be faster than that of the trawler; at least this is what we hoped would happen. However, the Lindholme drop was not approved by Southern Air Command, and they advised us that a Court-Republic helicopter from Port Elizabeth ('Rescue 402') was airborne. We were to establish communications with it as soon as possible and direct it to the ship in distress.

"At 16.15 'Rescue 402' was in the area and started hoisting survivors. The helicopter could only spend 30 minutes in the area. Due to the heavy swell and severe rocking motion of the vessel, the pilot also had some difficulty with the hoisting. After half an hour only four men had been lifted by the helicopter and they had to leave the area heading for Cape St. Francis. In the meantime, 'Rescue 404', from Mossel Bay, was en route to the area with an estimated arrival at 17.25. This chopper had some difficulty finding us, and overshot the search area by 12 miles, so we homed it in using green Verys and flares. At 17.30, by which time it was almost dark, 404 started hoisting and managed to take off six crew before suffering winch failure. We were advised that a vessel *Kuswag 3* was steaming for the area and estimating arrival at 22.00 hours. At 18.30 communication was established with *Kuswag 3*, and at 21.00, when she was 14 miles away, a green Very was fired to assist her with her homing to the area. At 21.53 she reported having the stricken vessel's lights in sight, and advised us that we were at liberty to return to Cape Town. We did so, landing at 23.30 hours with 800 gallons of fuel remaining after a flying time of ten hours. All of us on board the Shack had agreed that the vessel was of control, but the situation did not appear to be as desperate as the radio operator of the trawler had made it out to be. Nonetheless, Southern Air Command had maintained positive control throughout the search and all communications with the associated rescue units had worked well."

Japie Horn – pilot

"The following story of an encounter with the US Navy over the Indian Ocean in April 1980 is spread over two days. On the first day we were detailed to find an American task force in the Indian Ocean; it consisted of an aircraft carrier and two guided-missile destroyers. I think the squadron had already been out looking, but couldn't find them; so then we went out. In the afternoon we were at 3,000 feet heading west, and just about to go off-task, when the radar reported a contact at about 90 miles or so distance, 300 miles west of Cape Town. We investigated and saw that there were three ships, so we then started flying in between them to take photographs. Our rear camera door was open, and the old F95 camera was operating. The ships were steaming at about 20 knots in a 'vic' formation. There were some personnel out on the aircraft carrier's deck watching us, however on the two missile destroyers there were none. Halfway through the photo-runs, on one of the turns, a Sea King helicopter suddenly appeared. They tried to catch us, but although we were doing only about 140 to 150 knots, they couldn't. I don't think they could really match that speed; they could perhaps do 120 to 130 knots or so. They also took photographs of us, but we didn't know that then.

"Only about a month or three later, when I was the adjutant of the squadron, as well as the ops officer at Cape Town International, we got a letter through the intelligence service which noted: 'Here is what your aircraft did in our formation, and here are the photographs of the Shackleton' – very interesting. Anyway, we didn't think much of it; we were still laughing about it and thinking they couldn't catch us.

"After we had photographed them all we had just climbed away and set course for Cape Town, landing two or three hours later. I think it was a Thursday, because on the Friday, the people from Maritime Command, Southern Air Command at that stage, pitched up at the squadron and said they wanted to go and have a look at this task force. Jesus man, curiosity, I think, or just to get away from a desk, or possibly just to get into an aircraft I guess. So, fine, we scratched together a crew and off we went. The OC of the squadron later told me that they were trying to 'firewall' the information because of the tense political situation at the time. We couldn't agree on our route; via False Bay, or slinking out round the western side of the peninsula – I think we went out that way. Anyway, we got out there; over Robben Island, and we set course. We were flying at 180 degrees at about 2,000 or 3,000 feet or something, and then started looking for the ships. Their speed was a bit of a 'guestimation', but we were quite certain they were south of Cape Point, heading towards Iran. When we got to Slangkop lighthouse, on the western side of the peninsula, the

Top: 28 April 1980 1716 J MR.3 of 35 Squadron. Photo taken by the US Navy. (Japie Horn)
Below: 28 April 1980 USN task force taken by WO Barnard from Shack 1716. (Japie Horn)

radar reported three contacts, and if I remember correctly, bearing 160 at 75 miles. It was then decided that we should switch off the radar and descend to about 200 feet or lower – whose idea this was I don't know. It may have been either the OC or the guys from command, but I don't know what the bloody idea was. Anyway, I just flew along; it wasn't my show, I was just the co-pilot. Funnily enough, every time the OC wanted to do something he said, 'OK, you fly along with me'.

"So off we went on the radar, or the navigator's plot. At about 25 or 30 miles from their projected position, where they were supposed to be, we just pitched the aircraft up at about 2,500 feet and levelled off. Radar on, sector scan about 15 or 20 degrees either side of the nose. Obviously the US Navy guys picked it up because they were ready, and their ECMs (electronic countermeasures) were quite capable of distinguishing between any radars and so on. At what must have been about 20 to 17 miles we could see the three ships because their wakes were so evident. There was a north-westerly blowing so they were steaming downwind. They did an emergency turn – 45 degrees to the right – and in that emergency turn they launched an F-14 Tomcat (but we didn't know it at that stage!). At about 15 miles I suggested we turn away, because their emergency turn indicated they meant business, and we were provoking them as well. Their scan of us was almost like gunnery radar, so we made a turn to the right and began flying away. Our passengers had now all seen what they wanted to see and done what they wanted to do. Not long after that the guy in the tail said, 'Oh *******', there was something behind us, closing at very high speed. I looked through the window to the right and, yes, there was a black smoke trail – something was coming. So I turned up the ECMs on my radar. We had that sort of spark plug on the top (the 'Orange Harvest' aerial), and I could hear the gunnery/missile radar going 'glick, glick', and then it just locked onto us.

"Then the aircraft appeared, and I saw the Tomcat out on the right-hand side with its speed brakes still out, but then the brakes went in and the wings swung forward into the low-speed position, and there she sat. It was amazing to see something like that. Then they swung over to the other side of the aircraft and took pictures of us while we were taking pictures of them. We tried all the frequencies attempting to make contact with them…nothing. Then as we were moving away from the carrier formation they started to shift away slightly. All the guys were saying 'Let's turn back and see what happens'. The Tomcat moved back to his previous position on our right echelon, probably swearing at us, so we

F-14 Tomcat from USS Dwight D Eisenhower *formating on 35 Squadron MR.3, 8 December 1980. (Japie Horn)*

35 Squadron crew three in 1982. Standing: LTR Dawie Stegmann, Dudley Baines, Danie van der Merwe, Paul 'Swannie' Swanepoe, Japie Horn, Frans Fourie, Barry Berghege, K C Bird, André du Toit, and Peter 'PJ' le Grange. Crouching: LTR Petrus 'Miggie' Janson, Bryan Ferreira, and Tiro Vorster.

turned left and headed for home. He then disappeared behind us and went back to his ship. So, that was day two. The navigator said something he had heard on the radar suggested they were picking us up, but that must have been the ship, not the Tomcat.

"We also intercepted numerous Soviet task forces going around the Cape at different times, we had the Krestos and Makaros and early on, before my time, they had the Kiev aircraft carrier going around the Cape. Somehow I was instrumental in most of them, but it wasn't such a big story at that time.

"The was always drama with the Shackleton on 35 Squadron. Even on delivery when two stopped over at Brazzaville, one had to stay behind and there was a big rigmarole. There were also numerous incidents in-service including problems with the nose gear. Some were put down in the bushes next to the runway – they even built a hangar around one."

Rex Wickins – radio operator

"After I left the RAF I decided to return to South Africa. All ambition of working with my father at Houghton Garage was soon dispelled. I withdrew from the garage proposition and contemplated my future once again. After six months I panicked and fled back to what I knew, Shackletons and 35 Squadron in the SAAF. Back in Gibraltar in 1963, a flight of three new Shackletons for the South African Air Force had transited through on their way home to Cape Town; I had obviously fraternised with many of the SAAF crew members. One in particular was Flt Sgt Leon Bloemhof, and we became good friends. By 1971 he had risen to the rank of major, and had also been appointed a captain on 35 Squadron. He was to be my introduction to a straightforward passage, into the SAAF and on to 35 Squadron based in Cape Town.

"Before the posting to 35 I was obliged to endure three months of 'training' and kitting out back at Swartkops. The 11 years since parting company with Sgt Major 'Mickey Mouse' Bardenhorst and his torturous parade ground seemed like a lifetime.

The whole set-up felt decidedly naive and far from the professionalism of the RAF. I was taking a step backwards; even the equipment was largely out of date. It felt like I was in the army rather than the air force. As I had left for England Prime Minister Harold Macmillan had made his historic 'Wind of Change' speech, and now the noose was slowly beginning to tighten. Upgrading and co-operation with the RAF had ceased. Moving down to Cape Town, the situation distanced itself and 35 Squadron seemed removed from the iron fist being perpetrated by the rest of the air force, army and police, specifically in South-West Africa and Angola. As a maritime entity 35 Squadron never participated in any 'colonial policing', unlike the RAF where at times we had been rampant! I wrote on the back of a postcard sent from Aden to my brother in 1964, that we were bombing tribesmen, but I was actually practising for when I came home. Written in jest, but that was the mind-set of most white South Africans at the time.

"Today Cape Town has become an international tourist destination, huge alterations and extensions to the airport have occurred. Yet the four large hangars in which 35 Squadron was accommodated on the opposite side of the airport from the civilian air terminal, remain much as they were in 1972. Sanctions, specifically military, were in force, which severely restricted our operations. Airframe and engine hours were rationed, and we flew less and less, conserving ourselves for the search and rescue role more than anything else. Hanging around the squadron every day, doing very little started driving me up the wall. I took to walking the perimeters to stop myself going 'dilly' from boredom.

"There were a few interludes that helped break the monotony, one most notable was a flight to Robben Island. Interestingly it was instigated by the annual officers' mess dining-in night, an event that usually entails having something special on the menu. My mischievous flight engineer, Andy Anderson, had informed me with a wink, that crayfish was always on the menu. Where did all the crayfish come from? Robben Island no less. My knowledge of this world-famous speck in the sea off Cape Town was minimal. We were aware that 'terrible and dangerous terrorists' were incarcerated in a maximum-security prison on the island, and not much more than that. It was common knowledge that nobody would dare to go within a mile of its shore without endangering their lives. Without any human exploitation for years, the shore around the island was seething with crayfish. Andy recruited me amongst the divers. All we had to do was get there, no easy matter for the 'man in the street', but not a problem for us. We secured the services of a local 28 Squadron Dakota from Ysterplaat, which dropped us off on the prison airfield, keeping its engines running. It turned around and departed before you could blink.

"A warden in a Jeep met us and quickly drove us down to the seaward shore, far from prying eyes. We donned our wetsuits and goggles, and began to plunder the ocean floor filling a large number of hessian sacks with crayfish. Our departure was as hasty as our arrival. The warden was on hand to whisk us back a couple of hours later, but not before we had a full catch. Our Dak, having finished its mission, ducked back into Robben Island to pick us up. Still with engines running, the tail was spun around and we clambered in with our catch and were airborne in a flash. Gone in sixty seconds, to coin a phrase.

"Sgt Andy Anderson was always the instigator of mischievous or dubious proposals. One weekend, while duty sergeant, he decided we should help ourselves to a small amount of Avgas. For us, being the security, it would be a simple undertaking. I positioned my Lotus under the wing of a parked Shack, and was passed the end of a hosepipe, the other end having been inserted into one of the wing tanks by Andy. The knowledge of a flight engineer was crucial for this exercise, and I was encouraged to suck on the end of the hosepipe and then place it in the tank of the Lotus.

"Lack of experience was to be my downfall. On the first try I had not sucked hard enough, in fact only enough to encourage a small amount that settled in the curve of the pipe. 'Nee man, you must suck harder,' he extorted, which I did. Still naive to this way of filling my tank, I was slow off the mark, and received a mouthful of high-octane. This would be excellent for the Lotus, but not for my mouth. I felt as though I had been kicked in the teeth, my throat took immediate exception to the intrusion and clamped up like a duck's arse when it hits water. It was no joke! I couldn't breathe! I seriously thought my days had come to an end. My lungs were empty, and my throat refused to open and let in any air. It was no laughing matter, but I survived and eventually the Lotus had a full tank. My curiosity of how the high-octane fuel would affect the performance of the Lotus was satisfied, as well as how it affects the throat.

"Occasions arose, infrequently as they were, to complete a reconnaissance up the west coast as far as the Angolan border and a bit beyond. Some flights needed an overnight refuel at Windhoek in order to get home. All that was required of us was to report any Soviet or Cuban naval and maritime activity. Nothing spectacular, and as far as we were concerned, not much to get excited about. We had little

'Shack attack' at Cape Town airport – some flee, others freeze. (Rex Wickins)

idea of the purpose of our reports, and returned to base in due course. Only in the last few years, and after reading a number of books on the Border War and the war in Angola, did I realise the purpose of our reconnaissance. It is more than likely, except for a few senior officers, we all remained in ignorance of this considerable battle that lasted some 12 years.

"The writing was on the wall…or hangar in my case. 'Hanging around' was beyond my tolerance of inactivity. I decided to buy myself out of the SAAF, for an acceptable amount, around R700 if I remember. I was lured with an invitation from a good friend Clive Perks, to join him in a business venture back in Johannesburg. My flying days as part of a Shack crew were over. According to my logbooks I had accumulated a total of 4,008 hours and 30 minutes, which translates into 167 days or 23 weeks or six months on the unique, demanding, but dependable 'growling' beasts that have come to be regarded with great affection by all who flew in them. My last flight ever in a Shackleton was on 21 September 1972 in No. 1721 of 35 Squadron, and lasted just over two hours.

"No.35 Squadron's Shackletons were finally decommissioned in 1984. They had been dispersed, not quite ignominiously, but in different directions. One, 1723, ended up on top of a roadhouse situated close to the N1 road in Soweto, just outside Johannesburg. I have bored my family to death telling them each time we drive past, 'I flew in that aircraft once'. Two were destined for the SAAF Museum. A restored Shackleton of 35 Squadron was invited to visit an air show in the UK. The painfully restored 'Pelican 16' was on its way to participate in the 1994 Royal International Air Tattoo at Fairford, when it crashed in the Sahara Desert. [See Lionel Ashbury's account below.] Although it had been standing on static display for almost ten years it had been lovingly restored and at the time of the crash was in prime condition. En route the aircraft, after an engine fire, made a miraculous crash-land-

The Shackleton's last hurrah with 35 Squadron, 22 November 1984. (Japie Horn)

ing in the inky black of night in the Mauritanian desert. All the crew were able to exit almost unscathed, and were rescued within a few hours. The crash-landing had been made with the ground never in sight, the descent being accomplished by brilliant airmanship and with the aid of a radio altimeter. Virtually impossible to retrieve from its isolated and desolate position, it remains there as if in a graveyard. At least it will not be desecrated by being placed on top of a roadhouse!"

On 23 November 1984 the Shackletons were officially withdrawn from active service. In Cape Town a parade and flypast (by the last three airworthy aircraft) were held to mark their passing. In that same year 35 Squadron was awarded the Sword of Peace which was in recognition of their countless SAR operations undertaken during the previous 27 years.

*That was not quite the end for the SAAF Shacks as it was decided to retain an aircraft in flying condition at the SAAF Museum. Telecom operator **Lionel Ashbury** tells the story of 1722's refurbishment.*

"The whole concept of getting a retired Shackleton of the SAAF airworthy again actually commenced in 1991. The specific aircraft in mind was Shackleton 1722. This was one of the last three still airworthy and serviceable when they were phased out of service with 35 Squadron on 23 November 1984. The other two were Shackletons 1716 and 1721. On 4 December 1984 these two were eventually flown from Cape Town to Pretoria, where they were officially handed over to the main branch of the SAAF Museum at AFB Swartkop, the oldest air force base in the SAAF. Shackleton 1722 remained with 35 Squadron at D F Malan airport in Cape Town, and was frequently ground run by W/O1 (retired) Henry James 'Pottie' Potgieter,

Lionel Ashbury still looking after 1722. (Rex Wickins)

(affectionately known as Uncle Pottie), who kept her in pristine condition. He had been involved with the SAAF Shackletons since 1959 and was the longest-serving member of the SAAF who served on them.

"The idea of officially handing Shackleton 1722 over to the satellite branch of the SAAF Museum at AFB Ysterplaat, had been sparked off towards the latter part of 1991. A target delivery date was set for 6 December. In November of that year Uncle Pottie and his team began in all earnestness to render her fully airworthy again. After a number of high-speed runs on the cross-runway at D F Malan, she finally took to the skies again on 4 December 1991 for a test flight. It was exactly seven years to the day since a SAAF Shackleton had last flown. The test flight proved to be successful, and two days later, on 6 December, she was finally flown over to Ysterplaat.

'Pottie' 'Oom' Potgieter with 1722 in 2018. (Rex Wickins)

"She was stowed in a hangar for a year and a half at her new home before being removed to create space for other operational aircraft. She was exposed to the elements, Uncle Pottie was not going to have any of that! He requested that she be flown back to 35 Squadron where he had ample space in a hangar for her. He was adamant that he was not prepared to let 1722 be exposed to the elements, like the other two up in Pretoria; they had been quite badly bleached by the harsh sun of the Transvaal. By then he had already retired, having terminated his long service with the SAAF, in 1992. Shackleton 1722 was finally flown back to 35 Squadron on 4 June 1993. She remained and was flown on regular occasions until the squadron moved to Ysterplaat on 18 November 2002, and she remains there to this day."

On 24 September 2006, Shackleton 1722 made its last flight and since than it has been maintained in an airworthy condition, but restricted to periodic ground runs. The main reasons for the grounding decision were a combination of cost and a decreasing number of qualified air and ground crew.

*As Rex Wickins has said, there was an attempt to bring one aircraft to the UK for air show appearances. This was sadly thwarted by technical issues while it was on its way. **Lionel Ashbury** was one of those on board for the fated trip north that ended in the total loss of the aeroplane.*

1722 c.2006 with Milnerton Lighthouse in the background. She flew her last flight on 29 March 2007. (Japie Horn)

"I just happened to have been one of the 19 crew members on board Pelican 16. I was so looking forward to visiting the UK, which would have been my first trip abroad ever, it would have been a dream come true. Even today, I am yet to leave the African continent. Hopefully one day I might just get the opportunity again.

"The museum curator at the SAAF Museum at Ysterplaat, the late Ron Bussio, had the idea of getting a SAAF Shackleton serviceable to embark on a visit to Osh-kosh, in Wisconsin, USA, to attend the annual air show there. In early 1993 the idea was put forward to the then chief of the SAAF, the late Lt Gen James Kriel, during an informal discussion in a SAAF pub one evening. He was a former Shack-leton pilot, having been the OC of 35 Squadron and Ysterplaat, respectively. He liked the idea and pledged to give it his full support. However, it was not to be with Shackleton 1722, as she had only 80-odd hours fatigue life left on her main spar. This was the least of the three remaining Shackletons, whereas 1721 had 400-odd hours left and 1716 the most, with still in excess of 2,000 hours left. The latter was one of only two SAAF Shackletons that had ever undergone a complete re-spar and refit (the other one was 1717). They were the first two Shackletons that were rolled out to the SAAF at Woodford, England, in May 1957.

"It was therefore decided to prepare 1716 for the trip to Oshkosh. By then she had been on the ground for over eight years, so a lot of work and preparation lay ahead to render her serviceable and airworthy again. Uncle Pottie was elected to gather a team of retired and serving members who had served on Shackletons in the past. This included himself and they were nine in total who formed the resto-ration team. They were as follows:

W/O1 (Ret) Henry 'Pottie' Potgieter – ground crew chief and aircraft fitter
W/O1 (Ret) Vernon 'Gus' Güse – aircraft fitter
W/O1 (Ret) Gert 'Buks' Bronkhorst – aircraft fitter and ex-flight engineer
W/O1 Neville 'Pine' Pienaar – aircraft electrician
W/O2 Frans Fourie – first flight engineer and aircraft fitter
W/O2 Johan 'JP' van Zyl – second flight engineer and aircraft fitter
W/O2 (Ret) M J 'Pat' Boyd – aircraft fitter
Robert 'Bobby' Whitfield-Jones – avionics and instrument fitter from the
Atlas Man Group (AMG), affiliated to the SAAF
Kevin 'Spud' Murphy – avionics fitter from AMG

"About June 1993 the project started. The team would commute by SAAF transport aircraft, which varied from the C-130s of 28 Squadron, who ran a shuttle service between Pretoria and Cape Town twice a week, or the C-47TPs Dakotas of 35 Squadron. They would then spend a week or two at Swartkop working on 1716, return home and embark on a trip to Pretoria again a fortnight later. This continued all the way up to late January 1994. In the week prior to finalising the airworthy restoration, I accompanied the team with another fellow AEO W/O2 C W Ander-son. During that week we worked furiously, from dusk to dawn, to round off the final touches that would declare 1716 fit to take to the skies again.

"Then dawned 2 February 1994, the day that it was declared that 1716 was ready to be test flown. By then the two nominated pilots of Pelican 16, Maj Eric 'Oompie' Pienaar and Maj Peter Dagg, as well as the proposed navigator and mission commander, Maj Horace Blok, had already arrived in Pretoria for the test flight. It just so happened that there was an air show to be held on that day by the SAAF Museum at Swartkop. It started at 10.00 hours local time that morning. Because of this the Shackleton crew had to bide their time until it was completed, before embarking on the test flight. At 16.30 the show had come to a close however, very few of the spectators had departed for home. Somehow the word had spread that the Shackleton was yet to fly and the majority stood fast. Finally, the big moment arrived. The aircrew boarded, started her up and taxied to the holding point of the active runway. Buks Bronkhorst, Spud Murphy and myself remained behind to see them off and to drive the vehicles across to neighbouring Waterkloof, to the east, as that was where she was to land once the test flight had been completed. After they were given clearance to line up, they taxied her onto the runway. She stood there for probably three minutes, with engines running, ready to go, while everyone was waiting with bated breath for the take-off run. Then suddenly, the revs of the four Rolls-Royce Griffons increased to that remarkable roar, the brakes were released and off she thundered down the runway. As she rotated to get airborne, all the spectators spontaneously applauded and with great enthusiasm. One could sense their happiness and satisfaction which, no doubt, matched that of ours, who stayed behind on the ground. What a moment! One I will never forget as long as I may live.

"The test flight proved to be successful and after a low-level beat-up over Swartkop, she was flown to Waterkloof, and after another low-level beat-up she landed safely. The next morning, 3 February 1994, with all the crew members on board,

1716's first flight after restoration, Waterkloof, 3 February 1994. (Dave Lawrence via Adrian Balch)

she was airborne again bound for Cape Town for the first time since she left there
nine years and two months before. Having landing safely at D F Malan she was
taxied to the 35 Squadron dispersal. After shut-down, she and the crew were met
and welcomed back by a piper from the Cape Town Highlanders playing a lament,
along with fellow colleagues, friends and spouses of those who flew her home.

"In the months that followed every available pair of hands was called on to
assist with the tough and dedicated work that was the order of the day – we only
had five months left to complete everything. Meanwhile the appointed mission
commander of Pelican 16, Maj Horace Blok, was also working extremely hard
behind the scenes preparing for our trip to Oshkosh. By then, the date for the
departure from Cape Town had been set for Friday 8 July 1994, and was planned
to be at midnight. Maj Blok single-handedly planned and arranged every conceiv-
able item you could think for such a huge trip; including the planned route, stopovers, passports, visas, over-flight rights, accommodation and meal bookings, fuel
and landing fees, the required inoculations for each crew member, to name but a
few. Besides doing all this he still occasionally had to travel to Pretoria and back to
give presentations to the SAAF Board on the progress of the preparation. It was at
one of these meetings that he was shocked to learn that the trip to Oshkosh was
no longer approved. This was mainly because the board unanimously felt that the
long flight from Africa to Canada across the Atlantic Ocean, with an ageing aircraft,
was deemed not to be a safe and sound idea. However, in the interim, word had
reached the RAF authorities of the proposed trip. Upon learning this, they contacted Maj Blok and proposed a visit to the UK, en route to Oshkosh. This the SAAF
Board was fully aware of and when they saw the disappointment on Maj Blok's face,
they suggested a trip to the UK only instead, to attend the Royal International Air
Tattoo at Fairford, Gloucestershire in July. To him this was 'first prize' and he glad-
ly agreed with their suggestion, rather than not having any trip at all.

"Back at 35 Squadron, 1716 was thoroughly inspected from nose to tail, every
single Perspex window, nose canopy, cockpit canopy and tail cone were newly
replaced, complete with new rubber seals along the edges. She was given an overall fresh coat of paint. In the end, she looked as shiny and new as she must have
been when she was rolled out brand, spanking new, at Woodford.

"During the last few weeks leading up to the departure date the pilots started
their training, renewing their general flying ratings, instrument ratings and landings,
on type, in order to get their type ratings and bring them up to date again. In between the flying days, the avionics fitter Spud Murphy executed a modification to
install a GPS system. The control unit he installed at the navigators' station, and
the small fin antenna of the GPS he mounted on top of the Orange Harvest 'spark-
plug' antenna. The interior of the aircraft was also spruced up, each seat was fitted
with a brand-new sheepskin cover, albeit in white as opposed to the olive-green
ones that the seats were covered with before. Even the ceiling and side panels were
given a fresh coat of paint.

"Finally the date arrived for our departure. The crew of 19 members were briefed to report to the squadron at 21.30 hours on the evening of Thursday 7 July 1994. Ample time was left for each of us to be checked by customs for the departure, and have our passports and visas checked and confirmed. There were dozens of people waiting to see us off, fellow colleagues, family members and friends, all there to bid the crew good-bye. At approximately 23.30 we said our last farewells and boarded Pelican 16.

"We finally got airborne from Cape Town at 00:06 on Friday 8 July 1994. The first leg to the UK was scheduled to be a planned 13½ hours flight to Libreville, Gabon, for the first stopover. The route, flight durations and stopovers planned from Cape Town to the UK were as follows:

Friday 8 July 1994: Cape Town – Libreville, Gabon; 13½ hours; one night
Saturday 9 July 1994: Libreville – Abidjan, Ivory Coast; 5½ hours; two nights
Monday 11 July 1994: Abidjan – Lisbon, Portugal; 13½ hours; two nights
Wednesday 13 July 1994: Lisbon – Duxford, England; 4 hours

"The main events during our visit to the UK, were based on invitations to participate in the Flying Legends air show at Duxford, Cambridgeshire, followed by the Royal International Air Tattoo at Fairford. The reverse route of the above was planned to be followed on the return trip back to South Africa, for an arrival in Cape Town on 8 August 1994.

The following 19 people were on board Pelican 16:
Aircrew:
Maj Eric 'Oompie' (Little Uncle) Pienaar – pilot and aircraft commander
Maj Peter Dagg – co-pilot
Maj Jonathan Balladon – third pilot
Maj Hartog 'Horace' Blok – first navigator and mission commander
Maj Blake Vorster – second navigator
W/O2 Frans Fourie – first flight engineer
W/O2 Johan 'JP' van Zyl – second flight engineer
W/O1 Chris Viviers – telecom leader
Flt Sgt Fred Deutschmann – telecom operator
Sgt Lionel Ashbury – telecom operator

Ground crew and other key personnel:
Col Derrick Page – PRO and liaison officer
Capt Anthony 'Tony' Adonis – treasurer
W/O1 (Ret) Henry 'Pottie' Potgieter – ground crew chief and aircraft fitter
W/O1 (Ret) Vernon 'Gus' Güse – aircraft fitter
W/O1 (Ret) Gert 'Buks' Bronkhorst – aircraft fitter

W/O1 Neville 'Pine' Pienaar – aircraft electrician
Robert 'Bobby' Whitfield-Jones – avionics and instrument fitter
Kevin 'Spud' Murphy – avionics fitter
Ron Bussio – SAAF Museum curator

"Numerous changes took place during the selection of who was to embark on the trip, before the 19 members were decided upon and finalised. As an example, our OC at 35 Squadron at the time, Lt Col 'Cassie' Carstens, was initially included as third pilot, but due to his commitment as OC, his inclusion was declined. This was also the case with W/O2 Pat Boyd and my colleague W/O2 Andy Anderson. Andy was very disappointed at first, but in the end, with what happened to Pelican 16, he was rather delighted that he was not on board after all. Sadly, five members have since passed to higher service:

Frans Fourie – May 2001
Ron Bussio – June 2002
Eric 'Oompie' Pienaar – 17 December 2002
Vernon 'Gus' Güse – 20 December 2007
Fred Deutschmann – 15 March 2015

"Of the remaining 14 members, 13 still reside in South Africa, while Kevin Murphy, a born Irishman, and his wife emigrated to the UK in 2001.

"Pelican 16 left South Africa and headed north. We encountered problems going into Abidjan, which required an engine change which was successfully completed and we set off again, this time bound for Lisbon. Early in the morning of 13 July No. 4 engine started running hot and we headed west towards the coast in search of cooler air. Soon afterwards sparks were seen coming from between the two propellers on No. 3 engine. This was immediately feathered and a Mayday was transmitted. An attempt was made to restart No. 4, but very quickly it seriously overheated, with the temperatures going off the clock. The attempt to shut it down again resulted in the propellers only partially feathering. The aircraft now only had two engines running, and even with full power, there was little hope of remaining airborne. Blake Vorster did his best to navigate the rapidly descending aircraft away from high ground and the crew took up their crash positions."

In the words of third pilot **Jonathan Balladon**:

"There was a loud, tearing, grating bounce, followed by a relative silence as the motors were throttled back and we were airborne again. In that millisecond, I was at once surprised at the relatively gentle impact and expecting a sudden stop to come next. Then we touched again and the deceleration and noise came back…more violent this time but not as rough as I had imagined it would be. And then it stopped.

"There was no fire, the aircraft had remained largely intact and everyone evacuated it successfully; the worst injury was a gash to 'Pottie' Potgieter's head, which soon stopped bleeding. The crew were able to get a radio working and at 07.30 the next morning they were found by a French navy Atlantique patrol aircraft, which dropped first aid and emergency equipment and directed a UN patrol to our position. Three hours later more vehicles appeared to rescue all 19 of us. Poor old Pelican 16 was left to its desert home and still sits there to this day."

The crash site was near Agwanit in the Western Sahara, a territory disputed for years between Morocco and the Polisario Front, a Sahrawi rebel movement working for independence for the region. The Shackleton crew members were helped by the Polisario, even though South Africa did not recognise its government-in-exile until ten years later.

At the ceremony to mark the retirement of the Shackletons, the chief of the South African Defence Forces General Constand Viljoen, said "We will do everything in our power to obtain a suitable replacement for the Shackleton. As an interim measure however, 35 Squadron will be equipped with Dakota aircraft in order to supplement the Albatross reconnaissance aircraft (Piaggio 166). The squadron did indeed re-equip with C-47 Dakotas – locally referred to as 'Dakletons' – a seemingly backward step as they had a far shorter endurance, little in the way of MR equipment and no weapons-carrying ability.

After 1990, the squadron was also tasked with a transport role, and in 2018 it was still flying Dakotas, albeit slightly more modern C-47TP turboprop versions.

The sad remains of Pelican 16 at Agwanit, Western Sahara. (SAAF Museum)

FINALE

A great many Shackleton stories have come my way, so much so that even in two volumes there has not been room to include them all. To draw this volume to a close I decided to include two more contributions, one from the aircrew and one from the ground crew which, for me, sum up quite nicely the challenges the 'Boys' faced every day.

AN AIRCRAFT ROTATION FROM BALLYKELLY TO MAJUNGA IN 1968

Sqn Ldr Tony Smart – pilot 42 and 210 Squadrons

"There was a last-minute change from WR955 to WL800 due to problems with the 'prepared' aircraft. We had a full crew of ten, plus five ground engineers covering all the major trades – engine, airframe, instruments, radio and radar.

25 Oct Ballykelly – Gibraltar eight hours 15 minutes

"Propeller oil leak from No. 2. It was inspected by the engineers and we decided to continue to Malta, where a two-day stopover was planned, and spares would be available from the resident Shackleton squadron.

26 Oct Gibraltar – Malta five hours 50 minutes

"The leak continued, so new propeller seals were fitted to No. 2. Departure was delayed by diplomatic clearance problems for overflying Egypt on the leg from El Adem to Djibouti.

30 Oct Malta – El Adem three hours 50 minutes

"This was a refuelling stop for the next stage of our journey, the high-level flight to Djibouti. There was a severe leak from propeller No. 2, and the engine was shut down. HQ were informed by radio, and arrangements were made to despatch an Argosy transport aircraft from Malta to El Adem with a complete new propeller assembly, plus a crane to facilitate lifting. On arrival, our engineers did as much preparation as possible. As soon as the Argosy arrived, the propeller assembly was rapidly changed, and after ensuring that our diplomatic clearance was still valid, we departed for Djibouti. The squadron commander, Wg Cdr George Sherret (a navigator), had decided to fly with us from Malta to Djibouti, so was able to see the problems we were encountering.

30 Oct El Adem – Djibouti nine hours 50 minutes

"Due to the overflight of Egypt this leg had to be completed at high level (for a Shackleton), around 8,000 to 10,000 feet. After around five hours No.1 engine was shut down due to fluctuating low oil pressure, high temperatures and associated vibrations. On arrival it was inspected by our 'on board' engine fitter who confirmed the need for a replacement engine, and HQ arranged for one to be sent from Aden by Hercules. When it arrived it was fitted by our ground engineering team, with the help of the flight engineer and, following two air test flights, we departed for Mombasa.

6 Nov Djibouti air tests 40 minutes and 20 minutes

"Two air tests. The first one was unusually long, so obviously showed problems, but I can't recall what.

6 Nov Djibouti – Mombasa ten hours 25 minutes

"We departed late at night for our usual low-level flight around the Horn of Africa, avoiding Somalian airspace, and with clear instructions not to use Mogadishu as a diversion airfield (even then they were not considered to be friendly). Just after daybreak, we noticed oil pouring from the No. 1 engine propeller assembly onto the exhaust stubs, with associated puffs of smoke – the engine was shut down. A couple of hours later, due to oil pressure, temperature and rpm fluctuations, we shut down No. 3 engine and continued to Mombasa on the remaining two engines. No. 1 was restarted and kept at idle rpm for the landing in case of further problems. Post-flight inspection revealed that the problems with No. 3 could be rectified with our on-board spares, but that No. 1 required a new propeller assembly, and No. 2 and No. 4 had cracked cylinder blocks and would have to be replaced. So, we had arrived in Mombasa with no serviceable engines!

"The new prop and two replacement engines were sent from Singapore and took nearly two weeks to arrive. In the meantime the two engines were removed, but only after we managed to locate the only crane in Mombasa capable (allegedly) of lifting the Griffon. This was found at the docks and had to be driven, at about two miles an hour, to the airfield. As it turned out it couldn't really cope with a Griffon engine without tipping up, so we solved the problem by sitting a number of the crew members on the back to balance it! When the Hercules finally arrived from Singapore, the two engines and the propeller assembly were unloaded, the unserviceable items were put on board, and they departed for home.

"Over the next few days the new propeller assembly was fitted to No. 1, and the No. 2 and 4 engines installed. However the propeller assembly could not be fitted onto the No.4 engine, due to an incorrect thread on the prop shaft (this was a newly reconditioned engine from Rolls-Royce!), and so yet another engine was requested. This was eventually sent from Ballykelly on a Hercules, accompanied by an engineering staff officer from HQ to see 'what the hell was going on'. In their wisdom they sent an electrical specialist, when all our problems had been associated with the engines, but as it turned out this was not a bad thing. As I was briefing him on the problems we had encountered, the lead engineer (the engineer who had set off from Ballykelly as Cpl Croft, but who I had just had the great pleasure of informing him of his immediate promotion to sergeant), came in from the airport to tell me that the aircraft batteries had now gone flat. They could not be re-charged at the airport as they had no charging equipment that could deal with NiCad batteries.

"This was a great opportunity to show the visitor the problems we had been having – the local agent referred us to the docks (again), so a visit was made and arrangements made for the batteries to be charged – a process that cost us another day. The visiting staff officer returned to the UK on the Hercules, fully aware of 'what the hell had been going on', and his parting shot was to say that he was amazed we had managed as well as we had under the circumstances. Eventually all our work was completed, engine runs were carried out and the aircraft declared ready for air test.

25 Nov Mombasa air test ten minutes

"On take-off the temperature on the newly replaced No. 2 engine went off the clock, and it was immediately shut down. Inspection showed blocked coolant channels. Nothing could be done, so another engine was required (subsequent inspection of the engine revealed that the coolant channels were blocked with milling swarf – yet another engine fresh from refurbishment at Rolls-Royce!) I think THIS replacement came from Aden, and after fitting, a further air test was carried out.

10 Dec Mombasa air test 40 minutes

"I have no record of any particular problems, but some work was obviously required, as another air test was carried out the next day.

11 Dec Mombasa air test 45 minutes

"The aircraft was finally fully serviceable. During the time in Mombasa I had developed a quite severe case of 'Coral Ear', an infection caused by sand getting into the ear. This caused acute pain and loss of balance, and I was treated with antibiotics by the local UK naval surgeon. Climbing off the aircraft after the final air test I almost fell off the steps, and could not keep my balance. A quick visit to the navy doc, and he said there was no way I could fly for at least a week. My final signal (number 138) to HQ said in effect, 'WL800 now serviceable. Captain unable to fly for minimum seven days due to recurrence of previously reported ear infection.'

14 Dec Mombasa – Majunga four hours 45 minutes

"A new captain, Les Miller previously my co-pilot, arrived from Ballykelly via Nairobi, and I waved the aircraft and crew off to Majunga. I stayed on in Mombasa for a further week before getting the overnight train to Nairobi, then flew by Alitalia 707 to Antananarivo (the capital of Madagascar). I spent the night there, and then flew to Majunga on the local shuttle flight; along with some locals and their livestock (one cow, some sheep and numerous chickens!) On arrival at Majunga I submitted a full chronological report, from the time we left Ballykelly to the time the aircraft departed Mombasa – no questions were ever asked.

"In summary, we took 52 days to get the aircraft to Majunga, with an average speed of less than five miles an hour. Total flying time was 45 hours and 30 minutes, of which two hours and 35 minutes were air tests. We used nine engines; the four we set off with, No. 1 replaced in Djibouti, two No. 2s replaced in Mombasa, and two No. 4s replaced in Mombasa. No. 3 went all the way despite the shut-down! We also used one propeller oil seal set on No. 2 engine in Malta, one propeller assembly replaced on No. 2 engine in El Adem, and one propeller assembly replaced on No. 1 engine in Mombasa.

"This episode was not typical of my experience flying the Shackleton. In two tours, one on the Mk.3 with 42 Squadron at St. Mawgan and another on the Mk.2 with 210 Squadron at Ballykelly totalling around 2,500 flying hours, I experienced only a couple of engine problems resulting in shut-down. I think this does however highlight the value of a good crew and, perhaps even more so a good ground crew. We dealt with the problems in the air, but once we had landed it was down to the ground crew to get to work and attempt to ready the aircraft for the next flight, often working long hours under difficult conditions. For example, in those days Mombasa was not the modern airport it is today. There were no hangar facilities, so all work was done outside in all sorts of weather, from blazing sun to heavy rain, with rudimentary equipment – remember the inadequate crane?

"Our repeated requests for replacement engines must have caused headaches at headquarters in the UK. I'm sure they dreaded the arrival of another of my signals from Mombasa which would send them on another frantic search for yet another spare engine, but with good co-operation all round we got what we needed in the end."

J/T John May – engine fitter Trials Flight, 120 and 240 Squadrons

"Inter-squadron co-operation, or to put it another way, theft!

"What had been a beautiful spring day was drawing to a close early in 1953. This in itself was rare in this part of the UK as Ballykelly is situated in Northern Ireland; forecast area Rockall Malin – normally a very wet and windy place. I was at the time an engine fitter on the newly formed 240 Squadron, commanded by Sqn Ldr Sid Banks. He was a great navigator and man-manager, though in my experience a sometimes shaky pilot, flying with him as I did in Oxfords and Tiger Moths. Sgt Paddy Annett, and Cpl Ian Codner were in charge of the crew preparing our brand-new shiny Mk.2 Shackleton for a late-night take-off. The other engine fitter on duty with me, doing the pre-flight checks, was LAC Brian Farrell who came from St. Helens, Lancs.

"As it was to be a long flight a full fuel load of 3,292 gallons was required. Once fuelling was completed we then topped up the engine oil, which was loaded using the large oil bowser. As every qualified RAF tractor driver should know, by lining up the propellers in the Y configuration, and with the flaps fully up, you could safely drive the tractor and bowser between the inner and outer engines. The squadron tractor driver, 'Nobby' Clark, was a lazy airman who spent most of the time smoking, sleeping, or missing from the job.

"Now for the star of this story. Enter LAC Roy Light, late of Plymouth, my good friend of 60 plus years. Roy was an air wireless mechanic whose pre-flight check would take all of 30 seconds. That completed he had nothing to do for the next three to four hours until the flight departed. Being a very bright and active man, and easily bored, he was always willing to help – the caveat being not to get his hands dirty. However the rugby field, where he excelled, was a different matter and he used to come back plastered in mud from head to toe. Roy spotted that 'Nobby' was missing from his post on the David Brown tractor. This one, complete with spade anchor and winch, was a dangerous vehicle in the wrong hands. The tractor was already attached to the oil bowser and, as Roy loved driving tractors, this was an opportunity too good to miss. Roy set off, successfully driving the unit between the starboard engines and stopped, allowing Brian and me to top up the oil tanks.

"With Clark still missing, a now very confident Roy moved off around the nose of the aircraft to fill the port engines, thus completing the operation. At this stage of the pre-flight the bomb doors were open, allowing other trades access. Instead of driving the tractor between the inner and outer engines, Roy drove between the bomb doors and the inner port engine, leaving a ten-foot gash in the bomb door, just missing the undercarriage before stopping. Oops! Where at 2100 hours do you find a spare bomb door? This is where the second part of my first sentence makes sense. No. 269 Squadron were the other squadron based at Ballykelly. To keep operational, they had allowed one of their Mk.1 aircraft to become what was known as a 'Christmas tree'. Components were removed, and replaced with red labels to mark and record removed parts. In the breeze, the labels fluttered, hence the name Christmas tree. Apparently, there were 250 labels attached to this aircraft.

"Half of the pre-flight ground crew, with a bomb trolley, were dispatched to 'borrow' the bomb door from the 269 aircraft, whilst the riggers, with the aid of other trades, removed the damaged and unserviceable door. The replacement door was fitted and tested in less than two hours, achieved in the dark with the aid of torches, tractor headlights and muscle power, under the watchful eyes of Sgt Annett. Risk assessment and Health and Safety reports not needed! The aircraft's departure time was missed by less than an hour.

"As the ground crew had worked past midnight they were not required to report for duty until after lunch the following day. So it was that I was on duty to see the aircraft return and marshal it on to the pan later that afternoon. The only evidence to show what had happened the previous night was the tatty-looking port bomb door on 240 Squadron's gleaming white new Mk.2 Growler. The 'would-be' tractor driver, Roy Light, went on to a successful 30 plus years career in the Metropolitan

Police, instructing on motorcycles and powerful traffic cars. After such a disastrous start who would have thought that this would be the case?"

LEST WE FORGET

My wife Heather and I recently visited the 'Coastal Command church' situated right on the edge of what remains of St. Eval airfield in Cornwall. It is no surprise that the churchyard contains no fewer than 56 RAF graves, and once inside the church the care and attention paid to the memory of Coastal Command is all around you.

Here are the badges of all the 'Kipper Fleet' squadrons, and the Shackleton Association register of all those lost, over there is the font cover from the church at Changi, but of all the artefacts one very sobering one stands out. Mounted on the wall is the wooden cross from Sin Cowe Island which stood over the grave of Flt Sgt David Dancy, as described in Chapter Two. St. Eval church is a memorable place to visit, and brings home the debt we owe to the men and women of Coastal Command, wherever they may have served and in whatever role.

Dirty Avro Shackbat with a salt-caked
windscreen,
Butting out past Rockall in the mad March
days,
Looking for the Foxtrot,
Seeking out the Whiskey,
Long Atlantic rollers in dark greens and
greys.

Nothing on the radar, nothing on the Jez
buoys,
Sea state six to seven and the sub's gone
deep.
Back to Ballykelly
As the day is dawning,
Ten hours in the logbook and the Soviets
were asleep

The Sin Cowe Island cross in St. Eval church. (Steve Bond)

Brian Haining (with apologies to John Masefield)

So many stories, so many still to be told, so many yet to be discovered......

OPERATING UNITS BASED OUTSIDE THE UK

SQUADRONS

37 – 'Wise without eyes' Luqa 07.53–21.08.57, Khormaksar 21.08.57–07.09.67

38 – 'Before the dawn' Hal Far Luqa 09.53–10.65, 30.10.65–31.03.67

203 – 'East and West' Luqa 01.02.69–12.71

205 – 'First in Malaya' Changi 05.58–31.10.71

210 – 'Hovering in the heavens' Sharjah 01.11.70–15.11.71

224 – 'Faithful to a friend' Gibraltar 07.51–31.10.66

269 – 'We see all things' Gibraltar 01.01.52–24.03.52

OTHER UNITS

MARDET Sharjah (under Kinloss control) 08.67 – 01.11.70

SAAF 35 Squadron 'Shaya Amanzi' (Strike the Water) Ysterplaat 27.01.57 – 23.11.84

PRODUCTION LIST

Prototypes (3)
VW126, VW131, VW135

MR.1 (29)
VP254–VP268, VP281–VP294

MR.1A (47)
WB818–WB832, WB834–WB837, WB844–WB861, (WB862 cancelled), WG507–WG511, WG525–WG529

MR.2 (70)
WB833, WG530–WG533, WG553–WG558, WL737–WL759, WL785–WL801, WR951–WR969

MR.3 (34)
WR970–WR990, XF700–XF711, XF730, (XF732–XF734, XG912–XG924 all cancelled)

MR.3 SAAF (8)
1716–1723

Total built: 191

APPENDIX THREE

ACCIDENTS

All accidents to Shackleton aircraft based overseas, or which occurred overseas, and which resulted in the total loss of the aircraft.

12 Aug '51   VP283 224 Squadron
During conversion training at Gibraltar, approached too low, hit the runway and sheared off the undercarriage. Attempted a go around but ditched in the sea.

12 Feb '54   WL794 T 38 Squadron
Crashed into the sea off Gozo, Malta while exercising with a submarine. Ten killed. Sgt Norman Betts (air engineer), Sgt Percy Edlund (air signaller), Sgt James Henderson (air signaller), Sgt James Hennell (pilot), Sgt Peter Raddon (air signaller), Flt Sgt Wallis Rawlinson (air engineer), Sgt Dudley Skinner (air signaller), Master Nav Charles Sloan (navigator), Fg Off Albert Smallwood (navigator), and Flt Lt Raymond Stevenson (pilot).

14 Sep '57   WL792 K 224 Squadron
Crashed on the runway at Gibraltar following undercarriage collapse during an air display.

9 Dec '58   VP254 B 205 Squadron
Crashed in South China Sea 280 miles north of Labuan. Eleven killed. Sgt Peter Barnley (air signaller), Flt Lt Walter Bouttell (pilot), Flt Lt Stanley Bowater DFC AFC (co-pilot), Flt Sgt David Dancy DFC (air engineer), Fg Off Michael Jones (navigator), Sgt Peter Marshall (air signaller), Flt Lt Alan Moore (navigator), Flt Sgt Edward Owen (air signaller), Sgt John Sixsmith (air signaller), Master Sig James Stewart (air signaller), and Mr A R Miller (assistant police commissioner).

15 May '62   VP294 N 205 Squadron
Force-landed at Gan and damaged beyond repair.

8 Aug '63   1718 K 35 Squadron SAAF
Crashed in Wemmershook Mountains near Cape Town after striking a hill off its planned route during bad weather; 13 killed. Capt Thomas Silversten (co-pilot), 2nd Lt Charles (third pilot), Capt Jacques G Labuschagne (navigator), Lt Abraham Coetzee (second navigator), 2nd Lt George Smith (third navigator), CO Derek Strauss (flight engineer), WO2 Sydney Scully (second flight engineer), L/Cpl Marthienus Vorster (signals leader), Sgt David Sheasby (radio operator), L/Cpl Charl Viljoen

(second radio operator), L/Cpl Matthys Taljaard (third radio operator), L/Cpl Michel Bordreiss (fourth radio operator), and Airman Johannes Chamberlain.

4 Nov '67   WL786 E 205 Squadron

Ditched in the Indian Ocean 120 nm west of Lhokkrket, Sumatra, en route Gan–Changi following an engine failure and subsequent fire. Eight killed. Flt Sgt Roger Adams (AEOp), Flt Lt Hugh Blake (pilot), Fg Off Robert Bungay (pilot), Flt Lt Kenneth Greatorex (navigator), Plt Off David Love (navigator), Sgt David Morgan (air signaller), Flt Sgt Richard Rees (AEOp), and Flt Lt Ivor Stanley (AEOp).

1 Apr '68   WR956 Q Ballykelly Wing

Crash-landed at Ballykelly and struck off charge.

13 Jul '94   1716 J SAAF

Force-landed in the Western Sahara following double engine failure while en route to the UK. All 19 on board survived with only one minor injury.

OTHER PERSONNEL LOSSES

12 Aug '62   WG533 B 224 Squadron

Signaller Sgt Peter Gibbings fell from the aircraft near Gibraltar.

30 Nov '82   35 Squadron SAAF

Major Mike Bondesio died of a heart attack whilst piloting a Shackleton.

The total number of personnel who lost their lives in the Shackleton, including those based in the UK is 156, of which 44 were in the accidents listed above.

ABBREVIATIONS AND CODE NAMES

ADF	Automatic Direction Finder	DRC	Disappearing Radar Contact
AEO	Air Electronics Officer	ECM	Electronic Counter Measures
AEW	Airborne Early Warning		
A/F	After Flight	FEAF	Far East Air Force
AFB	Air Force Base	Fg Off	Flying Officer
Air Cdre	Air Commodore	FLOSY	Front for the Liberation of Occupied South Yemen
AM	Air Marshal		
ANZAC	Australia and New Zealand Army Corps	Flt Lt	Flight Lieutenant
		Flt Sgt	Flight Sergeant
AOC	Air Officer Commanding	GCA	Ground Controlled Approach
API	Air Position Indicator		
ASF	Aircraft Servicing Flight	Gp Capt	Group Captain
ASI	Air Speed Indicator	GR	General Reconnaissance
ASV	Air-to-Surface Vessel	HF	High Frequency
ASW	Anti-Submarine Warfare	HMAS	Her Majesty's Australian Ship
ATC	Air Traffic Control		
AUW	All-Up Weight	HMNZS	Her Majesty's New Zealand Ship
AVM	Air Vice-Marshal		
B/F	Before Flight	HMS	Her Majesty's Ship
Blue Silk	Code name for Doppler navigation equipment	HQ	Headquarters
		IED	Improvised Explosive Device
Blue Turquoise	MARDET Sharjah patrols		
BOAC	British Overseas Airways Corporation	IRA	Irish Republican Army
		JASS	Joint Anti-Submarine School
CENTO	Central Treaty Organisation		
		J/T	Junior Technician
Chf Tech	Chief Technician	KD	Khaki Drill
C-in-C	Commander-in-Chief	LAC	Leading Aircraftman
CLE	Container Light Equipment	LROFE	Long-Range Operational Flying Exercise
CMC	Chairman of the Mess Committee	MAEO	Master Air Electronics Officer
CO	Commanding Officer	MARDET	Maritime Reconnaissance Detachment
CofG	Centre of Gravity		
Cpl	Corporal	MARSO	Maritime Reconnaissance and Special Operations
DFC	Distinguished Flying Cross		
DFM	Distinguished Flying Medal	MCU	Marine Craft Unit
		MEAF	Middle East Air Force

Mk	Mark	SEATO	South East Asia Treaty Organisation
MoD	Ministry of Defence		
MOTU	Maritime Operational Training Unit	Sgt	Sergeant
		SITREP	Situation Report
MR	Maritime Reconnaissance	SNCO	Senior Non-Commissioned Officer
MU	Maintenance Unit		
NAAFI	Navy Army and Air Forces Institute		
		SOE	Special Operations Executive
NATO	North Atlantic Treaty Organisation		
		Sqn	Squadron
NCO	Non-Commissioned Officer	Sqn Ldr	Squadron Leader
		SSBN	Ballistic missile-armed nuclear submarine
NDB	Non-Directional Beacon		
NEAF	Near East Air Force	SSN	Nuclear submarine
NLF	National Liberation Front	TU	Translation Unit
OC	Officer Commanding	UDI	Unilateral Declaration of Independence
OCU	Operational Conversion Unit		
		USAF	United States Air Force
PAN	Priority As Needed	USN	United States Navy
PE	Petrol Electric	USS	United States Ship
PLE	Prudent Limit of Endurance	VHF	Very High Frequency
		VIP	Very Important Person
Plt Off	Pilot Officer	WFA	Wind Finding Attachment
POW	Prisoner of War	Wg Cdr	Wing Commander
PSP	Pressed Steel Planking	W/O	Warrant Officer
QFI	Qualified Flying Instructor	WOp	Wireless Operator
RAE	Royal Aircraft Establishment	WRAF	Women's Royal Air Force
		W/T	Wireless Telegraphy
RAF	Royal Air Force		
RAAF	Royal Australian Air Force		
RN	Royal Navy		
RNAS	Royal Naval Air Station		
RNZAF	Royal New Zealand Air Force		
RPM	Revolutions Per Minute		
SAAF	South African Air Force		
SAC	Senior Aircraftman		
SAR	Search and Rescue		
SARBE	Search and Rescue Beacon		
SAS	Special Air Service		
SASO	Senior Air Staff Officer		

SELECT BIBLIOGRAPHY

BOOKS AND JOURNALS

Ashworth, Chris, Avro's *Maritime Heavyweight: The Shackleton*, Aston, 1990
Delve, Ken, *The Source Book of the RAF*, Airlife, 1994
Fairbairn, Tony, *Action Stations Overseas*, Patrick Stephens, 1991
Jefford, Wg Cdr C G, *RAF Squadrons*, Airlife, 1988
Jones, Barry, *Avro Shackleton*, Crowood Press, 2002
Lake, Deborah, *Growling Over the Oceans: The Royal Air Force Avro Shackleton, the Men, the Missions 1951-1991*, Souvenir Press, 2010
Meekcoms, K J and Morgan, E B, *The British Aircraft Specifications File: British military and commercial aircraft specifications 1920-1949*, Air Britain, 1994
Sturtivant, Ray and Hamlin, John, *RAF Flying Training and Support Units since 1912*, Air Britain, 2007
Wilson, Keith, *Avro Shackleton Manual*, Haynes Publishing, 2015

The Growler, the quarterly journal of the Shackleton Association
The Story Behind the Cross, a booklet published by St. Eval church 2018

SQUADRON ASSOCIATES AND OTHER WEBSITES

37 Squadron (Dave McCandless) *www.37Aden.co.uk*
120 Squadron *www.cxx.org.uk*
201 Squadron *www.201Squadronassociation.com*
203 Squadron Yahoo! *Group groups.yahoo.com/neo/groups/203sqn/info*
206 Squadron: Coastal Command *www.coastalcommand206.com/home*
Coastal Command and Maritime Air Association *www.ccmaa.org.uk*
Radfan Hunters (Ray Deacon. Khormaksar operations including 37 Squadron) *www.radfanhunters.co.uk*
The unofficial website on the South African Air Force *www.saairforce.co.za/*

VOLUME 1 CORRECTIONS

Page 8: LORAN is Long Range Navigation (delete Astro)

Page 14: Sadly, Lossiemouth was missed off the map. It is located just east of Kinloss.

Page 49: The Soviet cruiser is Kynda class, not Kirov

Page 104. St.Mawgan did continue to hear the Growler after November 1970, as the last Mk.3s of 42 Squadron did not leave until September 1971

Appendix 1 Operating Units: 201 Squadron missing motto is 'Here and Everywhere'

Appendix 3 Accidents: 9 Dec '58 David Dancy's correct rank is Flt Sgt, not Flt Lt

INDEX

PERSONNEL

MISCELLANEOUS

EXERCISES

OPERATIONS